1973

THE SUPREME COURT

AND
FUNDAMENTAL FREEDOMS

CURRENT POLITICAL PROBLEMS

FRENCH POLITICS AND ALGERIA   William G. Andrews

CAPITALISM, DEMOCRACY,
AND THE SUPREME COURT   Wallace Mendelson

FREEDOM AND EMERGENCY POWERS
IN THE COLD WAR
          Robert S. Rankin and Winifred R. Dallmayr

THE REVIVAL OF DEMOCRATIC
THEORY   Neal Riemer

AMERICAN FOREIGN POLICY: BEYOND
UTOPIANISM AND REALISM   Donald Brandon

THE SUPREME COURT:
JUDICIAL PROCESS AND
JUDICIAL POLITICS   Arthur A. North, S.J.

THE SUPREME COURT AND
FUNDAMENTAL FREEDOMS,
second edition   George W. Spicer

GEORGE W. SPICER
UNIVERSITY OF VIRGINIA

THE SUPREME COURT
AND
FUNDAMENTAL FREEDOMS

SECOND EDITION

APPLETON
CENTURY
CROFTS

DIVISION OF MEREDITH CORPORATION

NEW YORK

for L. R. S.

PREFACE

The generous reception accorded the first edition of this book, published in 1959, has induced the author and the publisher to update it in a second edition. This, then, is an enlarged and revised version of the original volume. Again, the general purpose is to analyze in reasonably brief compass the role of the Supreme Court of the United States as guardian of those fundamental constitutional liberties which are assumed to be essential to the effective operation of free institutions. The structure and approach of the new edition remain essentially the same as in the first.

The principal change is the addition of a new chapter dealing with civil and criminal procedure. Special emphasis is given here to the extension of the "doctrine of absorption" to important procedural guarantees of the federal Bill of Rights. Extensive additions or revisions or both have been made in other chapters. Expansion of the rights of communication and association treated in the first edition has continued unabated in the succeeding years. Among the more recent expansions are those relating to the right of organized groups such as the NAACP to solicit legal counsel through their leaders; seditious libel; freedom to travel; the right to hear and read; and marital privacy. Along with these, attention has been given to new developments regarding motion picture censorship and the problem of obscenity. New cases relating to the complex problems of religious establishment and the free exercise of religion have also been analyzed. In the area of political and social equality, the principal additions relate to the Twenty-fourth Amendment and its interpretation by the Court, the Voting Rights Act of 1965, and its sustension by the Court, the apportionment cases, racial discrimination in privately owned public facilities, and the Civil Rights Act of 1964. In regard to the cold war and internal security the main new emphasis concerns the shifting position of the Warren Court.

In such an extensive revision I have become indebted to many people. Among these, I owe special thanks to Professor R. Taylor Cole, Advisory Editor, and one of his colleagues at Duke University for the exceptionally thorough examination and constructive criticism of the revised manuscript. Without their aid, the book would surely have been a poorer one. I am grateful to Mrs. Carole Haith and to Miss Ruth Ritchie for the good humor and efficiency with which they did battle with longhand manuscript that was something less than a thing of beauty and at no time a joy. In the closing days of the revision Mr. Dennis Dorin, a graduate student in my Civil Liberties seminar, aided me in the search for, and the abstraction of, last-minute cases. Finally, I am greatly indebted to various members of the staff of the publisher, Appleton-Century-Crofts, and especially to Walter J. Green.

However, not even these able and helpful people could save the author from all errors of fact and imperfections of judgment. I can only say that the book is a better one for what they did. For the rest I must take the responsibility. Again, it is hoped that the book will be useful to the interested general reader as well as to the student and scholar in the field of American government and constitutional law.

G. W. S.

CONTENTS

1

INTRODUCTION

PURPOSE OF STUDY

The purpose of this book is to analyze briefly the role of the Supreme Court of the United States as guardian of such fundamental rights of the individual as speech, press, assembly, religion, equal protection of the laws, and those procedural guarantees of the Bill of Rights which have been "absorbed" into the due process clause of the Fourteenth Amendment as limitations on the states.

Although the interests of liberty are peculiarly those of the individual, they may be equally important to the society of which he is a part. These liberties furnish the foundation of our democratic political society. Without them, political democracy could not survive. The freedom of the electoral process, as reflected in a widely based and uncorrupted suffrage upon which democratic government is directly grounded, would be a meaningless and hollow ritual without the freedom of discussion and continuing debate that is made possible by the underlying rights of free speech, free press, and free assembly. These are the indispensable means for disseminating among the people the ideas and information essential for intelligent self-government. Indeed, self-government implies acceptance and maintenance of these freedoms as conditions which enable the people to continue to govern themselves. As Carl Swisher strikingly expressed it, "no tenable principles of political liberty will permit political liberty to decree its own execution." [1]

Then, of course, there is the broader social interest in the freedom to pursue and discover truth upon which progress in all phases of life depends. Even if it may be argued that there is no obviously sacred right of the individual to speak, write, teach, publish, it can be demonstrated that it is generally helpful to the community to hear what men have to say, to read what they write, and to use what they discover. If these objectives are to be realized, ideas and information—good and bad—must have free access to the open marketplace of thought and communication and be free to compete there for acceptance. The community that is denied the opportunity for this exchange is denied political democracy; it is also denied progress. This idea was perhaps most strongly expressed by John Stuart Mill, in his famous *Essay on Liberty*, in 1859. Mill said:

. . . the peculiar evil of silencing the expression of an opinion is that it is robbing the human race; posterity as well as the existing generation; those who dissent from the opinion, still more than those who hold it. If the opinion is right, they are deprived of the opportunity of exchanging error for truth: if wrong, they lose what is almost as great a benefit, the clearer perception and livelier impression of truth, produced by its collision with error.

ROLE OF SUPREME COURT IN SAFEGUARDING THE BASES OF DEMOCRATIC GOVERNMENT

In the American constitutional system, as it has developed over the past century and a half, it is the responsibility of the Supreme Court, though not of the Court alone, to safeguard those values which are essential to the existence of constitutional democracy. For greater understanding and appreciation of what follows, it

[1] *The Growth of Constitutional Power in the United States* (Chicago, University of Chicago Press, 1946), p. 161.

should be recognized at the outset that the Court, in performing this task, inevitably formulates policy—that is, it performs a political function although in a very different way than does the legislature. The inception of this was at least as early as John Marshall's opinion in *Marbury* v. *Madison* in 1803, and it has continued to this day.

In this historic opinion Marshall enunciated what came to be described as the doctrine of "judicial review." Only in terms of the application of this doctrine can the American brand of constitutional law be meaningfully defined. As Professor Edward S. Corwin cogently states: [2]

As employed in this country, Constitutional Law signifies a body of rules resulting from the interpretation by a high Court of a written constitutional instrument in the course of disposing of cases in which the validity, in relation to the constitutional instrument, of some act of governmental power, state or national, has been challenged. This function . . . involves the power and duty on the part of the Court of pronouncing void any such act which does not square with its own reading of the Constitutional instrument.

The rationale of this judicial power was authoritatively declared by Chief Justice Marshall in the aforementioned opinion. On the much debated question whether it was intended by the framers of the Constitution that the Court should exercise this power, the Constitution itself is silent. Scholars and jurists differ in their interpretation of what the framers intended. It seems to be generally agreed, however, that a number of the most influential members of the Constitutional Convention of 1787 favored such a power and assumed that the Court would exercise it. Moreover, as Charles P. Curtis, Jr., said of the authors of the Constitution, "What they left unsaid, they left open for *us* to decide." [3]

It would contribute nothing to our present problem to attempt either to defend or to denounce the alleged partisan motives and political implications of the decision that a section of the Judiciary Act of 1789 was unconstitutional and, therefore, null and void. Certainly it would have been easy for the Court to con-

[2] *Constitution of the United States of America: Analysis and Interpretation* (Washington, Government Printing Office, 1953), Introduction, p. ix.
[3] *Lions Under the Throne* (Boston, Houghton Mifflin, 1947), p. 3.

strue the statutory provision as inapplicable to the situation before it. The fact is that it was held invalid by one who has come to be regarded as the greatest of the Chief Justices of the United States, and many of his admirers have considered the holding a master stroke of judicial statecraft.[4] On the other hand, others have regarded the decision as an unwarranted usurpation.

Whatever the merits of the respective arguments as to origin, the doctrine has long since become firmly established as the most distinctive characteristic of the American constitutional system, and, in the words of Woodrow Wilson, the Court is "the balance wheel of our whole constitutional system." [5] As conservative a jurist on the question of judicial review as Judge Learned Hand remarked that while "it is impossible to have any assurance how the Convention would have voted at the time . . . it was probable, if indeed it was not certain, that without some arbiter whose decision should be final, the whole system would have collapsed," [6] and he thinks that the Court is the best arbiter.

The full story of how the Court achieved this distinctive role cannot be told here. Suffice it to say that its strength and durability spring from the fact that the American people look to the Court as the ultimate guardian of their Constitution and the liberties guaranteed therein. Its strength lies in the support of the people, and over the long pull it reflects the public thought and public conscience. When it functions at its best, it also helps to frame and guide the public conscience. Indeed, its highest function on occasion may be to hold back irrational and prejudiced majorities until they can give more sober consideration to a question. The independence and prestige of the Court enable it to resist to a considerable degree the temporary passions and prejudices of the people.

Finally, then, it may be said that the Court, in the performance of its function of judicial review, is the arbiter of the federal system in the settlement of conflicts between the states and the national government; that it fixes the boundaries between the con-

---

[4] A. J. Beveridge, *Life of John Marshall* (Boston, Houghton Mifflin, 1919), Vol. III, pp. 142–143.

[5] *Constitutional Government in the United States* (New York, Columbia University Press, 1907), p. 142.

[6] *Saturday Review*, March 15, 1958, p. 16.

stitutional powers of the legislative and executive branches of the national government in proper cases; and that it is the guardian of individual liberty against both national and state governments.

The latter function has been its most important since 1937. Within this period, judicial review of legislative action has been largely confined to the field of civil liberties. In the judicial settlement of controversies arising here as elsewhere, the specific language of the Constitution offers little guidance. As Chief Justice Marshall remarked in *McCulloch* v. *Maryland*,[7] the nature of the Constitution requires that only its great outlines should be marked, its important objects designated, and the minor ingredients which compose those objects be deduced from the nature of the objects themselves.

In the performance of the function of deducing "minor ingredients," the Court necessarily exercises a wide discretion in interpreting and applying such a concept, for example, as due process of law. The interpretation of what the Constitution commands here has been of a changing nature, as the Court majority has developed this concept in the face of changing conditions and varying climates of opinion. First, due process was only a procedural safeguard; it simply guaranteed a fair trial. Near the end of the last century it was given a substantive content and was applied by the Court to protect property rights but not personal rights, at least not for another quarter of a century. Then, in 1925, the due process clause of the Fourteenth Amendment became the principal constitutional safeguard of individual freedom.

Thus, it is important to recognize that judges deciding civil liberties cases in such a constitutional context may choose from among many legally applicable formulas and techniques and that the choices made necessarily result in policy decisions. In such a situation the rules made by judges necessarily reflect their views, and they reflect, as Judge Jerome Frank has pointed out, "judicial compromises or adjustment between conflicting social interests, and thus express judgments of value or policy." [8]

Behind the intricate array of formulas that are applied with

---

[7] 4 Wheaton 315 (1819).
[8] *Courts on Trial: Myths and Reality in American Justice* (Princeton, Princeton University Press, 1949), p. 265.

varying degrees of emphasis in the cases lies a common problem of judicial interpretation which runs through all civil liberties controversies, namely, a conflict of interests, and the Court must of necessity make a choice between the values involved in this conflict. When, for example, the Court declared invalid a series of handbill ordinances forbidding the distribution of handbills on the streets, it was expressing the value judgment that free speech is more important to the community than the object of maintaining clean streets by this method.

As already indicated, none of this is to suggest that courts make policy in the same way as does the legislature. The legislature formally initiates policy, whereas the courts can only act retrospectively in specific cases involving bona fide antagonists. The formal content of legislative policy may be ascertained by an examination of the statutes, but judicial policy grows out of rulings in specific controversies, and its content can, as a rule, be determined only by a review of the totality of cases dealing with a given subject. Even then, the results are sometimes obscure and confusing.

Finally, it should be noted, the Court does not bear sole responsibility for the protection of individual liberties. The Congress, the state legislatures, the President, the governors, and the citizens all share in this responsibility. Yet, although the courts cannot do everything in this connection, they can and have done much. Moreover, as already indicated, the judges have, since at least the early 1920's, been our principal teachers in civil liberties. Their statements in explanation of their decisions are not infrequently more important than the decisions themselves. The eloquent statements of such justices as Holmes, Brandeis, Hughes, Black, Frankfurter, and others have been profoundly influential in developing a popular appreciation of constitutional liberties.

SCOPE OF STUDY

In subsequent chapters, attention will be given to the following matters: (1) the Court's development of civil liberties doctrine before 1937, (2) the Court's role in the expansion of the constitutional law of freedom of speech, press, and assembly in the decade after 1937, (3) the extension of protection of religious freedom under the First and Fourteenth Amendments, and the Court's struggle with the constitutional prohibition of the establishment of religion, (4) the Court's response to problems of social and political equality involved in racial discrimination and in the malapportionment of seats in legislative assemblies, (5) the Court's response to the problems of civil liberty and national security presented by the cold war, and (6) a summary of the Court's achievements.

2

HISTORICAL BACKGROUND

The high points in the Court's development of civil liberties principles before 1937 (the beginning of the period emphasized in this book), which are of major importance to subsequent expansion of civil liberties, are: (1) the judicial interpretation by which First Amendment freedoms were incorporated into the "liberty" of the due process clause of the Fourteenth Amendment, and thus made applicable to state action and subject to the supervision of the federal courts; (2) the enunciation of the "clear and present danger" test by Justice Holmes in the Schenck case [1] in 1919, and its refinement and expansion by Justice Brandeis with Holmes' support in the Whitney case [2] in 1927; (3) the formulation of the "bad tendency" test as a gloss upon the older "reasonable man" test in the Gitlow case [3] in 1925.

Much of the most significant of these developments was the first. Judicial high points in this development include the declaration of the Court in the Gitlow case that First Amendment freedoms are among the fundamental personal liberties "protected by due process clause of the Fourteenth Amendment from impairment by the States," and the case of *Near* v. *Minnesota* [4] which was the first case to hold invalid (in 1931) a state act because it

[1] *Schenck* v. *United States,* 249 U.S. 47 (1919).
[2] *Whitney* v. *California,* 247 U.S. 357 (1927).
[3] *Gitlow* v. *New York,* 268 U.S. 652 (1925).
[4] 283 U.S. 697 (1931).

violated First Amendment freedoms in its substantive provisions. These doctrines will be further analyzed and explained in this chapter.

Chapter 4 will emphasize the application of the clear and present danger test to a series of new and different situations in the decade after 1937—situations involving mainly the collision of First Amendment freedoms with the exercise of the police power of the state in fields of general welfare not closely related to the necessities of national security. It was in this area that the Court clarified and reinforced the clear and present danger test by the theory of "preferred status" of First Amendment freedoms. Under this theory, the Court majority raised the constitutional barriers against governmental regulations of speech, press, assembly, and religion. It placed the burden of proof on the government to establish the validity of an act, appearing on its face to restrict any of these freedoms, by showing that the exercise of the freedom created a clear and present danger of a substantive evil within the power of the legislature to forbid.

As thus reinforced, the clear and present danger test was applied to extend the protection of freedom of expression to such new situations as picketing, criticism of judicial conduct, the distribution of handbills and speech in public places. An examination of the cases will demonstrate that in these areas the Court tended to give maximum scope to freedom by holding restraint to the minimum imposed by clear and present danger. In some cases involving these questions, the Court so applied the clear and present danger doctrine as to suggest an absolutist concept of First Amendment freedoms.

Such a conception was, for example, expressed by Justice Black in *Bridges* v. *California* in these words: [5]

What finally emerges from the "clear and present danger" cases is a working principle that the substantive evils must be extremely serious and the degree of imminence extremely high before the utterance can be punished. These cases do not purport to mark the furthermost constitutional boundaries of protected expression, nor do we here. They

[5] 314 U.S. 252, 263 (1941).

do no more than recognize a minimum compulsion of the Bill of Rights. For the First Amendment does not speak equivocally. It prohibits any law abridging the freedom of speech or of the press. It must be taken as a command of the broadest scope that explicit language, read in the context of a liberty-loving society will allow.

It will be observed in what follows that explicit application of the clear and present danger test has been for the time being abandoned.

The Constitution as originally adopted contained no restriction upon freedom of expression and of religion except the prohibition of any religious qualification for holding office and a provision freeing the members of the House and the Senate from any responsibility for their utterances in their respective chambers except to the members thereof. Even though the First Amendment became a part of the fundamental law in 1791, it is interesting to note that the judicial development of the constitutional law of free speech and free press, as guaranteed by this amendment, did not begin until the end of World War I, and the course of development with respect to religious freedom was not substantially different. The explanation for this situation lies in the dual fact that the First Amendment, like other provisions of the federal Bill of Rights, was directed only toward the national government, not toward the states, and that Congress, with the one glaring exception of the Alien and Sedition Acts of 1798, avoided encroachment upon these liberties for more than a century and a quarter. Moreover, this legislation, which was never tested by the Supreme Court, was effectively repudiated in the election of 1800. Except, then, for the Executive suppression of criticism of governmental policies during the Civil War, the national government took no action raising freedom of expression issues until passage of the Espionage Act of 1917.

With our entrance into World War I, Congress, spurred on by the stimulus of popular hysteria, enacted the Espionage Act of 1917, imposing restrictions on speech for the first time since 1798. This time the Supreme Court was quickly drawn into the controversy and thus entered upon its uneven course in the development of freedom of communication doctrine.

EXPANDING SCOPE OF
FIRST AMENDMENT FREEDOMS

First Amendment freedoms, more particularly freedom of speech and press, have through recent judicial interpretation come to mean much more than was indicated for many years after the adoption of the amendment. For some time after the amendment's adoption, freedom of speech and press was interpreted by commentators and state courts to mean only freedom from previous *restraint* in the Blackstonian sense. Blackstone was, of course, stating a rule of the English Constitution as it was understood in 1769 when he wrote that "The liberty of the press is indeed essential to the nature of a free state; but this consists in laying no previous restraints upon publications, and not in freedom from censure for criminal matter when published," and if one "publishes what is improper, mischievous, or illegal, he must take the consequences of his own temerity." [6] To Blackstone this was the whole of freedom of expression. By the terms of this test, the government may impose no restraint before the words are spoken or printed but may punish after utterance or publication at its discretion.

Even Justice Holmes went so far, in 1907, as to declare that the First Amendment had enacted Blackstone's definition of freedom of expression. Said he in *Patterson* v. *Colorado:* [7]

The main purpose of such constitutional provisions is to prevent all such previous restraints upon publications as had been practiced by other governments, and they do not prevent the subsequent punishment of such as may be deemed contrary to the public welfare. The preliminary freedom extends to the false as well as to the true; the subsequent punishment may extend to the true as to the false.

It is, of course, well known that Justice Holmes later repudiated this view.

In 1931, Chief Justice Hughes, in *Near* v. *Minnesota*,[8] the

[6] *Commentaries*, Vol. IV, p. 151.
[7] 205 U.S. 454 (1907).
[8] 283 U.S. 697 (1931).

first great free press case decided by the Supreme Court, modified both sides of the Blackstonian formula. Admitting that immunity from previous restraint is deserving of special emphasis, that immunity, he declared, "cannot be deemed to exhaust the conception of the liberty guaranteed by the state and federal constitutions." Freedom to punish for publication could render liberty of the press "a mockery and a delusion." Thus, "It is now clear that if subsequent penalties may constitute abridgments under the First Amendment, it is also true that some forms of prior restraint may be perfectly proper." Although "prior restraint" has experienced a considerable diversity of interpretation and application in subsequent cases, the general tendency, especially in the more recent cases, has been to evaluate its operation in the light of particular circumstances confronting the Court.[9]

ABSORPTION OF
FIRST AMENDMENT FREEDOMS
INTO FOURTEENTH AMENDMENT

Although this study is primarily concerned with the period from 1937 to the present, the judicial developments of this period cannot be understood without some knowledge of earlier developments. Prior to 1937, the Supreme Court had made important advances in the area of civil liberties which prepared the way for the development of the constitutional law of civil liberty from that date on. Unquestionably the most significant of these advances was the judicial interpretation by which the First Amendment freedoms were included in the liberty of the due process of law clause of the Fourteenth Amendment, thus rendering state action in this realm subject to the supervision of the federal courts.

But for its application to the states through the Fourteenth Amendment, the First Amendment would be of relatively little

[9] See *Niemotko* v. *Maryland*, 340 U.S. 268; *Kunz* v. *New York*, 340 U.S. 290; *Feiner* v. *New York*, 340 U.S. 315.

significance. It has already been noted that no case involving federal restriction of freedom of expression reached the Supreme Court until the end of World War I. At this time there was a rapid flurry of cases growing out of the enactment by Congress of the Espionage Act of 1917 and the Sedition Act of 1918. Although some of these cases led to the enunciation of important free speech doctrines (to be considered later under the appropriate heading), no serious questions concerning the constitutionality of the statutes were raised. After this series of cases ended, no further cases involving federal restrictions of First Amendment rights reached the Court until World War II.

In the meantime, however, the Supreme Court's expansion of the due process clause of the Fourteenth Amendment to include the freedoms of the First Amendment had brought to the Court a constant stream of cases involving state restrictions of First Amendment freedoms. Thus, the First Amendment through the Fourteenth has become the focal point of judicial review.

The evolution of this doctrine, whereby the enforcement of First Amendment freedoms against the states was made effective through the Fourteenth Amendment, is one of the most interesting and important aspects of American constitutional jurisprudence. Although it seems reasonably clear that such application was the intention of the framers of the Fourteenth Amendment, the Supreme Court thwarted this development for more than a half century. In the famous Slaughter House Cases of 1873, the Court so narrowed the scope of the privileges and immunities clause as to render it virtually meaningless and scornfully rejected the argument that due process possessed a substantive meaning.

The Supreme Court rigidly adhered to this interpretation of the Fourteenth Amendment until the end of the nineteenth century. By judicial interpretation, the due process clause was given a substantive content in the late 1890's. Under this interpretation the substance or content of a state law must be reasonable in order to be constitutional. But the doctrine was first applied to safeguard property rights and the liberty of contract,[10] chiefly of corporations, from state police power in the form of social legis-

[10] See *Smyth v. Ames*, 169 U.S. 466 (1898); *Holden v. Hardy*, 169 U.S. 366 (1898); *Lochner v. New York*, 198 U.S. 45 (1905).

lation, and was destined to be rejected as the basis for the protection of civil liberties against state encroachment for another quarter century. This is ironical when it is remembered that the primary purpose of the Fourteenth Amendment was to safeguard the personal and civil rights of the Negroes who had been freed from slavery by the Thirteenth Amendment.

Indeed, as late as 1922, in *Prudential Life Insurance Co.* v. *Cheek*,[11] the Supreme Court bluntly asserted that "neither the Fourteenth Amendment nor any other provision of the Constitution imposes any restrictions upon the state about freedom of speech." It is clear then that for a quarter of a century the Court had readily accepted freedom of contract as a constitutionally guaranteed liberty, but had steadfastly refused to give an equal status to freedom of speech, press, assembly, and religion. Clearly the Court could not persist in this illogical and indefensible position. Some indication of what was to come was indicated in certain dissenting opinions. As early as 1907, Justice Harlan had concluded: "It is, I think, impossible to conceive of liberty as secured by the constitution against hostile action, whether by the nation or by the states, which does not embrace the right to enjoy free speech and the right to have a free press."[12] More pointedly, Mr. Justice Brandeis remarked in *Gilbert* v. *Minnesota*[13] in 1920: "I cannot believe that the liberty guaranteed by the Fourteenth Amendment includes only liberty to acquire and to enjoy property." In this case even the majority had assumed for the sake of argument that freedom of speech, guaranteed in the First Amendment, restricted state action, but it was found that if such a right did exist, it had not been violated in the case before the Court.

Three years later, and only one year after the outspoken declaration to the contrary in the Cheek case, the Court gave a clear indication that it was abandoning its reluctance to intervene in the encroachments of state governments upon fundamental personal freedoms. In *Meyer* v. *Nebraska*[14] in 1923, the Court held

11 259 U.S. 530 (1922).
12 *Patterson* v. *Colorado*, 205 U.S. 454 (1907).
13 254 U.S. 325, 343 (1920).
14 262 U.S. 390 (1923).

invalid a state law forbidding German language instruction because the due process clause of the Fourteenth Amendment protected both the right of the teacher to pursue his calling and the
right of the parents to control the education of their children.
Despite the continued emphasis upon property rights, the Court's
definition of the "liberty" protected by the Fourteenth Amendment went much further. Said Justice McReynolds for the Court:

Without doubt, it denotes not merely freedom from bodily restraint,
but also the right of the individual to contract, to engage in any of the
common occupations of life, to acquire useful knowledge, to marry,
establish a home and bring up children, to worship God according to
the dictates of his own conscience, and generally, to enjoy those privileges long recognized at common law as essential to the orderly pursuit
of happiness by free men.

Then, in 1925, the great reversal became complete and un-
mistakable in an almost casual manner. In *Gitlow* v. *New York*,[15]
the Court, sustaining New York's "criminal anarchy" law against
the claim of a New York Communist that it deprived him of freedom of speech and press in contravention of the due process of
law clause of the Fourteenth Amendment, made this significant
proposition: "For present purposes we may and do assume that
freedom of speech and of the press—which are protected by the
First Amendment from abridgment by Congress—are among the
fundamental personal rights and 'liberties' protected by the due
process clause of the Fourteenth Amendment from impairment by
the states."

The assumption here made found expression in explicit decisions over the next several years. Two years later, in *Fiske* v.
Kansas,[16] a statute similar to that involved in the Gitlow case was
held invalid as applied because it violated the due process clause
of the Fourteenth Amendment. This Kansas statute which, among
other things, provided for the punishment of any person who "advocates . . . or teaches the duty, necessity, propriety or expedi-
ency of crime, criminal syndicalism or sabotage" was applied by
the state court as covering a case involving only membership in,

---

[15] 268 U.S. 652 (1925).
[16] 274 U.S. 380 (1927).

and the securing of other members for, an organization whose constitution proclaimed the incompatibility of interests and the inevitability of the struggle between employers and workers until the ultimate triumph of the latter. The statute as thus applied was held by the Supreme Court to deprive the defendant of liberty without due process of law. The first state act to be held invalid because it violated First Amendment freedoms in its substantive provisions was the Minnesota "gag-press law," which provided for the padlocking by injunctive process of newspapers publishing "scandalous, malicious, defamatory or obscene" material. In holding this statute to be an unwarranted previous restraint on freedom of the press, Chief Justice Hughes declared for the Court in 1931: [17] "It is no longer open to doubt that the liberty of the press and of speech is within the liberty safeguarded from invasion by state action." In subsequent cases the Court has added freedom of assembly,[18] freedom of religion,[19] and establishment of religion [20] to the liberty guaranteed against state restraint.

Only those liberties which the Court regards as basic or fundamental have been absorbed into the due process clause of the Fourteenth Amendment. When the first edition of this study appeared in 1959, these included only freedom of religion, freedom of speech and press, freedom of assembly and petition, and according to some interpretations, the Sixth Amendment's requirement that an accused shall have the assistance of counsel in capital cases. Mr. Justice Cardozo, in a case decided in 1937, referred to these rights as "essential to a scheme of ordered liberty." They were regarded as so vital to the preservation of our democratic system as to stand upon "a different plane of social and moral values." For illustration, Mr. Cardozo said of freedom of thought and speech "that it is the matrix, the indispensable condition of nearly every other form of freedom." [21]

Many of the guarantees of the federal Bill of Rights, however, had been held not to be of such vital importance as "to be implicit

[17] Near v. Minnesota, 283 U.S. 697 (1931); see also Grosjean v. American Press Company, 297 U.S. 233 (1936).
[18] De Jonge v. Oregon, 299 U.S. 353 (1937).
[19] Cantwell v. Connecticut, 310 U.S. 296 (1940).
[20] Everson v. Board of Education, 330 U.S. (1947).
[21] Palko v. Connecticut, 302 U.S. 319 (1937).

in the concept of ordered liberty," and thus were not protected against state action by the Fourteenth Amendment. From 1884 on, the Supreme Court had rejected the contention that certain procedural guarantees of the federal Bill of Rights were binding upon the states. Nothing in the Fourteenth Amendment compelled a state to afford a person accused of crime a grand jury indictment,[22] or a jury trial,[23] or immunity from self-incrimination,[24] or freedom from double jeopardy.[25] Although these procedural rights are important, admitted Justice Cardozo in the Palko case, "they are not the very essence of a scheme of ordered liberty. To abolish them is not to violate a 'principle of justice so rooted in the traditions and conscience of our people as to be ranked as fundamental.' . . . Few would be so narrow or provincial as to maintain that a fair and enlightened system of justice would be impossible without them."

All this was changed in the years from 1961 to 1965. During this period, as chapter 3 will point out, the Supreme Court extended to state criminal proceedings the following guarantees provided by the Bill of Rights to defendants in federal courts: (1) the Fourth Amendment's protection against unreasonable searches and seizures; (2) the Sixth Amendment's guarantee of the right of counsel; (3) the Eighth Amendment's prohibition against cruel and unusual punishment; (4) the Fifth Amendment's protection against compulsory self-incrimination; and (5) the Sixth Amendment's guarantee of the right of confrontation of witnesses against one's self.

Through these holdings the Cardozo distinction in the Palko case between criminal procedural rights and First Amendment freedoms has been largely repudiated. The doctrine of selective absorption, set forth in the Palko case and there confined primarily to First Amendment rights, has been extended to the above procedural rights and may well be extended to others.

At this point, mention will be made of the three "doctrines" by which the various justices of the Court would justify the above mentioned extensions of federal judicial power. The first and the

---

[22] *Hurtado* v. *California*, 110 U.S. 516 (1884).
[23] *Maxwell* v. *Dow*, 176 U.S. 581 (1900).
[24] *Twining* v. *New Jersey*, 211 U.S. 78 (1908).
[25] *Palko* v. *Connecticut*, 302 U.S. 319 (1937).

most complex to state is the so-called "fair trial" rule, which was the rule applied almost exclusively by the Court from the early 1920's to 1961. This rule rejects the concept of "incorporation" of any part of the Bill of Rights into the due process clause of the Fourteenth Amendment. Instead it holds that this amendment directly, and independently of the Bill of Rights, imposes limitations on state criminal proceedings which are similar to some of the specific guarantees. However, these guarantees operate upon the states not because of any process of absorption from the federal Bill of Rights but because they are on all the facts of a given case essential to a fair trial. The rule, then, is that "fairness" must characterize state proceedings in order to satisfy the demands of due process.

This is essentially a "natural law" rule. If a procedural right is invoked in such circumstances "that it cannot be denied without violating those fundamental principles of liberty and justice which lie at the base of all our civil and political institutions," it is essential to a fair trial.

Such a rule allows the states more flexibility in criminal proceedings than any doctrine of absorption since they are not bound by federal standards in the application of specific procedural commands such as the right to counsel, confrontation of witnesses, immunity from self-incrimination, etc. These rights are required in state proceedings when all the facts show that a fair trial is impossible otherwise. For example, the right to counsel was essential to a fair trial in the Powell case because of the particular circumstances of the case, but it was not essential in *Betts* v. *Brady* because the circumstances were different.[26]

The second doctrine is that of "selective absorption" by which certain guarantees of the federal Bill of Rights are held to be of such a fundamental character that they have been "brought within the Fourteenth Amendment by a process of absorption." These guarantees are, in the language of the Court, so "essential to a scheme of ordered liberty" that they are implicit in the concept of liberty guaranteed against state abridgment by the due process clause of the Fourteenth Amendment. This, too, smacks of "natural law" theory, and Justice Black will have none of it.

[26] See p. 40.

The third doctrine is that of "wholesale incorporation," so ardently espoused by Justice Black since the Adamson case in 1947. This doctrine holds that it was the original purpose of the Fourteenth Amendment to make the entire Bill of Rights applicable to the states. Justice Black can see no basis for choosing between the guarantees of the Bill of Rights. They operate on the state simply because that was the purpose of the Fourteenth Amendment. This view has never been accepted by a majority of the Court.

Important as these changes are in extending the scope of federal judicial power in state proceedings, they apparently reflect no substantial change in judicial doctrine. The doctrine of "selective absorption" applied by the Court majority in the recent procedural cases is not essentially different from that enunciated by Justice Cardozo in Palko, when he declared that the guarantees selected by the Court "have been taken over from the earlier articles of the Federal Bill of Rights and brought within the Fourteenth Amendment by a process of absorption."

The new view of the Court majority is that the above mentioned procedural guarantees of the Bill of Rights are of such a fundamental nature as to be "essential to a scheme of ordered liberty," and are therefore obligatory upon the states through the due process clause of the Fourteenth Amendment. Thus the change is not in the essential nature of the doctrine but in the scope of its application—a change in the thinking of the Court as to what rights are so fundamental as to be "essential to a scheme of ordered liberty."

JUDICIAL TESTS DEVISED BY THE COURT

Although the guarantees of the First Amendment are expressed in the most sweeping and unequivocal terms, they have never been regarded as absolute, but are subject to restrictions for the protection of the public safety and welfare. Hence the Court has found it necessary to devise tests or standards and to create presumptions to guide it in striking the proper balance between the public interest and the private right alleged to be invaded in a given case.

This the Court has not found an easy task. In cases involving these freedoms, the Court's task of interpretation differs from that in many other cases. Here it is faced not merely with a question of whether a power has been granted to the national government or reserved to the states, in which case there is the presumption of constitutionality, but in cases involving freedom of speech and press, or of religion, the Court must interpret and apply a power granted to Congress, or more often one reserved to the states, and at the same time interpret and apply a constitutional limitation on governmental power. Power, of course, is essential to and inherent in government. Yet it is an essential of the American system of constitutional democracy that governmental power be limited. To make this principle doubly sure, the Bill of Rights and other amendments were added to the Constitution. Moreover, the difficulty of the Court's task has been increased by virtue of the fact that First Amendment freedoms, as indicated previously, have been regarded by the Court as peculiarly fundamental in a democratic society. Here, as will later be shown, the usual course of presumption of constitutionality is not so readily available.

Thus there was need for principles of judicial construction, and the Supreme Court, spurred on first by World War I espionage and sedition legislation and later by the new doctrine of "nationalization" enunciated in the Gitlow case, set about to establish them.

By 1925, the Court had formulated several such tests: (1) the "clear and present danger" test, (2) the "bad tendency" test, and (3) later, a supplement to clear and present danger known as "preferred status" of First Amendment freedoms. Interrelated with (1) and (2) is the test of "evil intent." Only the briefest consideration of these tests can be undertaken here.

Clear and Present Danger Test

In the first Supreme Court free speech case of *Schenck* v. *United States*,[27] decided shortly after the First World War, Mr. Justice

[27] 249 U.S. 47 (1919).

Holmes sought to set forth a standard for the Court in terms of the now famous clear and present danger doctrine. He said:

The question in every case is whether the words are used in such circumstances and are of such a nature as to create a clear and present danger that they will bring about the substantive evils that Congress has a right to prevent. It is a question of proximity and degree. When a nation is at war many things that might be said in time of peace are such a hindrance to its effort that their utterance will not be endured so long as men fight, and that no court could regard them as protected by any constitutional right.

In this case a clear and present danger was found to exist, and the doctrine was applied to sustain the application of the Espionage Act of 1917 to Schenck's distribution of antidraft leaflets to men who were subject to military service, urging them in intemperate and impassioned language to resist the draft.

The clear and present danger test was also at issue in *Abrams v. United States*,[28] in which the Court sustained the application of the Sedition Act of 1918 to the distribution of Marxist pamphlets urging the workers of the world to resist the Allied and American intervention against the Bolsheviki after the Russian revolution. Holmes, with the concurrence of Brandeis, dissented, insisting that no threat of clear and present danger to our safety had been shown. On this occasion Holmes states his theory much more sharply in these words: "I think that we should be eternally vigilant against attempts to check the expression of opinions that we loathe and believe to be fraught with death, unless they so imminently threaten immediate interference with the lawful and pressing purposes of the law that an immediate check is required to save the country."

It should be noted that in none of the cases decided before 1927 did Justices Holmes and Brandeis use the clear and present danger test for the purpose of challenging the constitutional validity of a federal or state statute. The constitutionality of the Sedition Act of 1918 was not questioned, nor was that of state statutes of a similar nature. It would seem clear, then, that Holmes' Schenck formula was meant only as a "rule of reason" to

[28] 250 U.S. 616 (1919).

guide administrative authorities and the courts in the application of the act, and not as a test of the power of Congress to enact substantive legislation. In the application of the law, Holmes and Brandeis sought to give freedom of expression the maximum scope by requiring the showing of a clear and present danger.

In 1927, however, in *Whitney* v. *California* [29] Justice Brandeis, with the support of Holmes, set forth the doctrine as the basis on which the power of the legislative body to limit freedom of expression could be challenged by evidence that there was no emergency sufficiently grave and imminent to warrant it. Here Brandeis asserted that a legislative declaration of the existence of a danger sufficiently serious to justify restrictions on speech and assembly did no more than create a "rebuttable presumption." If the Court found that the conditions alleged by the legislature did not exist, it should refuse to enforce the law on the ground that no clear and present danger existed. In other words, in a case where the validity of a statute is dependent upon the existence of certain conditions, the enactment of the statute will not, alone, establish the facts essential to its validity.

In this case Justice Brandeis, in a concurring opinion in which Holmes joined, restated and refined the clear and present danger doctrine in a masterly civil liberties statement. Although both voted with the majority to sustain the conviction of the defendant under the California Criminal Syndicalism Act, on the basis of evidence that tended to establish the existence of a conspiracy to commit serious crimes, they disagreed with the majority on the validity of a section of the act which not only made it a felony punishable by imprisonment to advocate, or teach, or practice criminal syndicalism (the overthrow of the government by violence), but was also aimed "at association with those who proposed to preach it."

In his restatement of the theory, Brandeis in part declared:

Fear of serious injury cannot alone justify suppression of free speech and assembly. . . . There must be reasonable ground to fear that serious evil will result if free speech is practiced. There must be reasonable ground to believe that the danger apprehended is imminent. There

[29] 274 U.S. 357 (1927).

must be reasonable ground to believe that the evil to be prevented is a serious one. . . . In order to support a finding of clear and present danger it must be shown either that immediate serious violence was to be expected or was advocated, or that the past conduct furnished reason to believe that advocacy was then contemplated. . . . No danger flowing from speech can be deemed clear and present, unless the incidence of the evil apprehended is so imminent that it may befall before there is opportunity for full discussion. . . .

Although Holmes and Brandeis were never again to speak of the clear and present danger test, and although for ten years after Whitney the Supreme Court made no specific reference to the test, the Whitney formula nevertheless set the pattern which the majority of the Court followed when it finally accepted and applied the doctrine for the first time in 1937 to protect the libertarian claims of the defendant in the case of *Herndon v. Lowry*.[30]

In the meantime a number of cases vigorously sustaining libertarian claims were decided without reference to clear and present danger. Moreover, these cases were of pioneer significance in the development of freedom of expression and freedom of assembly with respect to state encroachment. Three cases involved direct application of the tremendously important principle, first enunciated by the majority of the Court in the dictum of the Gitlow case, that the fundamental rights of the First Amendment are embodied in the concept of liberty guaranteed against state encroachment by the Fourteenth Amendment.[31]

The failure of the Supreme Court to recognize the clear and present danger test even by name for a decade raised doubt as to whether it was any longer valid as a component of judicial decision. Then, in the constitutionally significant year of 1937, the Court for the first time applied the doctrine to invalidate a statute limiting freedom of expression. Thus it will be seen that for the first eighteen years of its history the doctrine never enjoyed full acceptance by the Supreme Court, but in the period from 1937 to about 1946 the stone which had been rejected became the head of the corner, and was applied by the Court in a variety

[30] 301 U.S. 242 (1937).
[31] *Near v. Minnesota*, 283 U.S. 697 (1931); *Grosjean v. American Press Co.*, 297 U.S. 233 (1936); *De Jonge v. Oregon*, 299 U.S. 353 (1937).

of situations, which will be considered subsequently. But the doctrine never gained the approval of all the justices. Justice Frankfurter had been its most vigorous and consistent antagonist.

Bad Tendency Test

The bad tendency test which was applied by the Court in the Gitlow case, and by the majority of the Court in the Whitney case, was essentially antithetical to clear and present danger and consequently much less favorable to freedom of expression.

In *Gitlow* v. *New York*, the majority of the Court rejected Mr. Justice Holmes' clear and present danger test and sustained the application of the New York Criminal Anarchy Statute of 1902 to the publication by a Left-wing Socialist of a manifesto in which it was claimed that humanity could be saved from capitalism "only by the Communist Revolution." It was not claimed that the publication posed any immediate threat to the safety of New York State, but the majority ruled that even though publications and speeches themselves create no immediate danger, they may be punished by the legislature if they have a "tendency" to bring about results dangerous to public safety. Mr. Justice Sanford declared for the Court majority that it was "not open to question" that a state could punish utterances "tending to corrupt public morals, incite to crime, or disturb the public peace. . . ." It was enough "if the natural tendency and probable effect was to bring about the substantive evils which the legislative body might prevent." [32] Furthermore, "Every presumption is to be indulged in favor of the validity of the statute." Legislative conclusions are to be declared invalid only if they are clearly arbitrary and unreasonable.

The bad tendency test is, then, nothing more than a gloss upon an earlier standard of judicial review known as the "reasonable man" test. By this standard the Court must not strike down a legislative judgment expressed in a statute if a fair and "reasonable man" could have reached the same conclusion as the legislature. Before the Whitney case it was possible to reconcile this

[32] 268 U.S. 652, 671 (1925).

theory with clear and present danger by arguing that they were applicable to different circumstances. For example, Justice Sanford argued in Gitlow that the clear and present danger test had no application "where the legislative body itself has previously determined the danger of substantive evil arising from utterances of a specified character."

But after Brandeis and Holmes had restated clear and present danger in Whitney as a basis on which the constitutionality of a law abridging free speech and assembly could be challenged by evidence that there was no emergency justifying it, there was no way of reconciling clear and present danger and the reasonable man theory except by giving a preferential status to First Amendment freedoms.

Preferred Status Doctrine

It is interesting that Justice Holmes, who evolved the clear and present danger test, was also an ardent champion of the reasonable man test in cases involving economic regulation. In his famous dissent to *Lochner* v. *New York*,[33] he declared that he would not hold invalid a statute "unless it can be said that a rational and fair man necessarily would admit that the statute proposed would infringe fundamental principles as they have been understood by the traditions of our people and our law." Yet there is implicit in the application of clear and present danger to First Amendment freedoms alone a preference for a more liberal scope for these than for other constitutional rights.

Holmes never gave an explicit and satisfactory explanation of why legislation limiting First Amendment rights must pass the clear and present danger test, whereas other legislation must simply pass the test of reasonableness.[34] It remained for other justices later to provide the rationale for the Holmes doctrine. On the face of this, it could plausibly be argued that Justice Holmes was inconsistent. A more reasonable explanation, however, for the apparent paradox is that Holmes believed that his judicial

[33] 198 U.S. 45 (1905).
[34] See C. H. Pritchett, *Civil Liberties and the Vinson Court* (Chicago, University of Chicago Press, 1954), pp. 28ff.

function called for a more exacting standard of judicial review in cases dealing with First Amendment freedoms than in those concerning procedural rights and economic matters. Certainly a strong case can be made for this position.

If First Amendment freedoms are fundamental in the sense that Justice Cardozo argued in the Palko case, that is, in the sense that they are the bases of nearly all other freedoms, it would seem only logical for the Court to apply more exacting standards of review in cases dealing with those liberties than in economic cases. Furthermore, as Justice Stone indicated in his now famous footnote to *United States* v. *Carolene Products Co.*[35] in 1938, it would seem elementary to the principles of constitutional democracy that "legislation which restricts those political processes" by which undesirable legislation may be repealed should "be subjected to more exacting judicial scrutiny under the general prohibitions of the Fourteenth Amendment than are most other types of legislation." If, for example, a popular majority of today should impose controls on certain economic activities, another popular majority of tomorrow with a different view may remove such controls, so long as the political processes by which such changes are effected remain free and unobstructed. This is not so with legislation limiting freedom of expression and assembly. If the majority of the moment suppresses those with whom they disagree, the minority is precluded even from arguing that a wrong has been done and that improvements are possible. Obstruction of the democratic process is not self-corrective. There is reason, then, for a court to intervene to insure freedom of discussion of possible changes and improvements in the affairs of the people and not to intervene in behalf of one economic theory rather than another.

Justice Stone also suggested that similar considerations might enter into the review of statutes directed at religious, national, or racial minorities, that "prejudice against discrete and insular minorities may be a special condition which tends seriously to curtail the operation of those political processes ordinarily to be relied upon to protect minorities, and which may call for a correspondingly more searching judicial inquiry."

[35] 304 U.S. 144 (1938).

The idea thus backhandedly suggested by Justice Stone in 1938, and clearly implied by Justice Cardozo in 1937, had by 1939, in the first handbill cases, become the doctrine of a clear majority of the Court. Of legislative abridgment of the rights of free speech and press, Justice Roberts said in these cases: "Mere legislative preferences or beliefs respecting matters of public convenience may well support regulation directed at other personal activities, but be insufficient to justify such as diminishes the exercise of rights so vital to the maintenance of democratic institutions."

As further developed in other cases in the 1940's, the preferred status doctrine became the supplement to, and the rationale of, the clear and present danger test. The relationship of the two concepts is well illustrated by this statement of Justice Jackson in the second flag salute case.[36]

The right of a state to regulate, for example, a public utility may well include, so far as the due process test is concerned, power to impose all of the restrictions which a legislature may have a "rational basis" for adopting. But freedom of speech and press, of assembly, and of worship may not be infringed on such slender grounds. They are susceptible of restriction only to prevent grave and immediate danger to interests which the state may lawfully protect.

In the language of the cases, the doctrine of clear and present danger as reinforced by preferred status may be briefly stated as follows: The liberties protected by the First Amendment, and made applicable to the states through the Fourteenth Amendment, are so peculiarly important to the maintenance of democratic institutions that they enjoy a preferred status in our scale of constitutional values, and thus any legislative act which appears on its face to restrict any of those liberties is presumed to be unconstitutional, and the burden of proof is on those who defend such legislation to show that it is justified by clear and present danger to the public interest.[37]

[36] *West Virginia State Board of Education* v. *Barnette*, 319 U.S. 624 (1943).
[37] See Robert E. Cushman, "Civil Liberties," *American Political Science Review*, Vol. 42 (February, 1948), pp. 42–43.

The Test of Evil Intent

The state of the speaker's mind has usually been an important factor in the determination of the danger of speech. Sometimes coupled with, and sometimes distinct from, the bad tendency and clear and present danger tests, the Court has applied the test of evil intent. The cases give little clue as to how obvious the evil intent must be before it can be of constitutional significance, but the Court is apparently more likely to sustain the punishment of speech if the speaker clearly meant to bring about the substantive evil. Only a few examples of the application of this concept of evil intent can be given here.

In the Gitlow case, words having an evil tendency and uttered with evil intent were held to be punishable. In the previously mentioned case of *Fiske* v. *Kansas*, the Court reversed the conviction of an I.W.W. organizer under the Kansas antisyndicalism law on the ground that there was no evidence that the defendant intended to effect his industrial and political ends by violence or other unlawful means. Here it was not suggested that there was no clear and present danger that such an intent would have resulted in illegal action. Yet, in *Whitney* v. *California*, Justice Brandeis restated the clear and present danger test to include the intent to create such danger. Still a different combination of intent with other elements was illustrated in the Yates case, where the Court held that advocacy of violent overthrow of the government, even with intent to bring about violent overthrow, could not be punished under the Smith Act unless the language employed was calculated to incite to action.[38]

[38] See Chapter 8.

3

CIVIL RIGHTS AND CRIMINAL PROCEDURE: DOCTRINE OF ABSORPTION EXTENDED

Beginning in 1961, the doctrine of "absorption" has been progressively extended to important procedural guarantees of the Fourth, Fifth, Sixth, and Eighth Amendments. With benefit of hindsight it could now be argued that this process of procedural absorption began with *Powell* v. *Alabama* [1] in 1932.

At any rate, since 1961 the following provisions of the federal Bill of Rights have been held by the Supreme Court to be operative on the states through the due process clause of the Fourteenth Amendment: (1) the Fourth Amendment's protection against unreasonable searches and seizures (1961); (2) the Eighth Amendment's prohibition against cruel and unusual punishment (1962); (3) the Sixth Amendment's guarantee of the right to counsel (1963); (4) the Fifth Amendment's protection against compulsory self-incrimination (1964); and (5) the Sixth Amendment's guarantee of the right of confrontation of witnesses against one's self (1965).

It is the purpose of this chapter to analyze the Court's extension of the doctrine of absorption to the foregoing criminal proce-

[1] 287 U.S. 45 (1932).

dures and, as background, to set forth briefly the nature and scope of those guarantees prior to absorption into the Fourteenth Amendment as limitations on the states.

UNREASONABLE SEARCHES AND SEIZURES

The Fourth Amendment provides that "The right of the people to be secure in their persons, houses, papers, and effects against unreasonable searches and seizures, shall not be violated, and no warrant shall issue, but upon probable cause, supported by oath or affirmation, and particularly describing the place to be searched, and the persons or things to be seized." The general purpose of this constitutional provision has been well stated by the Supreme Court itself:

This was not done to shield criminals nor to make the home a safe haven for illegal activities. It was done that an objective mind might weigh the need to invade that privacy in order to enforce the law. The right of privacy was deemed too precious to entrust to the discretion of those whose job is the detection of crime and the arrest of criminals. Power is a heady thing; and history shows that police acting on their own cannot be trusted. And so the Constitution requires a magistrate to pass on the desires of the police before they violate the privacy of the home.[2]

Excellent as this statement is, it does not provide an answer to specific cases. The great majority of cases arising under the clause grow out of failure to secure a warrant at all, let alone the failure of a warrant to be specific in its description. Yet it has been long established that failure to secure a warrant does not necessarily void a search or seizure.

Among the exceptions to the rule that a search can only be conducted with a search warrant issued by a judicial officer are these: (1) In situations where delay resulting from the time required to secure a warrant would allow the suspect to escape, or to conceal weapons or contraband and thus make conviction im-

[2] *McDonald* v. *United States*, 335 U.S. 451, 455 (1948).

possible.[3] This situation has grown out of the widespread use of automobiles, boats, and airplanes for the conduct of criminal activity. In these cases the searching officer must show that he had probable cause to believe that the law was being violated. (2) A search may be made without a warrant as an adjunct to a lawful arrest. Such searches are deemed necessary, among other reasons, to protect the arresting officer against concealed weapons, to deprive the prisoner of means of escaping, and to prevent the destruction of evidence. Of course, an arrest must be made under an arrest warrant unless a crime is being committed in the view of the arresting officer. This exception includes the search of things under the immediate physical control of the prisoner.[4] It is an easy step to expand the exception still farther to include one's room or apartment. For example, in the Rabinowitz case a warrant had been issued for the arrest of Rabinowitz on the charge of selling fraudulently altered postage stamps. In connection with the arrest, the officers searched, without a warrant, his safe, desk, and filing cabinets, and they found 573 more fraudulent stamps. On this evidence he was convicted, and a divided Supreme Court upheld the conviction on the ground that the search was connected with a valid arrest. It was reasonable, because it was confined to the small business which was open to the public and was under the immediate control of the prisoner.[5]

In this case, dissenting Justices Frankfurter, Black, and Jackson saw the majority weakening the requirement of "absolute necessity" as the only valid ground for exception to the general rule of search warrants. This is only one of many cases illustrating the difficulty of establishing a guideline between legal and illegal searches. The problem has been one of insuring that the police will not overstep this line.

Perhaps the most extreme invasion of privacy has been made possible by modern technology and electronic development. The result of this is illustrated by the famous Olmstead case [6] of 1928. Here the Supreme Court held that no unreasonable search was

---

[3] *Carroll v. United States*, 267 U.S. 132 (1924).
[4] *Harris v. United States*, 331 U.S. 145 (1947).
[5] *United States v. Rabinowitz*, 339 U.S. 56 (1950).
[6] *Olmstead v. United States*, 277 U.S. 438 (1928).

involved in the police's tapping of a suspect's telephone lines from an outside building and recording his incriminating conversations. The Court found that there had been no search and seizure in this case because the premises of the suspects had not been entered and the evidence was secured solely through the sense of hearing. Thus, it seems that a search must involve an actual trespass, and a seizure must be of something tangible.

In later cases the Court construed a provision of the Communication Act, enacted by Congress in 1934, as forbidding the use in federal trials of evidence secured by wiretapping.[7] But wiretapping is primitive in comparison with more recent electronic achievements. There are "electronic eavesdropping" devices which make wiretapping unnecessary, and the use of these has been upheld on the reasoning of the Olmstead case.[8]

If, however, a device is used in a manner to cause a "physical intrusion" of the suspect's premises, the search is unconstitutional. In the Silverman case in 1961, police drove a "spike mike" into a hot air duct in the wall of a building and overheard conversations throughout the building. This was held to be an unreasonable search, and the evidence thus secured could not be used.[9]

It is now clear that one of the most difficult problems confronting the Court in the enforcement of the constitutional protection against unreasonable searches and seizures arises from the use of incriminating evidence secured through an illegal search. The immunity clause of the Fifth Amendment and the Fourth Amendment are intimately related, as the Court indicated in an important early case, because "unreasonable seizures" condemned in the Fourth Amendment are usually made for the purpose of compelling a person to give evidence against himself, which in a criminal case is condemned in the Fifth Amendment; and compelling one in a criminal case to be a witness against oneself sheds light on the question as to what is an unreasonable search and seizure under the Fourth Amendment.[10]

---

[7] *Nardone* v. *United States*, 302 U.S. 379 (1937);
  Nardone v. *United States*, 308 U.S. 338 (1939).
[8] *Goldman* v. *United States*, 316 U.S. 129 (1942);
  On Lee v. *United States*, 343 U.S. 747 (1952).
[9] *Silverman* v. *United States*, 365 U.S. 505 (1961).
[10] *Boyd* v. *United States*, 116 U.S. 616 (1886).

The Court thought that the seizure of a man's books and papers to be used as evidence against him was not substantially different from compelling him to be a witness against himself. Thus the notion of a search was extended to include a subpoena to produce evidence in court.

In 1914, the Court in the well-known Weeks case enunciated the rule that evidence secured by illegal searches must be excluded from use in federal trials.[11] This rule reflects the very practical notion that the most effective way to stay the police from illegal searches is to make the fruits of the search useless. It should be noted, however, that the Weeks exclusionary rule did not, for nearly a half-century, apply to evidence illegally seized by one not an official of the federal government or in some way connected therewith. Thus if evidence was stolen by a thief or illegally seized by a state officer and then presented "on a silver platter" to federal officers, it could be used in a federal court. But this so-called "silver platter" doctrine was repudiated by the Court in 1960.[12]

STATE SEARCHES AND SEIZURES AND THE EXCLUSIONARY RULE

Although the federal courts had ruled since 1914 that illegally seized evidence could not be admitted in a criminal trial, the principle of federalism complicated the problem in respect to the states. All of them forbade illegal searches, but they were free to allow the fruits of an illegal search to be used in evidence in a state trial. Most of them followed the English common law rule that material and relevant evidence is admissible regardless of how it is secured.

The first case in which the Court had occasion to rule on the application of the Fourth Amendment to the states was *Wolf v. Colorado* [13] in 1949. Although the Court in this case decided that the Fourth Amendment's protection against illegal searches and seizures was incorporated into the due process clause of the Four-

[11] *Weeks v. United States,* 232 U.S. 383 (1914).
[12] *Elkins v. United States,* 364 U.S. 206 (1960), see also *Benanti v. United States,* 355 U.S. 96 (1957).
[13] 338 U.S. 25 (1949).

teenth Amendment as a right "implicit in the concept of ordered liberty," it went on to hold by a five to four vote that the due process did not require state courts to exclude from criminal trials evidence obtained in violation of this fundamental right. Justice Frankfurter, for the majority, concluded that "most of the English speaking world does not regard as vital . . . the exclusion of evidence thus obtained." The Court was, therefore, reluctant "to treat this remedy as an essential ingredient of the right." Instead, he suggested the futile sanction of "private action and such protection as the internal discipline of the police, under the eyes of an alert public opinion, may afford."

This anomalous decision produced some anomalous results. As it turned out, state courts were not permitted to admit all illegally seized evidence regardless of the extremity of the police methods in securing it. There could be exceptions. Three cases illustrate the dilemma in which the Court had placed itself. In the Rochin narcotics case [14] the Court barred the use of evidence obtained by pumping a man's stomach for three morphine capsules which he had swallowed as officers broke into his room. Surely the Wolf rule was applicable here, but the Court thought the conduct of the police was too offensive for toleration by a civilized community. Justice Frankfurter, for a unanimous Court, invalidated Rochin's conviction on the ground that:

It is conduct that shocks the conscience. Illegally breaking into the privacy of the petitioner, the struggle to open his mouth and remove what was there, the forcible extraction of his stomach's contents—this course of proceeding by agents of government to obtain evidence is bound to offend even hardened sensibilities.

In *Irvine* v. *California* [15] the conduct of the police was also shocking, but not shocking enough to justify another exception to the Wolf rule. In this case the California police had made two illegal entries into a suspected bookmaker's house and installed a concealed microphone in the bedroom and the bedroom closet. Wires were strung through the roof to a neighboring garage from which police officers with listening devices followed the conversa-

[14] *Rochin* v. *California*, 347 U.S. 128 (1952).
[15] 347 U.S. 128 (1954).

tions of the occupants for more than a month. The Court severely castigated this conduct of the police but affirmed a conviction based on the fruits of the conduct. Justice Jackson remarked for the Court that the conduct of the police "was trespass and probably a burglary," but he insisted that the Court must adhere to the Wolf rule, for there had been no direct physical violence against the person of the accused here as there was in Rochin.

In a third case, *Breithaupt* v. *Abram*,[16] decided in 1957, it was shown that the police had considerable leeway even when the body of the accused was invaded. A physician, at the request of a state patrolman, took a sample of blood from an unconscious truck driver who had been involved in an accident in which three persons were killed. After his conviction for manslaughter, based in part on the blood sample, Breithaupt sought his release by habeas corpus, contending that the use of the involuntary blood test had deprived him of his liberty without due process of law. The Supreme Court, through Justice Clark, did not agree and emphasized that blood tests are "routine," that they are taken "under the protective eye of a physician," and that they are not brutal or offensive to a sense of justice. They do not shock the conscience. Furthermore, intoxication is a serious hazard to life on our highways. So, "as against the right of an individual that his person be held inviolable, even against so slight an intrusion as is involved in applying a blood test . . . , must be set the interest of society in the scientific determination of intoxication, one of the great causes of the mortal hazards of the road."

The dissenters have been unconvinced by this differentiation of Rochin and Breithaupt. The only distinction that they were able to discern was the necessity of using force on Rochin, but not on the unconscious Breithaupt, but they "cannot accept an analysis that would make physical resistance by a prisoner a prerequisite to the existence of his constitutional rights." They seem to have a point. The hazy, subjective discussion of the issue by the majority led Chief Justice Warren to remark that "Only personal reaction to the stomach pump and the blood test can distinguish them."

16 352 U.S. 432 (1957).

In the latest case (*Schmerber* v. *California,* 34 LW 4586, 1966) decided on June 20, 1966, the Court went beyond Breithaupt and held that such evidence was admissible even though the accused, on the advice of counsel, objected to the extraction of his blood.

The paradoxical situation created by the Wolf case was finally acknowledged by the Court in *Mapp* v. *Ohio* [17] and the decision of Wolf with respect to the admission of illegally seized evidence was overruled. The Court held "that all evidence obtained by searches and seizures in violation of the Constitution is, by that same authority, inadmissible in a state court. . . ."

"Having once recognized that the right to privacy embodied in the Fourth Amendment is enforceable against the states, and that the right to be secure against rude invasions of privacy by state officers is, therefore, constitutional in origin, we can no longer permit that right to remain an empty promise." Thus the Fourth Amendment's right of privacy against the states "is enforceable against them by the same sanction of exclusion as is used against the Federal Government."

ABSORPTION OF IMMUNITY FROM SELF-INCRIMINATION

From the reasoning of the Court in the Mapp case, it was only a short step to the absorption of the Fifth Amendment's immunity clause into the due process clause of the Fourteenth Amendment. This was accomplished in *Malloy* v. *Hogan.*[18] In this case a convicted gambler in Hartford, Connecticut, refused to answer in a state court questions relating to events in connection with his earlier arrest and conviction, "on the ground that it may tend to incriminate me." The state court adjudged him in contempt and committed him to prison until he was willing to answer the questions. His petition for habeas corpus was denied on the ground

[17] 367 U.S. 643 (1961).
[18] 378 U.S. 1 (1964).

that the Fifth Amendment's immunity clause was not applicable in state courts.

In reversing the state court, the Supreme Court held "that the Fifth Amendment's exception from the compulsory self-incrimination is also protected by the Fourteenth Amendment against abridgment by the states." Thus the doctrine enunciated in *Twining* v. *New Jersey* [19] in 1908 and reaffirmed in *Adamson* v. *California* [20] in 1947 was repudiated.

The new doctrine of absorption was extended in *Murphy* v. *Waterfront Commission* [21] by a holding that testimony compelled in a state proceeding under a state grant of immunity cannot be used in a federal case. Earlier cases had upheld the use of such testimony.[22] But now that the privilege against self-incrimination was applicable in state proceedings the Court could hold "that the constitutional privilege against self-incrimination protects a state witness against incrimination under federal as well as state law and a federal witness may not be compelled to give testimony which may be incriminating under federal law unless the compelled testimony and its fruits cannot be used in any manner by federal officials in connection with a criminal prosecution against him." A question not answered by the decision is whether the officials of one state may compel testimony incriminating under the laws of another state.

The principle that no accused person may be compelled to testify against himself in a state proceeding was reinforced in the 1965 case of *Griffin* v. *California*.[23] The Court pointed out that California could not punish a man for claiming his right to be silent by conducting a discussion about it before the jury. On the basis of *Malloy* v. *Hogan,* the Court held "that the Fifth Amendment in its direct application to the federal government and its bearing on the states by reason of the Fourteenth Amendment, forbids either comment by the prosecution on the accused's silence or instructions by the court that such silence is evidence of guilt."

[19] 211 U.S. 78 (1908).
[20] 372 U.S. 46 (1947).
[21] 378 U.S. 52 (1964).
[22] *Feldman* v. *United States,* 322 U.S. 487 (1944).
[23] 380 U.S. 609 (1965).

THE RIGHT TO COUNSEL
IN STATE PROCEEDINGS

The Sixth Amendment provides in part that "In all criminal prosecutions the accused shall enjoy the right . . . to have the assistance of counsel for his defence." For a century and a half this language was apparently taken to mean that the accused was entitled to employ and to be represented by his own counsel, but that it imposed no mandatory requirement on the courts to see that counsel was provided in all criminal trials. But in 1938, the Supreme Court, in the case of *Johnson* v. *Zerbst*,[24] held that "the Sixth Amendment withholds from federal courts, in all criminal proceedings, the power and authority to deprive an accused of his life or liberty unless he has or waives the assistance of counsel." This meant, of course, that an indigent defendant who could not afford a lawyer's fee could nevertheless demand that the court appoint counsel to represent him. In reaching this conclusion the Court reasoned that the "right to be heard would be, in many cases, of little avail if it did not comprehend the right to be heard by counsel." As indicated by the Court the right to counsel can be waived, but the waiver is not valid unless made intelligently and understandingly.

The rule here enunciated did not mean that state governments also must provide counsel for indigent defendants in all criminal cases. However, even before the Zerbst case a partial step toward this rule for state courts had been taken in the case of *Powell* v. *Alabama* [25] in 1932. This was the first of the famous Scottsboro Cases, and it involved seven ignorant and illiterate Negro boys who were charged with the rape of two white girls in an open car of a freight train moving through Alabama. Taken from the train near Scottsboro, they were placed on trial for their lives under very threatening conditions and with only the most casual and indifferent sort of legal assistance until within a few minutes after the trial began. When the case reached the Supreme

24 304 U.S. 458 (1938).
25 287 U.S. 45 (1932).

Court, after conviction of the defendants, the conviction was set aside as a denial of due process under the Fourteenth Amendment.

Rejecting the precedents of earlier cases [26] which held that certain procedural guarantees of the Bill of Rights were not essential to due process, the Court pointed out that the rule there laid down "is not without exceptions," that it "must yield to more compelling considerations whenever such considerations exist." This case presents one of those compelling considerations because "the right involved is of such a character that it cannot be denied without violating those 'fundamental principles of liberty and justice which lie at the base of all our civil and political institutions.'" This is so, the Court argued, because the right to be heard by counsel is essential to a fair hearing:

> Even the intelligent and educated layman has small and sometimes no skill in the science of law. . . . Left without the aid of counsel he may be put on trial without a proper charge, and convicted upon incompetent evidence, or evidence irrelevant to the issue or otherwise inadmissible. He lacks both the skill and knowledge adequately to prepare his defense, even though he have a perfect one. He requires the guiding hand of counsel at every stage in the proceeding against him.

It is important to note that in this case the Court (because of the youth, illiteracy, and ignorance of the defendants, the public hostility, their surveillance by military forces, and other adverse circumstances) did more than hold that "the failure of the trial court to give them reasonable time and opportunity to secure counsel was a clear denial of due process." The Court went further to hold that if these defendants were unable to employ counsel, even though the opportunity were offered them, the necessity of counsel in the circumstances of this case was so vital and imperative that the failure of the trial court to make an effective appointment of counsel was likewise a denial of due process."

There is broad language in the opinion which apparently led many to believe that the Court had laid down the principle that the Sixth Amendment's right to counsel was operative in all state criminal trials through the due process clause of the Fourteenth

[26] See page 17.

Amendment. Justice Cardozo's inclusion of it, along with freedom of speech, press, etc. in his list in the Palko opinion indicated that it had been "absorbed" into the due process clause of the Fourteenth Amendment. But the Court's own statement of its precise holding does not warrant this conclusion. The holding is carefully confined to the particular circumstances of the case and does not extend to other criminal prosecutions. Said the Court:

All that it is necessary now to decide, as we do decide, is that in a capital case, where the defendant is unable to employ counsel, and is incapable adequately of making his own defense because of ignorance, feeblemindedness, illiteracy, or the like, it is the duty of the court, whether requested or not, to assign counsel for him as a necessary requisite of due process of law; and that duty is not discharged by an assignment at such time or under such circumstances as to preclude the giving of effective aid in the preparation and trial of the case.

Ten years later the Court confined the Powell principle quite literally and rigidly to the particular facts of that case. In *Betts* v. *Brady* [27] the Court declared that due process required the aid of counsel only in capital cases, that is, those in which the death sentence might be imposed. In all other cases, including serious noncapital felonies, the duty to provide counsel for the defendant "depends upon the offense and a determination of the defendant's ability, in the light of his age, education, and the like, to defend himself without counsel."

Betts, who had been indicted for robbery in a Maryland state court, requested the trial judge to appoint counsel for him on the ground that he was without means to secure legal aid. The judge refused because it was not customary in that county to appoint counsel for indigent defendants except in cases of rape and murder. The Supreme Court, in affirming, concluded that the "appointment of counsel is not a fundamental right essential to a fair trial," and for this reason it refused to accept the argument that the Sixth Amendment guarantee of counsel for indigent federal defendants was "made obligatory upon the states by the Fourteenth Amendment." The rule to be applied in state cases was rather the "particular circumstances" rule which determined the

[27] 316 U.S. 455 (1942).

need for counsel on the basis of whether essential fairness had been denied in the case.

All this was overturned in the significant Gideon case [28] of 1963, whereby the Court unanimously overruled the Betts case and absorbed the Sixth Amendment right to counsel into the due process clause of the Fourteenth Amendment.

Charged in a Florida court with a noncapital felony, Gideon appeared without counsel and without funds and asked the court to appoint counsel for him. This was denied on the ground that the state law permitted appointment of counsel for indigent defendants in capital cases only. Denied habeas corpus after his conviction by the state supreme court, he petitioned the Supreme Court of the United States for review. In reversing the conviction, Justice Black, for the Court, thought the Betts court was wrong in its conclusion that "the appointment of counsel is not a fundamental right essential to a fair trial," and therefore operative on the states through the Fourteenth Amendment. He charged that the Betts court failed to follow the "ample precedents" in support of this principle; and he made the dubious declaration that "This same principle was recognized, explained, and applied in *Powell* v. *Alabama*. . . ." In this connection the Justice invoked the dicta of the Powell case and attempted to explain away the language quoted above in elucidation of the Court's precise holding.

Justice Clark, in a concurring opinion, made the pertinent point that the Court in Gideon is simply erasing an illogical distinction made in Betts. The Fourteenth Amendment, he asserted, requires due process for the deprivation of "liberty" and "life" alike, and there can be no constitutional "difference in the quality of the process based merely upon a supposed difference in the sanction involved."

Justice Harlan, also concurring, differed with the Court's analysis of the Powell case and rejected the doctrine of incorporation, insisting that due process simply requires the essentiality of a fair trial.

Two cases decided in 1964 extended the right established in Gideon to pretrial police investigations, and went a long way toward the effectuation of the dictum of *Powell* v. *Alabama* that

[28] *Gideon* v. *Wainwright*, 372 U.S. 335 (1963).

the accused "requires the guiding hand of counsel at every step in the proceedings against him." *Massiah* v. *United States* [29] related the requirement of counsel to the use of confessions in evidence and established the right of counsel at post-indictment interrogations. The Court held here that incriminating statements were not admissible in a federal court against an indicted defendant unless his lawyer had been present at the interrogation. It was proper for the federal officers to question the defendant under such circumstances, but the Court held "that the petitioner was denied the basic protections of the guarantee [Sixth Amendment right to counsel] when there was used against him at his trial evidence of his own incriminating words, which federal agents had deliberately elicited from him after he had been indicted and in the absence of counsel."

But does a man simply taken into custody, although not formally indicted, have the right to the presence of counsel during his interrogation by the police? The Escobedo case [30] gave an affirmative answer to this question. Escobedo was convicted of murder partly on the basis of a statement made in a pre-indictment police interrogation. He had retained counsel and repeatedly requested that he be permitted to consult with him during the interrogation, but this request was denied. Nor was he advised of his constitutional right to remain silent and to have counsel.

The Court held in a five to four decision that refusal by police to honor the defendant's request to consult with his attorney during the course of the interrogation constituted a denial of the "assistance of counsel" in violation of the Sixth Amendment made operative upon the states by the Fourteenth. The fact that the interrogation here was conducted before indictment made no difference. In the circumstances of the case, "no meaningful distinction can be drawn between interrogation of an accused before and after formal indictment." In fact, Escobedo had become the accused when the police started interrogating him in the absence of counsel. Apparently, then, the right to counsel begins as soon as the investigation ceases to be general and focuses on a particular suspect with a view to eliciting a confession.

[29] 377 U.S. 201 (1964).
[30] *Escobedo* v. *Illinois*, 378 U.S. 478 (1964).

Despite Justice Goldberg's emphatic confinement of the holding to the particular circumstances of the case and his pointing to the denial of Escobedo's request for his attorney as the vital point in the proceeding, the broad language of the opinion coupled with earlier and later rulings suggest that the case may have more far-reaching implications than indicated by the apparently narrow holding. Especially significant may be the Court's refusal to review a California decision that went considerably beyond the Escobedo rule.

In the Dorado case [31] the California court held that no valid confession could be taken unless the suspect had first been informed of his right to counsel and to remain silent. Unlike Escobedo the accused here had neither retained nor requested counsel, but the state court held that this did not justify the application of a rule of law different from that established in Escobedo. "The basic reasoning of Escobedo will not permit such a formalistic distinction." The right to counsel begins when police activities are no longer "purely investigatory but designed to elicit information from the suspect; the right does not originate in the accused assertion of it . . . Escobedo did not treat the request for counsel as the reason for the establishment of the right; it points out that the right had previously crystallized in the accusatory stage." To impose the requirement of a "request would discriminate against the defendant who does not know his rights."

The position of the California court was supported by the Supreme Court of the United States in *Miranda* v. *Arizona*, decided on June 13, 1966. Under this decision the immunity clause of the Fifth Amendment reaches into the police station house and requires that one suspected or accused of crime be adequately and effectively apprised of his rights of silence and of counsel; and that the exercise of those rights be fully honored. Such a warning must be in clear and unequivocal terms, and any waiver of these rights by the accused must be clear and intelligent. This means that in order fully to apprise an interrogated person of his rights, "it is necessary to warn him not only that he has the right to consult with an attorney, but also that if he is indigent a lawyer will

[31] *People* v. *Dorado*, 42 Cal. 169, 398 P. 2d. 36 (1965), cert. denied, 381 U.S. 937 (1965).

be appointed to represent him." The financial ability of the individual bears no relationship to the scope of these rights. (34 U.S.L.W. 4530–4532)

In view of these decisions, it was no surprise that on April 5, 1965, the Court declared, in *Pointer* v. *Texas*: [32] "We hold today that the Sixth Amendment's right of an accused to confront the witnesses against him is likewise a fundamental right and is made obligatory on the states by the Fourteenth Amendment"; and, of course, "It cannot be doubted at this late date that the right of cross-examination is included" in this right.

The chief witness against Pointer had made certain statements at a pretrial hearing at which Pointer, not being represented by counsel, could not effectively question him. A transcript of the statement of the witness, who after the hearing had left the state, was later admitted as evidence at the trial. A claim was made that the absence of counsel at the preliminary hearing violated the Fourteenth Amendment, but the case was decided solely on the confrontation issue.

Justices Harlan and Stewart concurred in the decision of the Court, but objected vigorously to the "selective incorporation" of the Bill of Rights into the Fourteenth Amendment. They would have left the Sixth Amendment entirely out of consideration and rested the reversal on the simple ground that the conviction deprived the defendant of liberty without due process of law under the Fourteenth Amendment. Justice Harlan thought the judgment "must be reversed because a right of confrontation is 'implicit in the concept of ordered liberty' . . . reflected in the due process clause of the Fourteenth Amendment independently of the Sixth."

CRUEL AND UNUSUAL PUNISHMENT

The Court came close to incorporating the Eighth Amendment prohibition against cruel and unusual punishment into the due

[32] 380 U.S. 400 (1965).

process clause of the Fourteenth Amendment in the famous electric chair case [33] of 1947. The petitioner in this case was placed in the electric chair and the switch was thrown, but because of some mechanical flaw, the current was not sufficient to cause death. He contended that the ordeal of a second preparation for execution would subject him to cruel and unusual punishment. The five-member majority of the Court assumed that the Eighth Amendment's prohibition against cruel and unusual punishment was binding on the states through the Fourteenth Amendment, but insisted that "the cruelty against which the Constitution protects . . . is cruelty inherent in the method of punishment," not "an unforeseeable accident."

In 1962 the Court struck down a California statute making it a misdemeanor for a person to "be addicted to the use of narcotics," and imposing a mandatory jail term of not less than ninety days. The trial court had interpreted the law as making it a crime either to use *or* to be addicted to narcotics. The Supreme Court held "that a state law which imprisons a person thus afflicted as a criminal, even though he has never touched any narcotic drug within the state or been guilty of any irregular behavior there, inflicts a cruel and unusual punishment in violation of the Fourteenth Amendment." [34] This, the Court argued, was no different from a statute making it a criminal offense for a person to be "mentally ill, or a leper, or to be afflicted with a venereal disease."

There was actually no mention of the incorporation doctrine in this opinion, but it would seem to be implicit, for it is difficult to see how this case can be distinguished from the foregoing cases on this point.

SUMMARY ANALYSIS

Since 1961 the Supreme Court has extended to state criminal proceedings five important guarantees provided by the Bill of Rights

[33] *Louisiana* ex rel. *Francis* v. *Resweber,* 329 U.S. 459 (1947).
[34] *Robinson* v. *California,* 370 U.S. 660 (1962).

to defendants in federal courts. In these cases the Court not only enunciated and applied new doctrine, but frequently overruled precedent in order to achieve the result.

As pointed out above, the Mapp case overruled *Wolf* v. *Colorado* and held that in a state criminal trial evidence secured in violation of the Fourth Amendment must be excluded. In the Gideon case, the Court overruled *Betts* v. *Brady* and held that counsel must be supplied, if requested, in state criminal proceedings, and not merely when special circumstances require such appointment, as in the Powell case. The right established in Gideon was later extended to pretrial police interrogations whether conducted before or after indictment. In Escobedo it was also held that where one has not been effectively warned of his right to remain silent in a pre-indictment police interrogation, he is entitled to counsel to enforce that right if he has retained and requested counsel.

Twining v. *New Jersey* and *Adamson* v. *California* were overruled by *Malloy* v. *Hogan,* which held that the privilege against self-incrimination must be applied in state proceedings in the same manner as in federal proceedings. In a second case, decided on the same day, the Court overruled *Feldman* v. *United States* in holding that testimony given in a state case under a grant of immunity may not be used in a federal proceeding.

In the spring of 1965, the Pointer Case, in extending the right of confrontation and cross-examination to state proceedings, overruled *West* v. *State of Louisiana* [35] and similar cases to the contrary.

Of course, these cases left many important questions unanswered. Perhaps the most important of these questions was whether the rulings apply retroactively. In *Linkletter* v. *Walker*,[36] decided in the spring of 1965, the Court ruled that the Mapp decision barring the use of illegally seized evidence in state criminal trials does not apply to prisoners whose convictions were made final prior to the decision. Justice Clark declared, for the Court, that the purpose of the Mapp decision would not now "be served by the wholesale release of the guilty victims. . . . To make the

[35] 194 U.S. 258.
[36] 381 U.S. 618 (1965).

rule of Mapp retrospective . . . would seriously disrupt the administration of justice."

In the case of *Johnson* v. *New Jersey*, decided on June 20, 1966, the Court also held that the Escobedo and Miranda cases affect only those cases in which the trial began after the dates on which these cases were decided (34 LW 4592–4595). But the Court pointed out that "while Escobedo and Miranda provide important new safeguards against the use of unreliable statements at trial, the non-retroactivity of these decisions will not preclude persons whose trials have already been completed from invoking the same safeguards as part of an involuntariness claim." On more pragmatic grounds the Court was again not mindful of the fact that "retroactive application of Escobedo and Miranda would seriously disrupt the administration of our criminal laws."

Theory of the New Procedural Cases

Before the cases of the early sixties when a state criminal proceeding was challenged as a deprivation of liberty without due process of law, the Court generally disposed of the question on the basis of a free wheeling "fair trial" rule under which the facts in each case were judged by a vague, undefined standard of fairness. The new theory of the Court majority is that the foregoing procedural guarantees of the Bill of Rights are of such a "fundamental" character that they are carried into state criminal cases by the Fourteenth Amendment; and they are applied accordingly to a single federal standard. It is this last point that Justices Harlan and Stewart find so objectionable. In the former's concurring opinion in the "confrontation" Pointer case he preferred the "fair trial" approach because it recognizes that the "Constitution tolerates, indeed encourages, differences between the methods used to effectuate legitimate federal and state concerns, subject to the requirements of fundamental fairness."

Justice Black rejects both of these approaches, contending instead that the Fourteenth Amendment was designed to apply the entire Bill of Rights to the states. Justices Harlan and Stewart have denounced both selective absorption and the Black full

incorporation theory on the ground that by applying these procedures to states in terms broader than necessary to decide the case
before it, the Court does violence to our federal system. In
Pointer v. *Texas* Justice Harlan declared: "The incorporation
doctrine, whether full blown or selective, are both historically and
constitutionally unsound and incompatible with the maintenance
of our federal system on even course."

Yet in the Pointer case he cited in support of his position that
the state judgment denying right of confrontation should be reversed, a passage from the Palko opinion which is generally regarded as the basis of selective absorption "For me this state
judgment must be reversed because a right of confrontation is
'implicit in the concept of ordered liberty' . . . reflected in the
Due Process Clause of the Fourteenth Amendment independently
of the Sixth."

Although there are differences among the justices as to the
theory by which the Fourteenth Amendment protects the procedural rights of individuals charged with, or suspected of, criminal
conduct, there is a general area of agreement in the cases that certain basic procedural rights are so fundamental to a free society
that they may not be denied the individual by either the state or
federal government under the Constitution.

The theory of selective absorption applied in the new procedural cases does not seem essentially different from the selective
absorption theory of the Palko case, except that it represents a
change in the thinking of the Court as to what rights are so fundamental as to be "essential to a scheme of ordered liberty."

Again one wonders why the Court cannot talk itself into
agreement on the single principle that certain procedural rights
are so essential to ordered liberty as to be implicit in the concept
of liberty guaranteed against state abridgment in the Fourteenth
Amendment.

Finally it may be noted that although the Black view of full
incorporation has never enjoyed the support of a majority of the
Court, the result desired by the justice is rapidly being achieved
through the process of selective absorption.

4

COMMUNICATION
AND ASSOCIATION

FREEDOM OF SPEECH AND PRESS:
CLEAR AND PRESENT DANGER TEST

As was pointed out in chapter 2, the Supreme Court, for the first time, in 1937, in the Herndon case applied the clear and present danger test to uphold the civil liberties claims of the defendant.[1] Here, the Court was faced with the conflicting claims of the clear and present danger test and the bad tendency test which the Court had applied in the Gitlow case. The Court set aside the conviction of Herndon under a Georgia anti-insurrection law for attempting to incite insurrection. The evidence on which Herndon was convicted in the state court consisted of his admission that he had held meetings for the purpose of recruiting membership for the Communist party and certain printed matter found in a box which he carried when arrested. In upholding the conviction the Georgia courts applied the tests of evil intent of the speaker and evil tendency of his words. The Supreme Court, however, found the act as applied bad because "The legislature of Georgia has not made membership in the Communist party unlawful by reason of its supposed dangerous tendency," and

[1] *Herndon v. Lowry*, 301 U.S. 242 (1937).

judge and jury had not found that the defendant's utterances constituted "a clear and present danger of forcible obstruction of a particular state function."

Mr. Justice Roberts, speaking for the majority of five, further declared:

The power of a state to abridge freedom of speech and assembly is the exception rather than the rule, and the penalizing even of utterances of a defined character must find its justification in a reasonable apprehension of danger to organized government. The judgment of the legislature is not unfettered. The limitation upon individual liberty must have appropriate relation to the safety of the state. Legislation which goes beyond this need violates the principle of the Constitution.

Thus for the first time a majority of the Court accepted and applied the doctrine of clear and present danger and embarked upon a course which, during the following decade, led to the acceptance of a near absolutist conception of First Amendment freedoms. In these years the doctrine was amplified and applied in a variety of new and unusual situations. This is not to suggest that clear and present danger was the sole test of free speech restriction. It was merely the principal one, and the one most consistently employed for libertarian results. Nor did its employment always embody the same judgment factors. Rather, it embodied a variety of factors given greater or lesser weight according to the circumstances of each case.

Labor Picketing as Freedom of Expression

One of the most interesting examples of judicial expression of the concept of freedom of speech is the inclusion of picketing within its protection as a means of persuasion and communication in labor disputes. The first indication that the Court might regard picketing as a form of free speech protected by the Fourteenth Amendment occurred in 1937 in *Senn* v. *Tile Layers Protective Union*,[2] which sustained the constitutionality of a Wisconsin statute legalizing peaceful picketing.

Three years later, in *Thornhill* v. *Alabama*[3] and *Carlson* v.

[2] 301 U.S. 468 (1937).
[3] 310 U.S. 98 (1940).

California [4] decided on the same day, the intimation of the Senn case that picketing is a form of free speech was confirmed. Applying the doctrine of clear and present danger, the Supreme Court invalidated statutes of Alabama and California against peaceful picketing, including the carrying of signs and banners. In the Thornhill case the Court held unconstitutional an Alabama statute forbidding peaceful picketing. Freedom of speech and press guaranteed by the Constitution includes "at least the liberty to discuss publicly and truthfully all matters of public concern without previous restraint or fear of subsequent punishment." Hence the Court concluded that, "In the circumstances of our times the dissemination of information concerning the facts of a labor dispute must be regarded as within the area of free discussion that is guaranteed by the Constitution." And the right to disseminate such information may be abridged only "where the clear danger of substantive evils arises under circumstances affording no opportunity to test the merits of ideas by competition for acceptance in the market of public opinion." Here the danger to the industrial concern was neither so serious nor so imminent as to warrant the sweeping interference with freedom of discussion that the statute prescribed.

In the Carlson case the Court, speaking through Mr. Justice Murphy, held that the display of signs and banners was a natural and appropriate method of publicizing the facts of a labor controversy and that it is consequently a part of freedom of the press protected against the action of the state by the Fourteenth Amendment.

Although these cases extended the protection of the Fourteenth Amendment to peaceful picketing as a form of free speech or press, they did not purport to free it from all restraint. The following term a sharply divided Supreme Court ruled that peaceful picketing may be enjoined if the labor dispute has been attended by serious and widespread violence. In *Milk Wagon Drivers Union* v. *Meadowmoor Dairies,* [5] the Court was confronted with the application of the Thornhill rule to the more complicated situation of a milk wagon drivers' strike in Chicago.

[4] 310 U.S. 106 (1940).
[5] 312 U.S. 287 (1941).

The case involved an injunction which had been secured by the dairy to restrain the union from interfering with the distribution of its milk. The Supreme Court of the United States, in an opinion by Mr. Justice Frankfurter, sustained this injunction. He found that the past violence had "given to the picketing a coercive effect" and that "acts which in isolation are peaceful may be part of a coercive thrust when entangled with acts of violence." In such a setting, "it could justifiably be concluded that the momentum of fear generated by past violence would survive even though future picketing might be wholly peaceful."

On the same day on which the Meadowmoor case was decided, the Court held that a state might not lawfully enjoin picketing because the picketers were not parties to an immediate labor dispute.[6] Justice Frankfurter declared in support of this conclusion that "A state cannot exclude workingmen from peacefully exercising the right of free communication by drawing the circle of economic competition between employers and workers so small as to contain only an employer and those directly employed by him."

The following year, in *Carpenters and Joiners Union* v. *Ritter's Cafe*,[7] the Court seemed to retreat somewhat from the broad principle laid down in the Thornhill case. In this case the union had been enjoined, under the Texas antitrust law, from picketing Ritter's restaurant because nonunion workers were employed by a contractor who was erecting a building for Ritter in another part of the city of Houston. The Texas court held that the picketing, which was peaceful, was being unlawfully carried on at a place remote from the scene of the actual dispute. Since the picketing took place at Ritter's restaurant rather than at the place where the building was being erected, it constituted an unlawful interference with his business. Mr. Justice Frankfurter, speaking for the majority of five, upheld the Texas court, and held that the union's right of free speech was not impaired by the injunction. His words were: "The recognition of peaceful picketing as an exercise of free speech does not imply that the states must be

[6] *American Federation of Labor* v. *Swing*, 312 U.S. 321 (1941).
[7] 315 U.S. 722 (1942).

without power to confine the sphere of communication to that directly related to the dispute."

On its face, this statement seems inconsistent with the rationalization of Mr. Frankfurter in the preceding case. The line of distinction drawn by the Court seems to be this: Here "Texas has deemed it desirable to insulate from the dispute an establishment which industrially has no connection with the dispute." The state has made no effort to safeguard other building enterprises of the contractor. In the Swing case, on the other hand, the circle was drawn around the employer and his immediate employees in the same industry. Hence "the circle of economic competition" may not be drawn between an employer and his immediate employees but may be drawn between discrete industries.

In 1943, however, in *Cafeteria Employees Union* v. *Angelos*,[8] the rule of the Thornhill case was extended to enterprises that had no employees.

Although the Thornhill doctrine had been mildly curtailed in the Meadowmoor and Ritter cases, its most serious shrinkage was produced by a series of cases in which the Court elaborated the principle that a state may forbid peaceful picketing conducted in violation of valid state law. The first of these cases was that of *Giboney* v. *Empire Storage and Ice Co.*,[9] in which the Court unanimously held that the state of Missouri might enjoin peaceful picketing that was designed to force the picketed persons to violate the valid antitrade-restraint law of the state. The avowed purpose of the picketing was to compel the ice company to agree to stop selling ice to nonunion peddlers in violation of the aforementioned statute.

The union's contention that the injunction against picketing adjacent to Empire's place of business was an unwarranted abridgment of its freedom of speech in attempting peacefully to publicize truthful facts about a labor dispute elicited from Mr. Justice Black this declaration for the unanimous Court: "It rarely has been suggested that constitutional freedom for speech and press extends its immunity to speech or writing used as an integral part of conduct in violation of a valid criminal statute.

[8] 320 U.S. 293 (1943).
[9] 336 U.S. 490 (1949).

We reject the contention now." Furthermore, this rule applies even where the public policy of the state is determined by the rulings of a court rather than by the legislature.

Three cases decided in the 1949 term of the Court further limited the right to picket as an element of freedom of speech. In *Hughes* v. *Superior Court of California*,[10] the Court held that the Fourteenth Amendment does not bar a state from the use of the injunction to restrain picketing of a place of business solely in order to force compliance with a demand that its employees be apportioned according to the racial origin of its customers. The demand was contrary to the policy of the state of California against racial discrimination in employment.

In *Building Service Employees International Union* v. *Gazzam*,[11] the Supreme Court held that the state of Washington might enjoin peaceful picketing designed to compel an employer to coerce his employees into joining the picketing union, in violation of the statutorily declared policy of the state that employers shall not coerce their employees' choice of a bargaining representative. The most significant of these cases was that of *International Teamsters Union* v. *Hanke*,[12] for here the picketing union was making no unlawful demands. The Court sustained a Washington state court injunction restraining picketing of businesses operated by the owners themselves without other employees for the purpose of compelling the observance of opening and closing hours set by the union. Once more, the Court declared through Justice Frankfurter that

. . . while picketing has an ingredient of communication, it cannot dogmatically be equated with the constitutionally protected freedom of speech. . . . The effort in the cases has been to strike a balance between the constitutional protection of the element of communication in picketing and "the power of the state to set the limits of permissible contest open to industrial combatants."

It seems clear that the ingredient of speech in this combination was substantially diminished in this case. To accomplish this required a narrow and ingenious construction of some earlier

10 339 U.S. 460 (1950).
11 339 U.S. 532 (1950).
12 339 U.S. 470 (1950).

cases.[13] These cases, according to Justice Frankfurter, merely established the rule "that a state could not proscribe picketing merely by setting artificial bounds, unreal in the light of modern circumstances, to what constitutes an industrial relationship or a labor dispute." [14] Although this case did not specifically overrule the Thornhill case, it is clear that it divested it of much of its constitutional vitality.

What, then, is the present status of labor picketing as freedom of expression? First, it is still true that indiscriminate curbing of peaceful picketing, by statute or injunction, is a denial of free speech in violation of the due process clause of the Fourteenth Amendment. But labor picketing is more than speech; it is an economic weapon, and as such it is subject to extensive regulation by the state with respect to both its methods and its purposes. Thus, for example, peaceful picketing may be restrained when conducted in a context of violence or when it is designed to thwart a validly declared state policy, whether the declaration emanates from the legislature or from the courts.

It is difficult to piece together from the foregoing cases any judicial philosophy, formula, or standard which has predictive value. "The essence of the problem of the picketing cases is to draw a line between the unquestioned privilege to discuss industrial relations freely and the far more limited right to exert the economic power of an organized group of workers held together by union discipline." [15] Peaceful picketing directed primarily to the general public is one thing, but peaceful picketing for the purpose of compelling an employer to violate a valid state policy is quite another thing. To hold the latter valid would be to give speech by means of picketing a preferred position over the more traditional forms of free speech.

Finally, it should also be noted that the institution of the closed shop is not entitled to the protection of the due process clause of the Fourteenth Amendment as an incident of the right of employees to assemble and associate together in labor organiza-

[13] *Senn* v. *Tile Layers Protective Union*, 301 U.S. 468 (1937); see also notes 6 and 9.

[14] 339 U.S. 470, 479–80 (1950).

[15] Archibald Cox, "Strikes, Picketing and the Constitution," *Vanderbilt Law Review*, Vol. 4 (April, 1951), p. 599.

tions. In *Lincoln Labor Union* v. *Northwestern Iron & Metal Co.*,[16] the Court declared that "The constitutional right of workers to assembly, to discuss and formulate plans for furthering their own self-interest in jobs cannot be construed as a constitutional guarantee that none shall get and hold jobs except those who will join in the assembly or will agree to abide by the assembly's plans."

Freedom of Expression and a Fair Trial: Contempt of Court

In a series of three cases [17] decided between 1941 and 1947, the Court held that discussion of pending litigation or criticism of past decisions was punishable by contempt procedure only in the face of a clear and present danger to the fair administration of justice. In none of these cases was the danger to the obstruction of justice so serious or so imminent as to warrant the restraint of freedom of speech and press. Nevertheless, in a more recent case,[18] which involved contempt committed by an attorney in the physical presence of the court, it was held that summary conviction and punishment were no denial of due process, even though the attorney's remarks were induced by "mildly provocative language from the bench."

In a 1962 case the Court reaffirmed the position first taken in 1941. In Wood v. Georgia,[19] a county sheriff publicly rebuked three local judges for what he contended was an appeal to racial prejudice for political purposes in charging a grand jury to investigate alleged bloc delivery of Negro votes. The sheriff, who was a candidate for reelection, stated among other things that "It is shocking to find a judge charging a grand jury in the style and language of a race baiting candidate for political office." For this criticism he was cited for contempt and convicted on the ground

[16] 355 U.S. 525, 531 (1949). See also *Auto Workers* v. *Wisconsin Employment Relations Board,* 336 U.S. 245 (1949); *American Federation of Labor* v. *American Sash and Door Co.,* 335 U.S. 538 (1949).

[17] *Bridges* v. *California,* 314 U.S. 252 (1941); *Pennekamp* v. *Florida,* 378 U.S. 331 (1946); *Craig* v. *Harney,* 331 U.S. 367 (1947).

[18] *Fisher* v. *Pace,* 336 U.S. 155 (1949).

[19] 370 U.S. 375 (1962).

that his remarks constituted "a clear and present danger to the administration of justice." The Supreme Court agreed with the sheriff that in the circumstances of the case there was no clear and present danger since he was a candidate for reelection and thought that the outcome would be influenced by the language of the judges in their charge to the grand jury. In reversing, the Court held that no showing of clear and present danger had been made.

In three of the preceding cases the Court was sharply divided, but despite this diversity among the justices, the general right of the press and of individuals to comment on and criticize pending judicial proceedings, as well as past judicial acts, seems well established. In determining whether a publication seriously threatens the administration of justice, consideration is given the supposition that the judge is a man "of reasonable fortitude" and is possessed of "a serenity that keeps him above the battle and the crowd."

Generally speaking, the position of the Court that wider judicial latitude should be permitted in the case of contempt committed in the immediate physical presence of the court would seem to be sensible. Contempt committed in the face of the judge presents a clearer and more imminent danger to the calm and unprejudiced administration of justice than does printed criticism from a point outside the courtroom.

Since all these cases involved state courts, it should be noted that the power of the federal courts to punish for contempt is limited by congressional statutes to misconduct in the presence of the courts, "or so near thereto as to obstruct the administration of justice," and the latest holding of the Supreme Court is that the word "near" indicates proximity in space and not a causal relationship.[20]

The conflict of interests presented in such cases as these confronts the Court with a dilemma, for there is involved a conflict not merely between public authority and private right but also between two important individual rights—the right to freedom of expression and the right to a fair and impartial trial by a court unimpeded by external pressure. In resolving the dilemma, the Court gave priority to freedom of expression because "the liberties

[20] Nye v. United States, 313 U.S. 33 (1941).

of the First Amendment . . . are too highly prized to be subjected to the hazards of summary contempt procedure."

The conflict between freedom of expression and a fair trial was presented in a different and more dramatic form in the case of *Billie Sol Estes* v. *Texas*.[21] Estes was convicted of swindling in a trial which was preceded by a two-day pretrial hearing which was carried to the public by radio and television. Ironically, the pretrial hearing was held to consider Estes' motion to prohibit television and radio broadcasting at the trial and to request that it be postponed.

At these hearings the courtroom was jammed with reporters, photographers, and television cameramen. The room was so crowded that at least thirty people were said to be standing in the aisles. Cables and wires were snaked across the floor and three microphones were on the judge's bench. Others were beamed at the jury box and the counsel table. The hearings were broadcast and televised live, and portions of the television tape were later shown on the regularly scheduled evening news programs. Four persons later selected as jurors in the trial proper had seen or heard at least part of the telecasts and broadcasts of the pretrial hearings, and some of the prosecution witnesses were in the courtroom during these hearings.

It is not surprising that the Court was sharply divided in this case. Five members agreed to reverse the conviction, but only four of them were willing to impose a blanket ban on the televising of state trials. Justice Harlan voted to reverse but preferred to put the case in a class by itself.

Justice Clark, in the opinion of "the Court," declared that the defendant had been deprived of his right under the Fourteenth Amendment to due process of law by the televising of his notorious, heavily publicized, and highly sensational criminal trial. In answer to the contention that the pretrial hearing could not be considered in determining the question before the Court, Justice Clark replied that "it may be more harmful than publicity during the trial for it may well set the community opinion as to guilt or innocence." He argued that such publicity could have a prej-

21 381 U.S. 532 (1965).

udicial effect on the jurors, the witnesses, the trial judge, and the defendant.

The dissenting justices conceded that if the scene at the pretrial hearing had been repeated before the jury in a courtroom, a fair trial could hardly have been afforded the defendant. But they did not consider the constitutional principle applicable to the earlier stage of the case because it was not a part of the trial before the jury.

The controlling vote, as previously indicated, was cast by Justice Harlan, who said that the Court's concern in this case was "only with a criminal trial of great notoriety, and not with criminal proceedings of a more or less routine nature." The essence of his reasoning is set forth in this passage:

The Estes trial was a heavily publicized and highly sensational affair. I therefore put aside all other types of cases. . . . The resolution of those further questions should await an appropriate case; the Court should proceed only step by step in this unplowed field. The opinion of the Court necessarily goes no farther, for only the four members of the majority who unreservedly join the Court's opinion would resolve those questions now.

Thus the major issue of whether the Constitution prohibits television in all criminal trials is still an open question. What does seem to be clear from the case, however, is that the Court will not permit television and radio to distort the judicial process into a form of sensational entertainment.

Freedom of Speech in Public Parks and Streets

The expansion of the area of judicial protection of civil liberties since the early 1930's has been especially notable with respect to the protection afforded those who wish to use the public parks and streets as forums for public discussion and the dissemination of propaganda. The extent of this development is strikingly illustrated by two Supreme Court cases separated by a period of 42 years. In the first case, decided in 1897, the Court unanimously sustained an ordinance of the city of Boston providing that "no person shall, in or upon any of the public grounds, make any public address . . . except in accordance with a permit of the mayor." Here, the Court took the position that for the legislature to forbid public speaking in a public park or highway was no more a violation of the rights of a member of the public than would be the refusal of the owner of a private house to permit it in his house.[22] In 1939 the Court held void on its face an ordinance of Jersey City, New Jersey, because it allowed the director of safety to refuse permits for public meetings on the basis of his opinion that such refusal would prevent riots, disorderly assemblages, or other disturbances.[23]

DISTRIBUTION OF "LITERATURE." In an interesting series of cases beginning in 1938, the right under the due process clause of the Fourteenth Amendment to distribute books, pamphlets, or leaflets on city streets and other public places without prior official permission or payment of a license tax was sustained as the proper exercise of freedom of the press. Parenthetically, it should be stated here that most of these cases also involve questions of religious freedom, and will receive further consideration later.

The first of the handbill cases was that of Lovell v. Griffin,[24] in which the Court invalidated a municipal ordinance of the city of Griffin, Georgia, which forbade the distribution of all "literature," in whatever form and whether sold or given away, without the written permission of the city manager. Lovell had been convicted, fined, and jailed for the distribution of religious tracts in violation of the ordinance. On appeal, the Supreme Court, through Chief Justice Hughes, held the ordinance invalid on its face, since "it strikes at the very foundation of the freedom of the press by subjecting it to license and censorship." Furthermore, the liberty of the press is not confined to newspapers and periodicals but embraces also pamphlets and leaflets. These, indeed, have been the historic weapons wielded in defense of liberty, as the pamphlets of Thomas Paine and others in our own fight for freedom abundantly attest. In its historical connotation, the press includes every form of publication which affords a medium of information and opinion. Moreover, freedom of the press extends to distribu-

22 *Davis* v. *Massachusetts*, 167 U.S. 43 (1897).
23 *Hague* v. *C.I.O.*, 307 U.S. 496 (1939).
24 303 U.S. 444 (1938).

tion of printed matter by persons other than the authors. Without freedom of circulation, publication would be of little value.

In subsequent cases the constitutional protection afforded the distribution of printed matter in streets and other public places was reaffirmed and extended to other situations. In *Schneider* v. *Irvington* [25] four cases involving the validity of municipal ordinances in four cities in as many states were merged. All the ordinances forbade the distribution of handbills in the streets or other public places; the Irvington ordinance went further and provided that "no one without a permit from the chief of police shall canvass, solicit, distribute circulars, or other matter, or call from house to house." Here was presented for the determination of the Court a sharp conflict between the traditional police power of the states to regulate in order to maintain the cleanliness, convenience, and good order of city streets and the fundamental right of freedom of the press. The ordinances were defended as reasonable police regulations to prevent littering of the streets and to protect the residents from the annoyance and danger of unrequested canvassing. With Mr. Justice McReynolds alone dissenting, the Court held all the ordinances void, as abridging freedom of speech and press guaranteed against the states by the Fourteenth Amendment. Said Justice Roberts for the Court: "Although a municipality may enact regulations in the interest of public safety, health, welfare or convenience, these may not abridge the individual liberties secured by the Constitution to those who wish to speak, write, print or circulate information or opinion." Certainly, cities have a duty to keep their streets clean and free from obstruction, but to accomplish this end they may not forbid a person rightfully on the street from handing "literature" to one willing to receive it. In some of these cases, recipients had thrown the leaflets on the sidewalk and the street with resultant littering of the street. Such offenders can undoubtedly be punished in the interest of preserving cleanliness and order in the streets, but this end may not be achieved by abridgment of those "fundamental rights and liberties," the "exercise of which lies at the foundation of free government by free men."

The Irvington, New Jersey, ordinance restricting house-to-house canvassing, which was not limited to commercial canvassing,

[25] 308 U.S. 147 (1939).

was violated by a person distributing religious tracts and was held by the Supreme Court to impose a prior censorship on the distribution of literature and the communication of opinion. This censorship, being subject to imposition at the discretion of police officials, makes the ordinance permitting it a violation of both free speech and free press. In *Martin* v. *Struthers* [26] in 1943, the same constitutional protection was successfully invoked against an ordinance making it unlawful for a distributor of handbills, circulars, or other advertising matter to ring door bells or knock on doors in order to summon the occupant to the door for the purpose of receiving such matter.

The Court pointed out that the dangers and abuses of this method of distribution can be easily "controlled by traditional legal methods," such as a regulation making it unlawful to ring the door bell of any householder who has appropriately warned that he is not to be disturbed. Thus, in *Breard* v. *Alexandria* [27] the Court sustained an ordinance forbidding door-to-door solicitation without the prior consent of the owners of the residences. Here constitutionality of the regulation depended "upon a balancing of the conveniences between some householders' desire for privacy and the publisher's right to distribute publications in the precise way that those soliciting for him think brings the best results."

This case was distinguished from the Struthers case on the ground that no commercial element was involved in the latter. The ordinance here covered only commercial advertising. It had previously been held that the right to distribute information or propagandist literature upon the public streets does not extend to commercial advertising. This is true even where commercial handbills carry a "public protest," which taken alone would be insurance from the restriction.[28]

The foregoing principle was extended even to the right to distribute religious literature in a company-owned town [29] or within a federal housing development without permission of the owners.[30]

[26] 319 U.S. 141 (1943).
[27] 341 U.S. 622 (1951).
[28] *Valentine* v. *Christensen*, 316 U.S. 52 (1942).
[29] *Marsh* v. *Alabama*, 326 U.S. 501 (1946).
[30] *Tucker* v. *Texas*, 326 U.S. 517 (1946).

In two other cases, the Supreme Court, reversing a previous decision,[31] held invalid municipal license taxes imposed on those who sell or distribute religious literature on the streets or from house to house [32] as previous restraint on freedom of the press and the free exercise of religion. Although such a tax may be imposed upon peddlers of nonreligious publications or other goods, religious activity may not be taxed at all. It enjoys a "preferred position" of complete immunity. This rule applies even to a person who makes his living entirely from the sale of religious books.[33]

SOUND TRUCKS. The two well-known sound truck cases show that technological progress can have a far-reaching and confusing effect upon the constitutional right of the individual to freedom of expression, as well as upon the power of government to regulate commerce and industry. The question presented here was whether the freedom of expression long afforded the natural voice applied to speech amplified by an electronic apparatus.

In the first of these cases a city ordinance of Lockport, New York, forbidding the use of sound amplification devices in public places, except with the permission of the chief of police, and prescribing no standards for the exercise of his discretion, was held unconstitutional on its face, since it established a previous restraint on the right of free speech in violation of the First Amendment made applicable to the states through the Fourteenth Amendment.[34] As indicated, the chief objection noted by the five-man majority was the absence of any standards defining the discretion of the chief of police. Furthermore, free speech protection extends to loudspeakers, declared Mr. Justice Douglas, because they "are today indispensable instruments of effective public speech. The sound truck has become an accepted method of political campaigning. It is the way people are reached."

[31] *Jones* v. *Opelika*, 316 U.S. 584 (1942).
[32] *Murdock* v. *Pennsylvania*, 319 U.S. 105 (1943).
[33] *Follett* v. *McCormick*, 321 U.S. 573 (1944); see also later cases in which the Court condemned licensing systems to control speech: *Kunz* v. *New York*, 340 U.S. 290, and *Niemotko* v. *Maryland*, 340 U.S. 268 (1951).
[34] *Saia* v. *New York*, 334 U.S. 558, 562 (1948).

Finally, Justice Douglas pointed out that, although courts in passing on the constitutionality of local regulations of the kind involved here must balance the various community interests, they should in that process "be mindful to keep the freedoms of the First Amendment in a preferred position."

Eight months after this decision another majority of five, comprising the former dissenters and Chief Justice Vinson, upheld the provision of a Trenton, New Jersey, ordinance making it unlawful for anyone to operate, for any purpose on the public streets, sound trucks or any amplifying device attached to a vehicle "emitting loud and raucous noises." [35] This ordinance, written in awkward and ambiguous language, is on its face more stringent than the Lockport ordinance, for it appears to be, in effect, a complete prohibition of electronic apparatus. Indeed, it was so interpreted by the state courts.[36] Nevertheless, the new Court majority held it to be a permissible exercise of legislative discretion to bar sound trucks with broadcasts of public interest, amplified to a loud and raucous volume, from the public ways of a municipality.

The judgment of the Court was announced by Justice Reed in an opinion which had the support of only the Chief Justice and Justice Burton. In the view of these three, the words "loud" and "raucous" were not so vague as to deny due process of law. The case was distinguished from Saia on the dubious mechanical basis that the Trenton ordinance, unlike the Lockport ordinance, did not vest uncontrolled discretion in the chief of police. The justice failed to point out that the Lockport ordinance at least insured the discussion of certain matters through loudspeakers, subject to permission by the chief of police. Justice Reed, however, insisted that the Trenton ordinance did not abridge the right guaranteed to every citizen to reach the mind of willing listeners and that "unrestrained use throughout a municipality of all sound amplification devices would be intolerable." Thus, he would seem to rest the decision upon the "loud and raucous" test, but this was not accepted by a majority of the justices. It is not clear, then,

---

[35] *Kovacs* v. *Cooper*, 336 U.S. 77 (1949).

[36] See C. H. Pritchett, *Civil Liberties and the Vinson Court* (Chicago, University of Chicago Press, 1954), p. 45.

whether sound trucks not emitting loud and raucous noises may be barred from the parks and streets.

Justices Jackson and Frankfurter, concurring, did not accept the loud and raucous test and apparently construed the ordinance to ban all sound trucks. Jackson agreed with Justice Black, who dissented, that the Saia decision struck down a more moderate exercise of the state's police power than the one here sustained and that this decision repudiates Saia. However, he thought that sound amplifying devices could be constitutionally regulated to any extent short of censorship of the contents of the broadcast. Justice Frankfurter thought that the terms on which sound trucks may be permitted to operate, if at all, should be left to the legislative judgment, so long as the legislature does not prescribe the ideas that may be noisily expressed or not expressed, nor discriminate among those who would thus disturb the public peace.

The sharp diversity of opinion among the justices of the Court in these two sound truck cases leaves the constitutional status of this new medium of communication unsettled and confused. As C. H. Pritchett aptly observes, "Justice Reed achieved the dubious distinction in the Kovacs case of writing an opinion for the Court to which five Justices objected, and of upholding a conviction on a different interpretation of local law from that of the state courts." [37]

At best only tentative conclusions can be drawn from these decisions. It is apparent that in general the use of sound amplifying devices is entitled to the protection of freedom of expression guaranteed by the Fourteenth Amendment, but volume of sound, time of broadcasting, and other conditions may be regulated by "narrowly drawn ordinances." An ordinance vesting arbitrary licensing power in a municipal official is clearly unconstitutional. But other cases will have to be decided before it is possible to say precisely how free speech doctrine applies to sound trucks.

Right of Privacy in Public Places

Although it is constitutional for a municipal ordinance to forbid "loud and raucous noises" from a sound truck on public streets,

[37] *Ibid.*, p. 46.

on the theory that "such distractions would be dangerous to traffic" and disturbing of the "quiet and tranquility so desirable for city-dwellers," there is no constitutional objection to the converse procedure of a street railway company amplifying radio programs through loud speakers in its passenger cars. The Public Utilities Commission of the District of Columbia, after an investigation and public hearings, issued an order permitting the Capital Transit Company, over the protest of some of its patrons, to receive and amplify radio programs consisting generally of ninety percent music, five percent announcements, and five percent commercial advertising. The Court held that neither the operation of the radio service nor the action of the commission permitting its operation is precluded by the federal Constitution.[38] In this connection Justice Burton emphasized the fact that an overwhelming majority of the passengers had approved of the programs.

Justice Douglas dissented on the ground that the practice of forcing people to listen to a radio program violated the due process right to privacy, which is, he asserted, "the beginning of all freedom."

Justice Reed had declared in the Kovacs case that "The right of free speech is guaranteed every citizen that he may reach the minds of willing listeners." But this apparently does not apply to those on the receiving end in a public place. In short, there is no right of privacy in a public place.

Motion Pictures and Freedom of Communication: Censorship

In 1952, the Supreme Court finally came to grips with the issue of motion picture censorship, which had long since become widely established. In 1915, the Court had held that a state law providing for the censorship of motion pictures was valid, on the theory that the showing of motion pictures is "a business pure and simple, originated and conducted for profit," and "not to be regarded as a

[38] *Public Utilities Commission of the District of Columbia* v. *Pollak,* 343 U.S. 451 (1952).

part of the press of the country or as organs of public opinion." [39]
This was long before the Court had become greatly concerned
with civil liberties issues, and in 1948 the Court said by way of
a dictum in a case involving another issue: "We have no doubt
that motion pictures, like newspapers and radio, are included in
the press whose freedom is guaranteed by the First Amendment." [40]

This dictum became the basis of the Court's ruling against
motion picture censorship in the so-called "Miracle case" in
1952.[41] In this case, provisions of the New York Education Law
which forbid the showing of any motion picture film without a
license, and authorize denial of a license on a censor's conclusion
that a film is "sacrilegious," were held invalid as a prior restraint
on freedom of speech and press under the Fourteenth Amendment. "It cannot be doubted," wrote Justice Clark for the unanimous Court, "that motion pictures are a significant medium for
the communication of ideas" in many different ways, and their
importance "is not lessened by the fact that they are designed
to entertain as well as to inform." Nor does it matter, contrary to
the position of the Court in Mutual Film Corporation, that the
motion picture enterprise is a large-scale business conducted for
private profit. The fact that books, and magazines are published
and sold for profit does not prevent them from being a form of
expression safeguarded by the First Amendment. The Court sees
no reason why operation for profit should alter the circumstances
for motion pictures. It apparently had had a different effect in
some of the handbill cases previously discussed.[42]

One week later, a Texas decision sustaining an ordinance of
the city of Marshall, which authorized a board of censors "to deny
a license for the showing of any motion picture which in its
opinion is of such a character as to be prejudicial to the best interest of the people" of the city, was reversed *per curiam* without
opinion on the authority of the Burstyn case and *Winters* v.

[39] *Mutual Film Corporation* v. *Industrial Commission*, 237 U.S. 230, 244
(1915).
[40] *United States* v. *Paramount Pictures, Inc.*, 334 U.S. 131, 166 (1948).
[41] *Joseph Burstyn* v. *Wilson*, 343 U.S. 495 (1952).
[42] *Valentine* v. *Christensen*, 316 U.S. 52, and *Breard* v. *Alexandria*, 341
U.S. 622.

New York, a decision in which a New York criminal statute had been invalidated on the ground of vagueness. Justice Frankfurter in a brief statement seemed to concur solely on the score of indefiniteness, but Justice Douglas in a concurring statement completely ignored the vagueness issue and saw prior restraint present in "a flagrant form" as the basis of invalidity. "If a board of censors can tell the American people what it is in their best interest to see or to read or to hear, then thought is regimented, authority substituted for liberty, and the great purpose of the First Amendment to keep uncontrolled the freedom of expression defeated." [43]

Early in 1954, in a *per curiam* opinion [44] the Court reversed judgments of the Court of Appeals of New York and the Supreme Court of Ohio, sustaining, respectively, a New York statute prohibiting the public showing of motion pictures "which were immoral" or which would "tend to corrupt morals," and an Ohio statute prohibiting the public exhibition of motion pictures which were not of a "moral, educational or amusing and harmless character." The New York case involved the refusal of a license for the showing of a motion picture entitled *La Ronde,* and the Ohio case, the denial of a license for a film called *M.* In its unanimous reversal, the Supreme Court of the United States merely cited the Burstyn case as authority. Thus the question of the standards of permissible censorship of motion pictures remained unresolved. Indeed, in the light of these opinions it would seem to be uncertain whether a majority of the Court found motion picture censorship invalid as a matter of principle or merely where standards of guilt are too vague.

In a case decided in 1959, the Court made somewhat clearer the basis of its decision, but still refused to say whether or not state censorship of motion pictures was valid. A provision of New York's education law forbids the licensing of motion pictures "which are immoral in that they portray acts of sexual immorality . . . as desirable, acceptable or proper patterns of behavior." The state had forbidden the showing of *Lady Chatterley's Lover* on the ground that such a showing violated the law in that adultery

---

[43] *Gelling v. Texas,* 343 U.S. 960, 961 (1952).
[44] *Superior Films, Inc. v. Dept. of Education,* 346 U.S. 587 (1954).

was "presented as being right and desirable for certain people under certain circumstances." It was on this ground alone that the Court of Appeals of New York sustained the denial of a license for the showing of the film.

In *Kingsley Corp.* v. *Regents of the University of New York* [45] the Supreme Court held the law as interpreted by the state court to be a clear violation of freedom of the press. Since the Court of Appeals of New York had rejected the notion that the film was obscene and there was no suggestion that it would itself operate as an incitement to illegal action, the Court found that: "What New York has done, therefore, is to prevent the exhibition of a motion picture because that picture advocates an idea—that adultery under certain circumstances may be proper behavior. Yet the First Amendment's basic guarantee is of freedom to advocate ideas. The State, quite simply, has thus struck at the very heart of constitutionally protected liberty."

Moreover, the censorship of the film cannot be defended on the ground that it portrays adultery as attractive. "This argument misconceives what it is that the Constitution protects. Its guarantee is not confined to the expression of ideas that are conventional or shared by a majority. It protects advocacy of the opinion that adultery may sometimes be proper, no less than advocacy of socialism or the single tax. And in the realm of ideas it protects expression which is eloquent no less than that which in unconvincing."

Although in none of the cases from Burstyn on had the Court sustained a program of censorship, it did assume in *Times Film Corp.* v. *City of Chicago* [46] in 1961, that a constitutionally valid film censorship law could be formulated. Chicago requires that films must be submitted before showing to the police commissioner, who is free to grant or withold a permit subject only to review by the mayor. The Times Film Corporation had refused flatly to submit the film *Don Juan*, contending that the requirement of review was administrative prior restraint and void on its face. The apparent object of the corporation was to force the Court to rule on the constitutionality of movie censorship as such.

[45] 360 U.S. 684 (1959).
[46] 365 U.S. 43 (1961).

The Court, however, refused to view the case in this light, but saw the case as presenting the question of whether an exhibitor has "complete and absolute freedom to exhibit at least once any and every kind of motion picture regardless of how obscene or offensive it may be." Thus the Court refused to rule that film censorship was necessarily unconstitutional. As seen by Chief Justice Warren, the Court had upheld "the principle of administrative censorship which is prior restraint in its purest and most far-reaching form."

Apparently the implications of this case were not so far-reaching as the Chief Justice had feared, for in *Freedman* v. *State of Maryland*.[47] Mr. Justice Brennan explained for a unanimous Court that Times Film Corporation had done no more than reject an absolute right against all prior restraint on the exhibition of motion pictures.

Although the Freedman case dealt only with the procedural adequacy of Maryland's system of censorship, the procedural standards set forth by the Court as necessary to avoid running afoul of the First Amendment would seem sufficiently onerous to discourage all censorship of motion pictures.

Stated briefly, the Court struck down the Maryland censorship statute because it did not sufficiently assure exhibitors a prompt judicial resolution of First Amendment claims. Freedman had exhibited the film, *Revenge at Daybreak,* without first submitting it to the state board of censors as required by law. He was convicted in the state court, and on his appeal to the Supreme Court he focused his charge of unconstitutionality of the statute "on the procedure for an initial decision by the censorship board, which, without any judicial fortification, effectively bars exhibition of any disapproved film, unless and until the exhibitor undertakes a time-consuming appeal to the Maryland courts and succeeds in having the board's decision reversed." The Court points out that in the only reported case indicating the length of time necessary to complete an appeal, the initial judicial determination consumed four months and final vindication of the picture on appeal required six months.

Applying the rule of the cases from Burstyn on, the Court held that "a noncriminal process which requires the prior sub-

47 380 U.S. 51 (1965).

mission of a film to a censor avoids constitutional infirmity only if it takes place under procedural safeguards designed to obviate the danger of a censorship system." The Court laid down these necessary safeguards: (1) the burden of showing that the film is not protected by the First Amendment rests upon the censor, not upon the exhibitor; (2) any restraint prior to judicial review can be imposed only long enough to preserve the status quo; (3) the procedure must assure a prompt final judicial determination of the issue, in order "to minimize the deterrent effect of an interim and possibly erroneous denial of a license." Thus, no longer can the censor simply deny a license and prevent the showing of a film unless the exhibitor is willing to undertake a long and costly siege of litigation. Instead, the licensing agency must either permit exhibition of the film or itself go promptly into the court to prevent it.

Mr. Justice Douglas declared in dissent, with Justice Black concurring, that "I would put an end to all forms and types of censorship and give full literal meaning to the command of the First Amendment."

In an earlier case [48] involving books, not films, the Court had declared that "any system of prior restraints of expression comes to this Court bearing a heavy presumption against constitutional validity . . . we have tolerated such a system only where it operated under judicial superintendence." In this case a Rhode Island statute had created a Commission to Encourage Morality in Youth which was given the duty, *inter alia*, of educating and informing the public with respect to indecent and obscene literature "tending to the corruption of the youth," and of investigating and recommending prosecution of all violations of the statute. The commission's practice, the Court pointed out, was to notify a distributor that certain designated books or magazines distributed by him had been found objectionable for sale and distribution to youth. A list of the "objectionable" publications was sent to local police departments. The Supreme Court held that Rhode Island had here subjected the distribution of publications to prior administrative censorship in violation of the Fourteenth Amendment.

[48] *Bantam Books, Inc.* v. *Sullivan*, 372 U.S. 58 (1963).

Again it should be emphasized that these are only procedural restrictions. The Court has never held nor said that state censorship of motion pictures is not constitutional. It is still apparent that films are more subject to censorship than books or newspapers, but the Court has not explained the basis of this implied distinction.

The Right to Hear and Read

In a novel censorship case [49] the Court in 1965 expanded the protective scope of the First Amendment in striking down an act of Congress which required the Postmaster-General to detain unsealed mail from a foreign country that appeared to be Communist political propaganda. The addressee was to be notified by card, and if he did not return the form card requesting the material within twenty days, it would be destroyed.

The addressees in this case clearly could not say that their freedom of expression under the First Amendment had been directly violated. They could only argue that freedom of speech and press includes the right to receive ideas, even if the speakers and writers—in this case the Chinese Communists—are not protected by the First Amendment. The Court agreed that the amendment guarantees the right to hear and read, but rested its holding "on the narrow ground that the addressee in order to receive his mail must request in writing that it be delivered. This amounts in our judgment to an unconstitutional abridgment of the addressee's First Amendment rights." This affirmative obligation the government may not impose on him.

It may be noted that this case marks the first time in the history of the First Amendment that it had been invoked by the Supreme Court to declare an act of Congress unconstitutional.

Obscenity and Freedom of Expression

In the field of public morality, the Court held invalid in *Winters* v. *United States* [50] the exercise of the police power of the state of

[49] *Lamont v. Postmaster General*, 14 L. Ed. 2nd 398 (1965).
[50] 333 U.S. 507, 514–15, 535 (1948).

New York in a statute which made it a crime to "print, publish or distribute . . . any printed matter principally made up of criminal views, or pictures or stories of deeds of bloodshed, lust, or crime." The state courts construed the statute "as prohibiting such massing of accounts of deeds of bloodshed and lust as to incite to crimes against the person." Even as thus construed, the Supreme Court by a six to three vote held the act invalid on the ground that it was so vague and indefinite as to violate procedural due process under the Fourteenth Amendment. It did not define the forbidden acts with such precision as to exclude a legitimate exercise of the right of free speech and press. Why the Court could not trust itself to strike down such encroachments upon these freedoms when presented to it is not made clear.

Justice Frankfurter, in a dissenting opinion in which Justices Burton and Jackson joined, respectfully suggested that the Court had been led into error by confusing the lack of certainty with respect to the outcome of different prosecutions for similar conduct with the lack of definiteness in the prohibition of the law. The former uncertainties will remain so long as judges are fallible, but they do not deprive persons of due process of law.

On the other hand, such terms as "obscene" and "lewd" may be employed in a criminal statute because, through a long history in the law, they have presumably acquired a reasonably definite meaning. Nevertheless, the Court experiences extreme difficulty in the determination of cases involving censorship or punishment of obscene publications. And oddly enough, this difficulty springs from the virtual impossibility of defining obscenity. Cases decided in the 1956 term of the Court illustrate this difficulty.

In *Roth* v. *United States* [51] and *Alberts* v. *California*, combined for the hearing, the Court decided that obscenity is not protected by the First Amendment against federal proscription, nor by the due process clause of the Fourteenth Amendment against state proscription. This is true because obscenity, like libel, is bad in itself, and therefore does not fall within the protection of free expression under the clear and present danger test. Obscene expressions are in the nature of verbal action and by their very utterance inflict harm upon those to whom they are addressed.

[51] 354 U.S. 476 (1957).

Consequently, they may be punished without regard to probable effect upon the conduct of others.

Justice Brennan, for the Court, found the ". . . rejection of obscenity as utterly without redeeming social importance," and he concluded that material which tends to incite lustful thoughts may be suppressed without evidence that it will probably lead to antisocial conduct. The test of obscenity applied was "whether to the average person, applying contemporary community standards, the dominant theme of the material taken as a whole appeals to prurient interest." This was deemed to define obscenity with sufficient clarity so that the constitutionally protected area for discussion of sex, which is not to be confused with obscenity, would be adequately safeguarded.

It was on this standard that the Court in *Roth* v. *United States* sustained a federal statute forbidding the transportation through the mails of "obscene, lewd, lascivious, indecent, filthy or vile" materials, and in *Alberts* v. *California* a statute forbidding the writing or production of "obscene or indecent" matter. Thus, in these cases the Court decided for the first time that a "sufficiently explicit" obscenity statute was constitutional.[52]

Justice Harlan, dissenting in Roth, thought the Court's sweeping generalization about obscenity's being outside constitutional protection begged the question before the Court. He would have had the Court construe the federal statute, in order to make it constitutional, as reaching only "hard-core pornography." He found that the material here involved did not qualify under his test.

In *Butler* v. *Michigan*,[53] a statute which defined as a misdemeanor making available to the general reading public any book containing obscene language, "tending to the corruption of the morals of youth," was struck down by the Court because it was "not reasonably restricted to the evil with which it is said to deal." Adults may not be restricted to reading matter fit only for children. "Surely," said Justice Frankfurter, "this is to burn the house to roast the pig."

In *Smith* v. *California*[54] the proprietor of a bookstore was

---

[52] See *Doubleday & Co.* v. *New York*, 335 U.S. 848 (1948).
[53] 352 U.S. 380 (1957).
[54] 361 U.S. 147 (1959).

convicted in municipal court for violation of a Los Angeles City ordinance which made it a crime for any person to have in his possession any obscene or indecent writing or book in any place of business where books are sold or kept for sale. Both the municipal court and the affirming appellate court defined the offense as consisting solely of possession. Knowledge of content of the book was not an element of the offense. Thus California had here imposed an absolutely criminal responsibility on the bookseller not to have obscene books in his shop.

In reversing this conviction the Supreme Court reasoned that such criminal liability without knowledge of contents would restrict the sale of books to those actually inspected by the bookseller and that this would restrict the dissemination of constitutionally protected material along with obscene material.

The Court continued its unsuccessful effort to define obscenity in *Manual Enterprises, Inc. v. Day*.[55] In this case, three magazines containing photographs of nude males designed to appeal to homosexuals had been declared obscene and hence nonmailable by the Post Office Department. In an action to enjoin the enforcement of the order, the Court held that the magazines could not be barred from the mails because they were not so patently "offensive on their face as to offend current community standards of decency." Further, the Court held that obscenity under the federal statute requires proof of two distinct elements: (1) "patent offensiveness" and (2) "prurient interest appeal." These two elements must be conjoined in the same material before it can be enjoined as obscene. The Court said that the Roth decision was meant to strengthen obscenity standards and render convictions more difficult. It had not meant to say that anything appealing to prurient interest was necessarily obscene. Furthermore, the "indecency" of such material must be "self-demonstrating" in order to meet the test of obscenity.

In 1964 the Court was again presented the opportunity of further clarifying the elusive issue of obscenity, but despite peripheral advances, the essential standard for the determination of obscenity remains vague and elusive. In *Jacobellis v. Ohio* [56] the Court undertook a clarification or reinterpretation of the

55 370 U.S. 478 (1962).
56 378 U.S. 184 (1964).

Roth standard. Jacobellis, manager of a motion picture theatre in Cleveland Heights, Ohio, was convicted on two counts of possessing and exhibiting an obscene film in violation of the Ohio code. The conviction, affirmed by the Supreme Court of Ohio, was reversed by a vote of six to three in the Supreme Court of the United States. The majority justices wrote four opinions. Mr. Justice Brennan, joined by Justice Goldberg, in "the opinion of the Court," found the film, *Les Amants*, not obscene under the Roth-Alberts test. Mr. Justice Stewart concurred on the theory that Roth-Alberts and later *per curiam* decisions had established that only hard-core pornography, which he thought *Les Amants* was not, could be forbidden. Justice White concurred without opinion. Justices Black and Douglas concurred on the ground that the First Amendment as it operates upon the states through the Fourteenth forbids all obscenity convictions.

In the principal opinion Mr. Justice Brennan, although conceding that application of an obscenity law to suppress a motion picture requires ascertaining the "dim and uncertain line that often separates obscenity from constitutionally protected expression," nevertheless insisted that it is the duty of the Court "to apply the applicable rules of law upon the basis of an independent review of the facts of each case." This being the first case involving a full discussion of an allegedly obscene work in a state obscenity case since the leading Roth-Alberts case in 1957, the Court took a fresh look at the Roth test. Recognizing that this test— "whether to the average person, applying contemporary community standards, the dominant theme of the material taken as a whole appeals to prurient interest"—leaves something to be desired, the Court nevertheless thought that any substitute would raise equally difficult problems and decided to stay with the test.

However, Mr. Justice Brennan sought to place the Roth test in sharper focus by adding a corollary, suggested by the Kingsley case.[57] Since a work cannot be proscribed unless it is "utterly without redeeming social importance," material that deals with sex in a manner that advocates ideas, or that has any literary, scientific, or artistic value or any other form of social importance may not be held obscene and denied constitutional protection.

[57] 360 U.S. 684 (1959).

Prurient appeal, then, of itself is not enough to withhold a work from constitutional protection. The justice ruled that any weighing of a work's value against its prurient appeal would be inconsistent with the principle that it may not be proscribed unless it is utterly without social importance. Furthermore, before material can be proscribed under this test, it must be found to go substantially beyond customary limits of candor in description or representation.

Confusion was confounded by the latest obscenity decisions of the Court in which a minority of the justices held that the manner and form in which a book or other publication is published, advertised, or distributed may be considered in determining whether a publication is obscene. For example, in the Ginzburg case, Mr. Justice Brennan, speaking also for Justices Fortas and White and Chief Justice Warren, declared that a federal prosecution for advertising and mailing books and magazines that were created and exploited entirely to "pander" to prurient interests is not barred by the First Amendment even though the same material in other contexts might be protected. Thus the conduct of the purveyor of allegedly obscene material is, according to this position, relevant to the determination of the social value of the material itself. (*Ginzburg* et al. v. *United States*, No. 42, October Term, 1965; *Mishkin* v. *New York*, No. 49, October Term, 1965; *Memoirs* v. *Massachusetts*, No. 368, October Term, 1965).

Perhaps the most significant expansion or reinterpretation of the Roth test was the Court's declaration that the reference to the "contemporary community standards" by which the issue of obscenity is to be judged are not the standards of the particular community from which the case arises, but those of the nation as a whole. Under this test, then, the concept of obscenity would vary in meaning from time to time but not from place to place at any given time within the nation.

What, then, is the judicial test of obscenity? In so far as there may be said to be a test, it may be stated as follows: "Any material is obscene if it is utterly lacking in redeeming social importance and if its dominant appeal, judged by contemporary national standards, is to prurient interest of the average person, and in its description or representation goes substantially beyond customary limits of candor; or is exploited in such manner as to appeal solely to prurient interests."

It is not clear what the difference is, if any, between this revised Brennan test and Mr. Justice Stewart's "hard-core pornography." Neither justice has succeeded in defining his terms. Justice Stewart could only say "I know it when I see it, and the motion picture involved in this case is not that." The result is that Jacobellis still leaves the relevant tests so subjective and lacking in clear definition as to offer little help in determining the obscenity of a specific work.

Freedom of Expression and Public Order

Perhaps the most extreme and divergent application of the clear and present danger test to uphold or deny libertarian claims relates to exercise of the state police power to maintain public order and safety and to protect public morality. It is, of course, clear that not all speech is protected under the First and Fourteenth Amendments. In *Chaplinsky* v. *New Hampshire*,[58] a case in which the conviction of the petitioner, under a New Hampshire statute providing that "no person shall address any offensive, derisive or annoying word to any person who is lawfully in any street or other public place, nor call him by any offensive or derisive name," etc., was sustained, Mr. Justice Murphy made this statement:

There are certain well-defined and narrowly limited classes of speech, the prevention and punishment of which have never been thought to raise any constitutional problem. These include the lewd and obscene, the profane, the libelous, and the insulting or "fighting" words—those which by their very utterance inflict injury or tend to incite an immediate breach of the peace. It has been well observed that such are no essential part of any exposition of ideas, and are of such slight social values as a step to truth that any benefit that may be derived from them is clearly outweighed by the social interest in order and morality.

This was the view generally followed by the Court before application of the clear and present danger test to such situations in the 1940's. Nevertheless, Justice Douglas, with little considera-

58 315 U.S. 568, 571, 572 (1942).

tion of the facts of the case, set forth an absolutist conception of free speech in *Terminiello* v. *Chicago* [59] in 1949, which was calculated seriously to restrict the power of local government to maintain public order. The Court by a five to four vote reversed a conviction under an ordinance which, as interpreted by the municipal court, permitted punishment for breach of the peace of speech which "stirs the public to anger, invites disputes, brings about a condition of unrest, or creates a disturbance." The case stemmed from an extremely inflammatory address by an irrepressible rabble-rouser, attacking in a long string of insulting and fighting epithets the members of various racial and political groups and government officials, in an auditorium guarded by the police from a threatening mob on the outside. Apparently rejecting the "fighting words" theory of the Chaplinsky case, Justice Douglas wrote for the narrow majority that "A function of free speech under our system of government is to invite dispute," and that it may serve its purpose best when it "induces a condition of unrest . . . or even stirs people to anger." For this reason, the justice concluded, "freedom of speech, though not absolute . . . is nevertheless protected against censorship or punishment, unless shown likely to produce a clear and present danger of a serious substantive evil that rises far above public convenience, annoyance, or unrest."

In a hard-hitting dissenting opinion, Justice Jackson argued that the Court had abandoned the conception of "fighting words" and "clear and present danger" embodied in earlier cases and had substituted in their place "a dogma of absolute freedom for irresponsible and provocative utterance which almost completely sterilizes the power of local authorities to keep the peace against this kind of tactics." He concluded with the observation that the Court had gone far toward "accepting the doctrine that civil liberty means the removal of all restraints from these crowds" and with the warning to his brethren that, "if the Court does not temper its doctrinaire logic with a little practical wisdom, it will convert the constitutional Bill of Rights into a suicide pact."

It is difficult to reconcile the position of the Court in this case

[59] 337 U.S. 1, 4 (1949).

with the holding in *Feiner* v. *New York*,[60] decided early in 1951. Feiner, a university student, made a speech from a box on a street corner in Syracuse, New York, in which he applied the appellation "bum" to the President of the United States and to several lesser officials. It was also alleged, but disputed, that he urged the Negroes in his audience to rise up in arms and fight for their rights. It was generally agreed that the speaker stirred up "a little excitement." When one of his auditors, with the aid of an epithet reflecting on Feiner's ancestry, threatened violence against him if the police did not pull him down from the box, the police intervened, and after two unheeded requests that Feiner stop speaking, arrested him on a charge of disorderly conduct. He was later convicted by the local trial court, and the conviction was affirmed by two state appellate courts. Relying upon the findings of these state courts that danger to public order was threatened, the Supreme Court of the United States, through Chief Justice Vinson, expressed confidence that the arrest had been made solely "for the preservation of order and protection of the general welfare," and with no thought of curbing the expression of the petitioner's opinions. It is significant that the Chief Justice explicitly stated that Feiner was not arrested or convicted for what he said, but rather because of the reaction of some of his listeners to the speech. Feiner was nevertheless found guilty of inciting to riot and of deliberately defying police officers and was sent to prison. This is, indeed, a hazardous formula for those who would exercise their freedom of speech on street corners. Police suppression is simply dependent upon the willingness of someone in the audience to create a disturbance.

Justice Black thought that the policeman's action in arresting Feiner without explanation was a "deliberate defiance" of official duty, as well as of the constitutional right of free speech. Justice Douglas, also in dissent, argued that it was the duty of the police to protect Feiner from the threatening auditor and that by failing to do so they threw their weight on the side of those who sought to break up the meeting, thereby becoming "the new censors of speech."

Efforts by Negroes and on behalf of Negroes to eliminate

[60] 340 U.S. 315 (1951).

racially discriminatory practices of state and local governments have, in the 1960's, led to other cases involving clashing claims of public order and freedom of communication. In 1963 [61] a group of 187 Negro students were arrested and convicted of the common law crime of breach of peace by South Carolina state courts because they marched to the State House in Columbia, assembled there in an area open to the general public, and there expressed their grievances "to the citizens of South Carolina along with the legislative bodies of South Carolina." They expressed "our feelings and dissatisfaction with the present condition of discriminatory actions against Negroes" and said that they would like racially discriminatory laws "removed."

The record as examined by the Supreme Court of the United States presented no evidence of any disorder either on the part of the petitioners or of the assembled onlookers. There was no obstruction of pedestrian or vehicular traffic within the State House grounds. Police protection at the scene was ample to meet any foreseeable possibility of disorder. Nevertheless, the police authorities warned the petitioners that they would be arrested if they did not disperse within fifteen minutes. Instead of dispersing, they sang "The Star-Spangled Banner" and other patriotic and religious songs to the accompaniment of clapping hands and stamping feet, and they listened to what the city manager called a "religion harangue" by one of their leaders. When the fifteen minutes had expired, they were arrested and marched to jail. On the above evidence they were convicted of breach of the peace and given a fine or jail sentence by the state court.

After "an independent examination of the whole record," the Supreme Court declared, "it is clear to us that in arresting, convicting, and punishing the petitioners under the circumstances disclosed by this record, South Carolina infringed the petitioners' constitutionally protected rights of free speech, free assembly, and freedom of petition for redress of their grievances. . . . The circumstances in this case reflect an exercise of these basic constitutional rights in their most pristine and classic form."

For similar conduct, a minister, the Reverend L. B. Cox, was convicted in Baton Rouge, Louisiana, for the violation of a breach

[61] *Edwards* v. *South Carolina*, 372 U.S. 229 (1963).

of peace statute.[62] In reversing, the Supreme Court declared, "It is clear to us that on the facts of this case, which are strikingly similar to those present in *Edwards* v. *South Carolina*, Louisiana infringed appellant's right of free speech and free assembly by convicting him under this statute." The minister's offense consisted in leading some two thousand student demonstrators in a street parade in Baton Rouge and in appealing to them to sit in at the lunch counters of several stores if they were not served. The sheriff testified that the only aspect of the conduct to which he objected was "the inflamatory manner in which he [Cox] addressed the crowd and told them to go on up town, go to four places on the protest list, sit down, and if they don't feed you, sit there for one hour." The Court was not convinced that this part of Cox's speech divested the demonstration of its protected character under the free speech and assembly guarantees of the Constitution. The Court found that the entire assembly, from its beginning until its dispersal by tear gas, was orderly and well-behaved. This was confirmed, said the Court, by a film of the events taken by a television news photographer.

Freedom of speech and association *vis à vis* the maintenance of public order were further extended in *Dombrowski* v. *Pfister* [63] where the Court held that federal courts may enjoin state criminal prosecutions when they find that the state laws being enforced are in violation of the defendant's constitutionally protected freedom of speech. The decision was rendered in a case brought by Dombrowski and other officers of the Southern Conference Educational Fund. Invoking the Civil Rights Act,[64] they sought declaratory relief and an injunction restraining state officials from prosecuting and threatening to prosecute them for alleged violations of the Louisiana Subversive Activities and Communist Control Law. The S.C.E.F., which had been active in fostering civil rights for Negroes in Louisiana, charged that the state had been using unconstitutional state subversive laws to harass it in its civil rights activities.

Prior to this case, it had been the general practice for federal

[62] *Cox* v. *Louisiana*, 379 U.S. 536 (1965).
[63] 380 U.S. 479 (1965).
[64] 42 U.S. C. Section 1983.

courts to refrain from intervening in such cases until the defendants were tried in the state courts and their appeals decided by the highest court of the state. Indeed, the U.S. district court had, in this case, dismissed the complaint on the ground that it should abstain pending interpretation of the statutes in the state courts. But the Supreme Court agreed with appellants that the statutes on their face violated the First and Fourteenth Amendments' guarantees of freedom of expression because: (1) the definition of "subversive organization" was too broad and vague, and (2) the S.C.E.F. had not been given a hearing before it was declared a "Communist front" group.

The district court erred in holding that the complaint failed to allege sufficient irreparable injury to justify equitable relief, because the allegations in the complaint set forth a situation in which criminal prosecutions will not insure vindication of constitutional rights. The complaint alleges, among other things, that "the threats to enforce the statutes . . . are not made with any expectation of securing valid convictions, but rather are part of a plan to employ arrests, seizures, and threats of prosecution under color of the statutes to harass appellants and discourage them and their supporters from asserting and attempting to vindicate the constitutional rights of Negro citizens of Louisiana." Instances of such harassment already experienced by the S.C.E.F. are cited.

The Right to Solicit Counsel as Freedom of Expression

In NAACP v. Button [65] in 1963, the Court expanded the scope of freedom of expression and association by holding that the organization had a First Amendment right to use and to urge its members to use the services of lawyers and courts to protect its right to promote its ideas against segregation. The case involved a 1956 amendment to the Virginia law outlawing the solicitation of legal business in the form of "running" or "capping," a regulation allegedly designed to curb unethical and nonprofessional conduct

[65] 371 U.S. 415 (1963).

by attorneys. The amendment (Chapter 33, Acts of Assembly 1956) included in the definition of "runner" or "capper" an agent "for any organization or association which employs, retains or compensates any attorney at law in connection with any judicial proceeding in which it has no pecuniary right or liability." The Supreme Court held unconstitutional the application of this amended law to the NAACP.

In its consideration of this case the Court was obviously not unmindful of the fact that the legislation at issue was a part of Virginia's "massive resistance" program against desegregation. Against the contention of the state that "solicitation" of litigation is outside the area of freedoms protected by the First Amendment, the Court had two answers: one is that a state cannot foreclose the exercise of constitutional rights by mere labels; and the second is that abstract discussion is not the only kind of communication that the Constitution protects. It also protects vigorous advocacy of lawful ends against governmental intrusion. The Court, therefore, considered the issue in the context of NAACP objectives, and in this context litigation is not just a means of settling private conflicts, but "a means for achieving the lawful objectives of equality of treatment," by all levels of government, "for members of the Negro community."

Pointing out that "there is no longer any doubt that the First and Fourteenth Amendments protect certain forms of orderly group activity" such as "the right to engage in association for the advancement of beliefs and ideas" [66] and freedom from "compelled disclosure of a person's political association," [67] the Court concluded that for the NAACP litigation is a form of political expression and that for such a group "association for litigation may be the most effective form of political association."

Said the Court, "Groups which find themselves unable to achieve their objectives through the ballot frequently turn to the courts. . . . The NAACP is not a conventional political party; but the litigation it assists . . . makes possible the distinctive contribution of a minority group to the ideas and beliefs of our society. For such a group, association for litigation may be the

[66] NAACP v. *Alabama* ex rel. *Patterson,* 357 U.S. 449.
[67] *Bates* v. *Little Rock,* 361 U.S. 516.

most effective form of political association." [68] The statute, by
making such conduct punishable, presents "the gravest danger
of smothering all discussion looking to the eventual institution of
litigation on behalf of the rights of members of an unpopular
minority."

Justice Harlan, for himself, Clark, and Stewart, filed a dissenting opinion in which he saw the amended Virginia statute as
no more than a reasonable exertion of the state's right to maintain
proper standards of legal practice. He agreed that litigation is a
proper and constitutional method whereby organized groups may
protect their right of political association, but the right is not absolute. ". . . litigation, whether or not associated with the attempt to vindicate constitutional rights, is *conduct*; it is speech
plus. Although the State surely may not broadly prohibit individuals with a common interest from joining together to petition a
court for redress of their grievances, it is equally certain that the
State may impose reasonable regulations limiting the permissible
form of litigation and the manner of legal representation within
its borders." By balancing the interest of the state in regulating
legal practice against the effect of the regulation on the individual
rights of the NAACP members, he concluded that the Virginia
regulation was reasonable.[69]

In 1964 the Court extended the doctrine of the Button case
by ruling that a labor union has a constitutionally protected right
to advise its members to seek, in employer liability cases, the
counsel of particular lawyers." [70]

Freedom of Expression versus Seditious Libel

On March 9, 1964, a striking innovation was made by the Supreme
Court in *The New York Times* v. *Sullivan*.[71] In this case, freedom
to criticize the official conduct of public officials was held to be

[68] *NAACP* v. *Button*, 371 U.S. 415, 429–30 (1963).

[69] For a thorough critical analysis of the opinions in this case, see
R. H. Birkby and Walter F. Murphy, "Interest Group Conflict in the
Judicial Arena: The First Amendment and Group Access to the Courts,"
Texas Law Review, October, 1964, pp. 1030–1048.

[70] *Brotherhood* v. *Virginia*, 377 U.S. 1 (1964).

[71] 376 U.S. 255 (1964).

protected against state civil libel laws by the First and Fourteenth Amendments unless the criticism is knowingly false and malicious. The case arose from an allegedly libelous advertisement in *The New York Times*. In the state court, Sullivan, a commissioner of the city of Montgomery, Alabama, had won a libel judgment for $500,000 against *The New York Times* and four Negro ministers for the *Times'* publication of an advertisement allegedly libeling certain unnamed officials. The Supreme Court, in dismissing the judgment, held that the First and Fourteenth Amendments limit the power of the state to impose sanctions, through civil action, for criticism of the conduct of public officials "unless false statements are made with actual malice."

It seems clear from the circumstances and the Court's discussion of this case that the justices believed that Alabama officials, in their determination to thwart Negro rights, sought to use the libel laws to punish their opponents. This, no doubt, explains in part why the Supreme Court here entered an area of the common law which had usually been left to the interpretation of state courts. Furthermore, a number of cases had strongly suggested by way of dicta that libel is outside the protection of the First Amendment.[72] But in this case, the Court, as in *NAACP* v. *Button*,[73] was unwilling to be governed by labels and refused to permit the door to be closed against its scrutiny of the libel judgment of the state court. Said the Court: ". . . libel can claim no talismanic immunity from constitutional limitations. It must be measured by standards that satisfy the First Amendment." [74]

Thus the Court held that "the rule of law applied by the Alabama courts is constitutionally deficient for failure to provide the safeguards for freedom of speech and of the press that are required by the First and Fourteenth Amendments in a libel action brought by a public official against critics of his official conduct." The Court further ruled that under these safeguards the evidence presented in the case was constitutionally insufficient to support

[72] *Chaplinsky* v. *New Hampshire*, 315 U.S. 568 (1942), *Near* v. *Minnesota*, 283 U.S. 697 (1931), *Pennekamp* v. *Florida*, 328 U.S. 331 (1946), *Beauharnais* v. *Illinois*, 343 U.S. 250 (1952), *Roth* v. *United States* 345 U.S. 476 (1957), *NAACP* v. *Button*, 371 U.S. 415 (1963).

[73] 371 U.S. 415 (1963).

[74] *The New York Times* v. *Sullivan*, 376 U.S. at 269.

the state court judgment. The proposition of the state court that "The Fourteenth Amendment is directed against state action and not private action," has no application to this case. Although it involves a civil suit between private parties, the courts of the state have applied a rule of law which the petitioners contend unconstitutionally restricts freedom of speech and press. The test is to be found not in the form in which state power has been applied or in the label given it, but whether such power has in fact been exercised.

It is also immaterial in the circumstances of this case that the allegedly libelous statements were published in the form of a paid "commercial" advertisement. "It communicated information, expressed opinion, recited grievances, protested claimed abuses, and sought financial support on behalf of a movement whose existence and objectives are matters of the highest public interest and concern." The fact that space for such expressions was sold is as immaterial as the fact that newspapers and books are sold. Any other conclusion would close off an important outlet for the dissemination of information and ideas by persons who have no access to publishing facilities.

Sullivan's reliance on statements of the Supreme Court to the effect that the Constitution does not protect libelous publications is not permitted to foreclose the inquiry in this case for the reason that none of the cases has sustained the use of libel laws to impose sanctions upon criticism of the official conduct of public officials. On the other hand, the general principle that freedom of expression upon public questions is secured by the First Amendment has long been settled. After citing many cases in support of this proposition the Court comes to the heart of its opinion: "Thus we consider this case against the background of a profound national commitment to the principle that debate on public issues should be uninhibited, robust, and wide-open, and that it may well include vehement, caustic, and sometimes unpleasantly sharp attacks on government and public officials." The only remaining question then is whether the advertisement forfeits its constitutional protection by virtue of the falsity of some of its factual statements and by its alleged defamation of Sullivan. To the first part of this question, the Court replies that a certain amount of error is inevitable in the free debate if it is to have the "breathing space" that it needs to survive. The interest of the public here far outweighs the interest of the public officials involved. Neither does injury to official reputation justify repression of speech that would otherwise be free. Thus neither factual error nor defamatory content nor the two in combination remove criticism of official conduct from constitutional protection unless the object of such criticism proves that it was made with "actual malice—that is, with knowledge that it was false or with reckless disregard of whether it was or not." In the *Times* case the Court concluded that the facts did not support a finding of malice.

Perhaps the most remarkable aspect of the Court's opinion in the *Times* case is the support it draws from the controversy over the Sedition Act of 1798, "which first crystallized a national awareness of the central meaning of the First Amendment." Of course the Sedition Act, as the Court admits, was never tested in the Supreme Court, but "The attack upon its validity has carried the day in the court of history." Furthermore, the constitutional limitations implicit in the history of the Sedition Act are not limited to Congress alone, but apply also to the states through incorporation into the due process clause of the Fourteenth Amendment. This is, indeed, novel and strong doctrine.

In the following term (November, 1964), the Court, in the case of *Garrison* v. *Louisiana*,[75] extended *The New York Times* rule to cases of criminal libel and held that the "rule also limits state power to impose criminal sanction for criticism of the official conduct of public officials."

The Court in a unanimous decision reversed the conviction of Jim Garrison, the district attorney of Orleans Parish, Louisiana, on a charge of criminal defamation growing out of Garrison's criticism of the official conduct of eight judges of the Criminal District Court of Orleans Parish. The Court saw no merit in the argument that since criminal libel statutes serve different interests from those of civil libel laws, they should not be subject to the same limitations with respect to freedom of speech and press. The constitutional guarantees of these freedoms "compel application of the

[75] 379 U.S. 64 (1964).

same standard to the criminal remedy." The First and Fourteenth Amendments put speech concerning public affairs in a special position, for such speech "is more than self-expression; it is the essence of self-government."

What are the implications of these rulings for freedom of expression doctrine? Have they wrought a revolution? Or must they be interpreted in relation to the situations out of which they arose? Professor Harry Kalven, Jr., in a thoughtful essay, sees in the Court's "emphasis on the Sedition Act of 1798 as the key to the meaning of the First Amendment," the probability of a new constitutional doctrine of free speech and press. The Court's apparent finding of the clue to "the central meaning of the First Amendment" in the historic controversy over seditious libel leads him to believe that the Court has produced "an opinion that may prove to be the best and most important it has ever produced in the realm of freedom of speech." [76] He seems to foresee the probable abandonment of the clear and present danger test and the balancing theory. Perhaps so, but the observation may be premature. As to clear and present danger, its explicit application has never been essential to libertarian decisions, as previous pages of this book have observed. The balancing theory, which certainly involves an implicit recognition of the imminence and gravity of danger threatened by the free exercise of speech, has not always been easy to isolate in the opinions of the Court, but the only alternative to it is the theory of absolutism of First Amendment freedoms.

It should be noted that the Court in these two cases was unwilling to apply such an absolutist concept to the criticism of public officials, although Justices Black, Douglas, and Goldberg would have done so. The majority was careful to emphasize that "the knowingly false statement and the false statement made with reckless disregard of the truth, do not enjoy constitutional protection." This view of the majority was based on the conviction that "the known lie" and "calculated falsehood" are no essential

[76] See his, "*The New York Times* Case: A note on 'The Central Meaning of the First Amendment,'" *The Supreme Court Review* 1964, P. B. Kurland, ed., pp. 191–221.

part of any exposition of ideas, and "are of such slight social value as a step to truth that any benefit that may be derived from them is clearly outweighed by the social interest in order and morality."

The reason for the Court's extension of the scope of freedom of expression in the *Times* case seems to have been dictated by two related situations: first, the Court believed that Alabama was using its libel laws to curb Negroes in the enjoyment of their established constitutional rights. It is strongly noted that the *Times* advertisement was concerned with the support of "a movement whose existence and objectives are matters of the highest public interest and concern." The second situation involves "a profound national commitment to the principle that debate on public issues should be uninhibited," especially where the official conduct of public officials is concerned. Thus without any reference to clear and present danger, the Court, in effect, places criticism of public officials without malice in a preferred position.

FREEDOM TO TRAVEL: DENIAL OF PASSPORTS

In a series of cases decided between 1958 and 1965, the Court has recognized the right to travel abroad as a part of the liberty of which citizens cannot be deprived without due process of law under the Fifth Amendment, and it has held that such a right may not be restricted because of the citizen's political beliefs or associations, but only in order to protect our national security.

In *Kent* et al. v. *Dulles*,[77] the Court in a five to four decision (Justices Clark, Burton, Harlan, and Whittaker dissenting) held that the Secretary of State was not authorized under the Passport Act of 1926 and the Immigration and Nationality Act of 1952 to deny passports to petitioners because of their alleged Communistic beliefs and associations and their refusal to file affidavits concerning present or past membership in the Communist party. The Court pointed out that although the Secretary has broad power under the law to issue passports, this power has been con-

[77] 357 U.S. 116 (1958).

strued generally to authorize refusal of a passport only when the applicant (1) is not a citizen or a person owing allegiance to the United States, or (2) was engaging in criminal or unlawful conduct. The petitioners do not fall under either of these categories. Although the Court does not reach the question of constitutionality in this case, it strongly hints that Congress is without constitutional authority to deny passports on the grounds here claimed by the Secretary of State. Said the Court: ". . . we deal here with a constitutional right of the citizen, a right which we must assume Congress will be faithful to respect. We would be faced with important constitutional questions were we to hold that Congress by [this legislation] had given the Secretary authority to withhold passports to citizens because of their beliefs or associations."

In *Aptheker* et al. v. *Secretary of State*,[78] passports were revoked under Section 6 of the Subversive Activities Control Act of 1950, which provides that when a Communist organization is registered or under final order to register, it shall be unlawful for any member with knowledge or notice thereof to apply for or use a passport. The Court held that Section 6 is unconstitutional on its face, because it too broadly and indiscriminately trespasses the liberty guaranteed by the Fifth Amendment. In support of this holding, the Court gives this characterization of the law: its proscriptions include both knowing and unknowing members; it renders irrelevant the member's degree of activity in the organization and his commitment to its purpose; it establishes an irrebuttable presumption that those who are members of the specified organizations will, if given passports, engage in subversive activities; the prohibition applies regardless of the purpose for which an individual wishes to travel; it applies to a member regardless of the security sensitivity of the area in which he wishes to travel. "The section therefore," the Court concludes, "is patently not a regulation narrowly drawn to prevent the supposed evil, . . . yet here as elsewhere precision must be the touchstone of legislation so affecting basic freedoms."

Perhaps the most interesting aspect of this case is the novel effort of Mr. Justice Goldberg to apply earlier evolved First

[78] 378 U.S. 500 (1964).

Amendment rules—such as preferred status and reversal of presumption—to the right of foreign travel which was held to be a part of the liberty implicit in the Fifth Amendment. The Justice believed that this case, like *NAACP* v. *Button*,[79] involves freedoms that "are delicate and vulnerable, as well as supremely precious in our society," and that the Court's approach to restraining legislation should be the same here as there. Furthermore, "since freedom of travel is a constitutional liberty closely related to rights of free speech and association, we believe that appellants in this case should be required to assume the burden of demonstrating that Congress could not have written a statute constitutionally prohibiting their travel." If this is a First Amendment case, as Justice Goldberg comes close to saying it is, the Court might have avoided doctrinal confusion and spared itself some clumsy craftsmanship by pitching its decision entirely on First Amendment grounds.

However, the right to travel abroad is not an absolute right. It can be limited when considerations of foreign policy or national security justify it. In *Zemel* v. *Rush*,[80] decided on May 9, 1965, the Court ruled that the Secretary of State was authorized under the Passport Act of 1926 to deny a passport to Louis Zemel, who desired to go to Cuba to satisfy his curiosity and to become a better-informed citizen, and that the exercise of that authority was constitutionally permissible. The Chief Justice, for the majority of six, construed the broad language of the Passport Act of 1926 to include authority on the part of the Secretary of State to lay down area-restriction in the use of passports.[81]

In distinguishing this case from Dulles and Aptheker, the Chief Justice points out that refusal to validate Zemel's passport "does not result from any expression or association on his part"; he is not being forced to choose between membership in an organization and freedom to travel. His passport was simply rendered ineffective with respect to travel to Cuba "because of foreign policy considerations affecting all citizens"; and this was no interference

[79] 371 U.S. 415 (1963).
[80] 381 U.S. 1 (1965).
[81] The language is: "The Secretary of State may grant and issue passports . . . under such rules as the President shall designate and prescribe for and on behalf of the United States. . . ."

with First Amendment rights as he alleged. "The right to speak and publish does not carry with it the unrestrained right to gather information."

True, *Kent* v. *Dulles* held that the right to travel is a part of the liberty of which the citizen cannot be deprived without due process of law under the Fifth Amendment, but this does not mean that under no circumstances can liberty be inhibited.

MARITAL PRIVACY AND THE BILL OF RIGHTS

One of the most extraordinary decisions rendered in the 1964 term of the Court came on the final day of the term. In *Griswold* v. *Connecticut*,[82] the Court struck down the 1879 Connecticut statute which made it a punishable offense for "any person" to use any drug or device "for the purpose of preventing conception." Under the state's aiding and abetting statute "any person who assists, abets" or causes anyone else to commit the above offense "may be prosecuted and punished as if he were the principal offender."

Twice before, the Planned Parenthood League of Connecticut had challenged this law before the Supreme Court, but on both occasions the Court found no justiciable cause of action. In a 1943 case [83] the Court found that a physician had no standing to challenge the law on the ground that it prevented him from advising his patients. The patients and not he had been injured, said the Court. In 1961,[84] the Court refused to rule on a claim by a group of women that they were unable to get birth control information. Here, the Court said that no real controversy existed because the law had not been enforced, and thus the issue was prematurely raised.

After the Poe case, a Mrs. Griswold, executive director of the league, and Dr. C. Lee Buxton, a professor at the Yale University Medical School, set up a birth control clinic in New Haven,

[82] 381 U.S. 479 (1965).
[83] *Tileston* v. *Ullman*, 318 U.S. 44, 46 (1943).
[84] *Poe* v. *Ullman*, 367 U.S. 497 (1961).

whereupon they were arrested, tried, convicted, and fined one hundred dollars each, and the clinic was closed. Thus they finally confronted the Court with a genuine controversy to decide.

The act was held to be in violation of the right of marital privacy implicit in "several" provisions of the Constitution. Mr. Justice Douglas, writing for the majority, could point to no specific guarantee of the right of privacy in the Constitution, but neither is there an express guarantee of the right to distribute literature, the right to read, the right to travel, the right to teach, the right of association, and freedom of inquiry, yet all of these rights and others have been held to be implicit in the First Amendment as necessary in making the express guarantee fully meaningful. For example, in NAACP v. Alabama,[85] the Court held the "freedom to associate and privacy in one's associations" to be protected as "a peripheral First Amendment right."

Prior cases suggested to Mr. Justice Douglas that specific guarantees of the Bill of Rights have penumbras "formed by emanations from those guarantees that help give them life and substance." Some of these guarantees—such as the First, Third, Fourth, and Ninth Amendments, and the immunity from self-incrimination clause of the Fifth Amendment—"create zones of privacy."

The present case, Justice Douglas concluded, "concerns a relationship lying within the zone of privacy created by several constitutional guarantees. And it concerns a law which, in forbidding the use of contraceptives rather than regulating their manufacture or sale, seeks to achieve its goals by means having a maximum destructive import upon that relationship."

There were three concurring opinions and two vigorous dissenting opinions. Mr. Justice Harlan, concurring in the judgment of the Court, thought that the law "infringes the due process clause of the Fourteenth Amendment because the enactment violates basic values 'implicit in the concept of ordered liberty.' "[86] He does not agree that the relevant inquiry in this case is dependent upon the first eight amendments "or any of their radiations." The due process clause of the Fourteenth Amendment stands on its own merit.

---

[85] 357 U.S. 449, 662 (1958).
[86] Quoting Palko v. State of Connecticut, 302 U.S. 319, 325 (1937).

Mr. Justice White was content to say simply that the law as applied to married couples deprives them of liberty without due process of law.

Mr. Justice Goldberg, joined by Chief Justice Warren and Justice Brennan, concurred in both the judgment and opinion of the Court, but added that the right of marital privacy is also one of the unspecified "fundamental rights" protected by the Ninth Amendment. That amendment provides that the enumeration of certain rights in the Constitution "shall not be construed to deny or disparage others retained by the people." Apparently not content with the Court's mere reference to the Ninth Amendment as a source of penumbral radiation of the right of marital privacy, Justice Goldberg adds his own extraordinary opinion "to emphasize the relevance of that Amendment to the Court's holding." He labors valiantly to this end, but with something less than illuminating results.

He denies that his interpretation of this amendment broadens the powers of the Court. On this point he is misunderstood, he insists. He does not accept Black's position that the entire Bill of Rights is incorporated in the Fourteenth Amendment as restriction on the states, and he does "not mean to imply that the Ninth Amendment is applied against the states by the Fourteenth." Nor does he mean to say "that the Ninth Amendment constitutes an independent source of rights protected from infringement by either the states or the Federal Government." Then, what is the point?

"Rather, the Ninth Amendment shows a belief of the Constitution's authors that fundamental rights exist that are not expressly enumerated in the first eight amendments and an intent that the list of rights included there not be exhaustive." One wonders why Mr. Justice Goldberg felt impelled to add so much to the vagueness and complexity already existent in the Court's opinion. One also wonders why the majority justices could not talk themselves into agreement on the principle that the statute violated the right of marital privacy implicit in the concept of liberty guaranteed against state abridgment in the due process clause of the Fourteenth Amendment.

The foregoing arguments brought strong dissents from Justices Black and Stewart. In essence, the right of privacy "created by several fundamental constitutional guarantees" is something which they are unable to find "in the Bill of Rights, in any other part of the Constitution, or in any case ever before decided by this Court."

RIGHT OF ASSEMBLY AND PETITION

Nature of the Right

One of the basic rights of every American under the First Amendment and the due process clause of the Fourteenth Amendment of the Constitution is the right to assemble with others for the purpose of discussing problems of common interest and of protesting against actions and policies of government deemed to be unjust, or unwise, or calling for positive action by government deemed to be in the public interest.

Throughout a large part of its history the right of petition was regarded as primary to the right of assembly, the latter being a subordinate and ancillary right. Today, however, the right of assembly is fundamental. In *De Jonge* v. *Oregon*, the first case in which the right of assembly was held by the Supreme Court to be included in the "liberty" guaranteed against state abridgment by the due process clause of the Fourteenth Amendment, the Court declared that

. . . peaceable assembly is a right cognate to those of free speech and free press and is equally fundamental. . . . For the right is one that cannot be denied without violating those fundamental principles of liberty and justice which lie at the base of all civil and political institutions—principles which the Fourteenth Amendment embodies in the general terms of its due process clause.

Therefore, the Court went on, "The holding of meetings for peaceable political action cannot be proscribed. Those who assist in the conduct of such meetings cannot be branded as criminals on that score." If the right of assembly is to be preserved, the question is not under whose auspices the meeting is held, but what is its purpose; not one of the relationship of the speakers, "but whether their utterances transcend the bounds of the freedom of speech which the Constitution protects." [87] Here, then, the Court flatly rejected the concept of guilt by association.

In the case from which these quotations come, De Jonge, a member of the Communist party, was convicted in the state court for violation of the Oregon Syndicalism Act, which defined criminal syndicalism as "the doctrine which advocates crime, physical violence, sabotage, or any unlawful acts or methods as a means of accomplishing or effecting industrial or political change or revolution." The act also punishes various acts promotive of criminal syndicalism such as "presiding at or assisting in conducting a meeting of such an organization, society or group." On the undisputed evidence, De Jonge spoke at a meeting in Portland called by the Communist party; he did not discuss criminal syndicalism but rather a current maritime strike. For this he was arrested, convicted, and sentenced to seven years in prison. Speaking through Chief Justice Hughes, the Supreme Court held that De Jonge had been deprived of freedom of assembly and speech without due process of law. The Court pointed out that under the interpretation which had been given the Oregon statute, no meeting of the Communist party, however innocent the topic of discussion, would be lawful. This, held the Court, amounted to an arbitrary infringement of the right of freedom of assembly.

Federal Restraints

Attempts by government to regulate peaceful assembly of the people, as with freedom of speech and press, pose issues of sharp conflict between the importance of preserving freedom of communication and the necessity of maintaining public order and safety. The banning of such offenses as breach of peace, disorderly conduct, nuisances, and obstruction of public ways has operated to restrict the right of people to assemble for the exchange of ideas. To draw the line between legal and illegal regulation here is not always an easy task for the Court.

[87] *De Jonge* v. *Oregon*, 299 U.S. 353, 364, 365 (1937).

Restrictions by the national government have been less frequent in recent years than formerly.[88] Nevertheless, petitions for the repeal of the World War I espionage and sedition laws and against military recruitment have been punished by imprisonment. Especially unsuccessful have been processions or marches for the presentation of petitions in the national capital. In 1894 General Coxey's armies of unemployed marched on Washington, only to see their leaders arrested for walking on the grass around the Capitol. In 1932 the march of the veterans on Washington to petition for bonus legislation met with a stern rebuke. The Administration, considering the march a threat to the Constitution, called on the army to expel the bonus marchers from the capital and burn their camp.[89]

State Restraints

Before the doctrine of absorption of First Amendment freedoms into the concept of liberty guaranteed against state abridgment by the due process clause of the Fourteenth Amendment had been enunciated, it had been thought that there was no federal constitutional barrier to state or local regulation, or even prohibition, of meetings in public places. However, as has been seen, the existence of such a barrier was forecast in the Gitlow case in 1925 and definitely established for freedom of assembly in the De Jonge case in 1937.

One of the principal methods by which state and local governments have attempted to restrict meetings in public places has been requirement of a permit. Some of these regulations have been honest efforts to prevent interference with traffic, to give police protection to the gatherings when needed, or to maintain public order. At other times, however, the regulations have been rooted in prejudice and vindictiveness. On the whole, the Supreme Court has dealt sternly with the latter.

In *Hague* v. *C.I.O.*,[90] decided in 1939, the question at issue

[88] See *The Constitution of the United States of America*, Annotated, 82d Cong., 2d Sess., Sen. Doc. 170 (Washington, Government Printing Office, 1953), pp. 806–807.

[89] *Ibid.*

[90] 307 U.S. 496 (1939).

was the validity of a Jersey City, New Jersey, ordinance requiring a permit for public assemblies in the streets, parks, or public buildings of the city, and authorizing the director of public safety to refuse to issue such a permit if, after investigation of all the facts and circumstances pertinent to the application, he believes it proper to refuse in order to prevent riots, disturbances, or disorderly assemblage.

The Chief of Police of Jersey City, acting under the foregoing ordinance, denied the C.I.O. the right to hold lawful meetings in Jersey City on the alleged ground that the members were Communists or comprised Communist organizations. When the case reached the Supreme Court, it was held by a majority of five to two that the ordinance was void on its face, since it allowed the director of public safety to refuse permits for public meetings on his mere opinion that such refusal would prevent riots, disturbances, and disorderly assemblages.

In the principal opinion, Mr. Justice Roberts made this significant statement relative to the place of freedom of assembly in the American democratic system:

Freedom of assembly is an essential element of the American democratic system. At the root of this case lies the question of the *value* in American life of the citizen's right to meet face to face with others for the discussion of their ideas and problems—religious, political, economic or social. Public debate and discussion take many forms including the spoken and the printed word, the radio and the screen. But assemblies face to face perform a function of vital significance in the American system, and are no less important at the present time for the education of the public and the formation of opinion than they have been in our past history. The right of assembly lies at the foundation of our system of government.

In *Bridges* v. *California* [91] it was held that a telegram sent to the Secretary of Labor, strongly assailing the action of a state court in a pending case, was entitled to protection under the Fourteenth Amendment as an exercise of the right of petition. In 1945, a state statute requiring union officials to register before soliciting union membership was found to violate the right of peaceful assembly.[92]

[91] 314 U.S. 257 (1941).
[92] *Thomas* v. *Collins*, 323 U.S. 516 (1945).

A few years later, however, a closely divided Court sustained an order of a state employment relations board forbidding the calling of special union meetings during working hours,[93] and in June, 1951, the Court in a six to three decision held that a conspiracy to break up by force and threats of force a meeting called to protest against the Marshall Plan did not afford a right of action against the conspirators under the Ku Klux Klan Act of 1871.[94]

The three dissenters, speaking through Justice Burton, argued that Congress could punish a conspiracy of private persons that had as its purpose the denial of a federally created constitutional right.

Lobbying and the Right of Petition

Conflict of interest is again sharply involved in the widespread practice of lobbying, one of the most important expressions of the right of petition, and the persistent popular demand for restrictive regulation of this weapon of organized group interests. With the tremendous growth of organized special interest groups since the beginning of this century, the professional lobby has become the chief weapon of these groups for influencing governmental policy. Much criticism has developed concerning the methods and purposes of the organized interests, as they operate through their professional lobbyists.

Starting early in the present century, many states enacted legislation to regulate lobbyists. On the national level, there have been no less than four congressional investigations of lobbying activities. A more recent one has been by a Committee of the House of Representatives authorized by the Eighty-first Congress in 1950.[95] In 1946 Congress passed the Federal Regulation of Lobbying Act, under which more than two thousand lobbyists have registered and some five hundred organizations have reported lobbying contributions and expenditures.

[93] Auto Workers v. Wisconsin Employment Relations Board, 336 U.S. 245 (1949).

[94] Collins v. Hardyman, 341 U.S. 651, 663 (1951).

[95] See General Interim Report of the House Select Committee on Lobbying Activities, 81st Cong., 2d Sess. (Washington, Government Printing Office, 1950).

This act requires certain designated reports to be made to Congress by every person receiving contributions or expending money for the purpose of influencing, directly or indirectly, the passage or defeat of any legislation by Congress. The act also requires every person who engages, for pay or for any consideration, to attempt to influence the passage or defeat of any legislation by Congress to register with the Clerk of the House and the Secretary of the Senate and to make certain disclosures concerning himself and his employer or the interest in whose behalf he is acting.[96]

In the case of *United States* v. *Rumely* decided in 1953, in which the Lobbying Act was indirectly involved, the Court ruled through Justice Frankfurter that "as a matter of English" the phrase "lobbying activities" means representations made directly "to Congress, its members or its committees" and does not embrace attempts to direct the thinking of the community. The next year, in *United States* v. *Harriss*,[97] the Court upheld the constitutionality of the act. Chief Justice Warren, referring to the Rumely case, argued that the language of the act was meant to refer to lobbying in the sense of "direct communication with members of Congress on pending or proposed federal legislation," and not to attempt to influence Congress indirectly through an appeal to public opinion.

Construed in this manner, the statute does not violate the First Amendment guarantees of free speech, press, and assembly. In support of this conclusion, the Chief Justice reasons that if the American ideal of government by elected representatives is to be fully realized, the individual members of Congress must be able to distinguish between the pressures of special interests "masquerading as proponents of the public weal" and the voice of the people. Congress, by this legislation, he continues, is not seeking to forbid these pressures; it is seeking rather "a modicum of information" as to "who is being hired, who is putting up the money, and how much." To forbid Congress to do this is to deny it the power of self-protection.

---

[96] 2 U.S.C. Sections 264, 266.
[97] 347 U.S. 612 (1954).

SUMMARY ANALYSIS

Expansion of Scope of Protection

In the cases covered in this chapter, the exercise of freedom has, for the most part, collided with the police power of the state in fields of general welfare not closely related to the necessities of national security. In this sphere, the Court broadened the scope of protection of freedom to include new situations such as picketing, criticism of judicial conduct, the distribution of handbills and other printed materials in public places, the operation of sound trucks in public places, and motion pictures. In the period and area discussed, the Court generally tended to give maximum scope to freedom.

PICKETING. The Court in the initial case of *Thornhill* v. *Alabama* held that a statute which forbade all picketing, whether peaceful or not, was void on its face. It will be recalled that this holding was modified in subsequent cases. However, picketing is still regarded as speech, and indiscriminate curbing of peaceful picketing is an unconstitutional restraint of freedom of speech. However, picketing is also an economic weapon and, as such, is subject to regulation by the state as to both methods and purposes. Thus peaceful picketing may be restrained if the labor dispute has in the past been attended by violence, extends beyond the industry involved in the dispute, or if its purpose is to force violation by the employer of a validly declared state policy.

Although the more recent cases have tended to minimize the element of speech in picketing and to accentuate the element of economic coercion, peaceful picketing directed primarily toward the purpose of informing the public of the facts of a labor dispute still enjoys the status and protection of free speech. The problem confronting the Court in picketing cases is that of drawing a line between the clear right to publicize and discuss industrial relations and the much more limited right of an organized group of workers to exert their economic power.

CONTEMPT OF COURT. In a series of cases decided in the 1940's, the general right of the press and of individuals to criticize pending judicial proceedings, as well as past judicial acts, was upheld. Such a right, however, does not extend to contempt committed in the physical presence of the court. The sharp division of the justices in this group of cases was no doubt due to the fact that they involve a conflict not merely between public authority and private right, but also between two important private rights, namely, freedom of expression and the right to a fair trial. The majority of the Court resolved the dilemma by the application of the doctrine of preferred status to freedom of expression.

FREE SPEECH IN PUBLIC PLACES. The scope of free speech in public places was extended by a series of cases upholding the orderly distribution of handbills, pamphlets, and other materials on the streets and in other public places, and the sale of religious or noncommercial literature in public places, without prior official permission or payment of a license tax.

The most confusing and unsatisfactory aspect of this development involves the attempt to apply the free speech doctrine to speech amplified by electronic devices. In the Saia case an ordinance requiring a license from the chief of police for the use of sound amplification devices was held to vest unrestrained discretion in the officer, and therefore amounted to previous restraint of speech. In Kovacs, the Court sustained an ordinance forbidding the operation of any sound truck emitting "loud and raucous" noises. Yet, part of the majority of five construed the ambiguous ordinance as banning all sound trucks. Hence it is impossible to say precisely what the application of free speech doctrine to sound trucks is. Wading through the confusing diversity of judicial opinion, we may tentatively state this much: Generally, the use of sound amplification devices is protected as freedom of expression by the Fourteenth Amendment, but volume of sound, time of broadcasting, and other conditions may be regulated by "narrowly drawn ordinances." An ordinance vesting unrestrained licensing power in an official is clearly invalid.

MOTION PICTURES. In the case of the *Miracle* the Supreme Court extended the protection of freedom of expression to motion pictures. It will be recalled that up to the *Miracle* decision in 1952, there had been in force (since 1915) a decision that motion pictures are mere entertainment and not entitled to guarantees of freedom of expression. The *Miracle* ruling, holding invalid as prior restraint on freedom of expression the provision of a New York statute authorizing denial of a license to show a motion picture on a censor's judgment that the film is "sacrilegious," apparently does not preclude a state from censoring motion pictures "under a clearly drawn statute designed and applied to prevent the showing of obscene films."

In the absence of a claim of obscenity a state may not prevent the exhibition of a motion picture merely because it advocates an idea, even the idea that adultery in certain circumstances may be proper behavior. Furthermore, First Amendment protection is not confined to ideas that are conventional or shared by a majority. However, there is no absolute right against all prior restraint in the exhibition of a motion picture regardless of how obscene and offensive it may be. But an exhibitor is entitled to a prompt judicial resolution of any First Amendment claim, and the burden of showing that a film is not protected by the First Amendment rests upon the censor. Any system of prior restraint comes to the Court bearing a heavy burden of presumption of constitutional invalidity.

OBSCENITY. A state may not punish mere possession of obscene books and magazines by a bookseller without regard to his knowledge of their content. To do this would be to restrict the dissemination of constitutionally protected material along with the unprotected in violation of the First and Fourteenth Amendments.

Magazines may not be barred from the mails on the ground of obscenity unless they are so patently offensive on their face as to offend current community standards of decency and to appeal to prurient interest.

No material can be held obscene unless it is utterly lacking in social importance, and unless its dominant appeal, judged by contemporary national standards, is to the prurient interest of the average person. Furthermore, the description or representation of such material must go substantially beyond customary limits of candor.

Other Expansions of Freedom of Expression

The right to hear and read implicit in the First Amendment forbids the government to impose upon an addressee the positive obligation to request that unsealed mail from foreign countries, thought to be Communist propaganda, be delivered to him. Freedom of speech and press includes the right to receive ideas, even if the speakers and writers are not protected by the First Amendment.

Radio and television coverage may be barred from a heavily publicized and highly sensational criminal trial, and such prohibition may be extended to a pretrial hearing, but this prohibition extends no further than to cases similar to the Estes case. Sensational publicity in such a case could have a prejudicial effect on all parties connected with the trial.

It is recognized that the right to travel abroad is a part of the liberty of the individual of which he may not be deprived without due process of law under the Fifth Amendment; and such a right may not be restricted because of a person's political beliefs or associations. Restriction on travel to certain regions may, however, be imposed in order to protect our national security.

The Court has expanded the scope of freedom of expression and association to include the right of the NAACP to use and to urge its members to use the services of lawyers and courts to protect their rights to disseminate and promote their ideas against segregation.

The First and Fourteenth Amendments limit the power of a state to impose civil or criminal sanctions for criticism of the official conduct of public officials unless false statements are made with actual malice. Libel, civil or criminal, "can claim no talismanic immunity"; it must be measured by First Amendment standards.

A state law forbidding the use of contraceptives, as applied to married couples, violates the right of "marital privacy" implicit in "several" provisions of the Constitution, such as, for example, the First, Fourth, and Fifth Amendments.

Judicial Criteria

If there is any conclusion which emerges clearly from the foregoing consideration of free speech cases, it is that they have not been decided by the application of a tidy formula or even a set of formulas. In every case the Court is confronted with a set of competing interests or values, and its decision will, in the final analysis, rest upon its evaluation of the relative importance of these conflicting interests, tempered by the several justices' conception of their proper judicial function. Hence, few generalizations are possible on the basis of these decisions, and predictions are hazardous. However, the following observations can be made with respect to the Court's handling of the free speech cases considered in this chapter.

In expanding the area of protection of freedom of expression to include new fields since 1937, the Court has generally given wide scope to the exercise of freedom. In this enterprise it has employed an elaborate array of intellectual devices to support its decisions. For approximately a decade following 1937, the most effective device employed by the Court to uphold libertarian claims was the clear and present danger test. Both the nature of the cases and the attitude of the Court operated to give clear and present danger a strong libertarian thrust in this period. As previously noted, the cases of this period involved, for the most part, the conflict of the exercise of freedom of expression with the peace, good order, and convenience of the community as distinguished from the requirements of national security. Moreover, the majority of the justices in this period seemed to be fired with an evangelical zeal for libertarian values.

Since the early 1950's, however, the Court has extended the free expression coverage of the First and Fourteenth Amendments without the aid of "clear and present danger."

The problem facing the Court in these cases is to reconcile the interest of the speaker and the community in the free expression of ideas with the protection of the public peace and of the primary uses of streets, parks, and other public facilities. In weighing the conflicting values involved in this process, a justice is necessarily guided by his conception of the judicial function and of the duties imposed upon him by the nature of this function. For example, Justice Frankfurter, with his strong attachments to the reasonable man theory would support the legislative judgment on the need for restraint unless it were clearly "unreasonable," whereas Justice Black would uphold the free speech claim unless the speech posed a clear, imminent, and serious danger to the public interest.

Although it is clearly impossible to isolate each of the values that each justice may have applied to the decision of a case, what happens in the determination of free speech cases of the kind examined in this chapter may be described as follows: The nature of the speech and the circumstances in which the utterance takes place are weighed or balanced against the need for restraint, the scope, method, and time of the restraint in relation to freedom of expression. To elaborate briefly on these factors, there are certain types of speech which have never been considered as entitled to constitutional protection because they effect injury without contributing anything to the process of rational discussion. These include the lewd and obscene, and the insulting or fighting words. Circumstances in which utterances take place may render otherwise innocent words dangerous and punishable. As Justice Holmes suggested in his famous Schenck opinion, it is one thing falsely to shout fire on a lonely hilltop, but it is quite another thing to shout fire in a crowded theater. Speech in the latter situation poses a threat of imminent and serious danger to the public safety. Speech that incites to crime is likewise beyond the pale of constitutional protection.

As to repressive regulation, it cannot be so broad in its scope or vague in its terms as to trap the innocent as well as the guilty. The law must prescribe for the guidance of administrators and courts reasonably clear and ascertainable standards of guilt and afford the citizen fair notice of what is forbidden. It makes a difference if a statute is narrowly drawn and directed to the specific evil aimed at or if it is drawn in such broad and vague terms as to encompass speech that is constitutionally protected.

Closely related to this problem is the question of the method by which freedom of expression is restrained in the public interest. This is well illustrated by the handbill cases previously considered. These cases do not hold that a community may not prevent the littering of its streets, but rather that the constitutional method of achieving this end is to punish those who litter the streets and not to ban all distribution of handbills.

Also, the time of impact of a restraining statute on speech is important. The position of previous restraint in our constitutional tradition is, of course, well known. The evil of previous restraint arises from the fact that it gags the speaker in advance, for fear that he will abuse freedom of speech if he is allowed to exercise it. This has generally been viewed by the Court as a very different matter from punishing speech that clearly and immediately threatens vital interests of the community. The weakness of prior restraint is that it deals with what may be rather than with what is or has been. In the 1940's the Court tended to condemn previous restraint on its face as a matter of course, but in the early 1950's the Court moved away from this on-its-face condemnation of previous restraint. The latter movement is reflected in the cases of *Breard* v. *Alexandria* and *Poulos* v. *New Hampshire* where prior restraint was upheld. Thus previous restraint is still viewed with a suspicious judicial eye, but it is no longer condemned out of hand.

The Heyday of Clear and Present Danger

Both the nature of the cases and the attitude of the Court operated to give clear and present danger a strong libertarian thrust in the decade preceding the cold war. It was during these years that the test was clarified and reinforced by the theory of the preferred status of First Amendment freedoms. As thus strengthened, the clear and present danger test was employed by the Court to extend the protection of freedom of expression to include new situations such as picketing, criticism of judicial conduct, and speech in public places by means of sound trucks.

As previously noted, these cases involved for the most part the conflict of the exercise of freedom of expression with the peace, good order, and convenience of the community as distinguished from the requirements of national security. Here, the Court tended to sustain the claims of freedom in the absence of immediate and serious danger to the public interest.

5

FREEDOM OF RELIGION

FREE EXERCISE OF RELIGION

The victory for free exercise of religion signalized by the adoption of the First Amendment in 1791 was not seriously challenged in the first century and a half of our constitutional history, and hence there was little occasion for the Supreme Court to intervene in defense of the freedom formalized in 1791.

It was, of course, well known that the clause in the First Amendment that "Congress shall make no law . . . prohibiting the free exercise" of religion limited only federal action and did not apply to state restrictions of First Amendment freedoms.[1] Indeed, it was long thought that the due process clause of the Fourteenth Amendment imposed no such limitations upon state action. As indicated in chapter 2, the Supreme Court in 1922 declared that "neither the Fourteenth Amendment nor any other provision of the Constitution imposes restrictions upon the state about freedom of speech."[2] The logic of this declaration, of course, applies to freedom of religion and other First Amendment freedoms. Thus, the Supreme Court could exercise its jurisdiction to safeguard a claimed violation of religious freedom only if the violation was committed by an agency of the federal government.

[1] *Permoli* v. *New Orleans*, 44 U.S. 589, 609 (1845).
[2] *Prudential Life Insurance Co.* v. *Cheek*, 259 U.S. 530 (1922).

Federal Restraints

The decisions of the Supreme Court involving congressional power over religious freedom, as limited by the free exercise clause of the First Amendment, have concerned, for the most part, laws relating to the practice or advocacy of polygamy as a doctrine of the Mormon Church and conscientious objection to military service.[3] It was in these cases that the Court first delineated in broad strokes the nature and scope of the "free exercise" right.

In its first consideration of this right, the Court sustained a federal statute forbidding bigamy as a crime in the Territory of Utah. To the plea of the defendant that the act denied him the free exercise of his religious beliefs as a Mormon, the Court answered that although "Congress was deprived of all legislative power over mere opinion," it was left "free to reach actions which were in violation of social duties or subversive of good order." [4] Religious belief could not be pleaded against an overt act made criminal by the law of the land. Laws may not interfere with religious beliefs or opinions, but they may interfere with religious practices. To allow conduct in violation of law to be excused on the ground of religious belief "would be to make the professed doctrines of religious belief superior to the law of the land, and in effect to permit every citizen to become a law unto himself." [5]

It was the purpose of the free exercise clause of the First Amendment to allow everyone under the jurisdiction of the United States to hold such beliefs respecting his relation to the Deity and his obligations thereunder as meet the approval of his judgment and conscience and to express his beliefs in such form as he may think proper, so long as there is no injury to the rights of others.[6] This includes the right to teach and propagate any religious doctrine "which does not violate the laws of morality and property and does not infringe personal rights." [7]

[3] *Hamilton* v. *Regents*, 293 U.S. 245 (1934) and *Arver* v. *United States* 245 U.S. 366 (1918).
[4] *Reynolds* v. *United States*, 98 U.S. 145 (1878).
[5] *Ibid.*, 167.
[6] *Davis* v. *Beason*, 133 Wall. 333 (1890) and *Watson* v. *Jones*, 13 Wall. 679 (1871).
[7] *Ibid.*

Nor can religious belief be cited to obtain exemption from legally imposed obligations of general application, such as military service. Thus there is no constitutional right which relieves conscientious objectors from military service.[8] Nevertheless, Congress may as an act of grace grant such immunity. In 1918 the Court summarily rejected, as completely unsound, the argument that the Selective Service Act was repugnant to the religious freedom clause of the First Amendment because of the exemption granted to ministers of religion, theological students, and members of sects whose beliefs deny the moral right to engage in war.[9]

In a series of cases,[10] starting in 1929 the Court on three successive occasions first construed the Naturalization Act so as to deny the privilege of naturalization to those who, because of religious belief or other conscientious scruples, refused to promise to bear arms in defense of the United States. Yet, in *Girouard* v. *United States*,[11] in 1946, these decisions were overruled, and the Court held that conscientious objection to bearing arms did not constitute a lack of attachment to the United States. In admitting Girouard to citizenship, the Court stated that it was unwilling to assume that Congress in passing the Naturalization Act had intended to repudiate our long-standing tradition of religious liberty by barring from citizenship those who conscientiously objected to military service on religious grounds. The language of the oath did not require that interpretation. This decision was reaffirmed and extended in *Colmstaedt* v. *Immigration and Naturalization Service*,[12] where refusal on religious grounds to participate in the production of munitions or to deliver them to combat troops did not disqualify an applicant for naturalization.

Of course, it is not to be inferred from the last two cases that Congress is without constitutional power to make religiously inspired pacifism a barrier to citizenship. On the contrary, Congress has complete power to grant or withhold the privilege of naturalization on any grounds, or for no reason at all, that it sees fit.

[8] *Hamilton* v. *Regents*, 293 U.S. 245 (1934).
[9] *Arver* v. *United States* 245 U.S. 366 (1918).
[10] *United States* v. *Schwimmer*, 279 U.S. 644 (1929); *United States* v. *MacIntosh*, 283 U.S. 605 (1931); *United States* v. *Bland*, 283 U.S. 636 (1931).
[11] 328 U.S. 61 (1946).
[12] 339 U.S. 901 (1950).

These doctrines have been reaffirmed and sharpened in a more recent case involving state action. In *Cantwell* v. *Connecticut*, the Court declared that freedom of conscience and freedom to adhere to such forms of worship as the individual may choose cannot be restricted by law. But the state will protect him in the exercise of his chosen form of religion. "Thus the Amendment embraces two concepts—freedom to believe and freedom to act. The first is absolute, but in the nature of things, the second cannot be." [13]

In the language of the cases, the rule for the guidance of congressional action may be summarized as follows. One has the right to practice any religious principle and to teach any religious doctrine which does not violate the laws established by society for the good order and morality of the community, and which does not restrict or injure the personal rights of others.

State and Local Restraints

It was, of course, not until after it had been determined that the specific inhibitions of the First Amendment were applicable to the states through the due process clause of the Fourteenth Amendment that the Supreme Court became the guardian of religious liberty against the states. Since 1937, nearly all religious freedom cases have arisen from state rather than federal action. Indeed, it was not until after the Supreme Court had made this important determination that there reached the Court a sufficient number of cases from which there could be developed a constitutional law of religious freedom in any substantial sense. Thus, it is not an exaggeration to say that the constitutional law of religious freedom, for the most part, has evolved out of court decisions since the middle 1930's. Obviously, the incorporation of religious freedom into the "liberty" protected by the Fourteenth Amendment against state deprivation was an inseparable part of the significant evolution that brought the other First Amendment freedoms within the scope of the concept. Because of the relatively limited area for federal restrictions on religious freedom, it may be said that the relevant clause of the First Amend-

[13] 310 U.S. 296, 303, 304 (1940).

ment has found its chief value through incorporation into the Fourteenth Amendment.[14]

The decision of the Supreme Court to review state restrictions on religious freedom brought forth a veritable rash of cases by a small but aggressive religious sect known as Jehovah's Witnesses. A summary of these and other cases involving state encroachment on the free exercise of religion follows. Although the Fourteenth Amendment had been a part of the Constitution for nearly three quarters of a century, it was not until 1940 that the Supreme Court handed down the first decision squarely holding that the religious freedom embraced in the First Amendment is equally protected against state action by the due process clause of the Fourteenth Amendment. To be sure, several earlier Witness cases [15] had established the right to distribute religious literature on the streets and in public places without prior permission of any public officer, but these cases were decided under freedom of speech and press guarantees, without consideration of freedom of religion.

In *Cantwell* v. *Connecticut*,[16] decided in May, 1940, the Court specifically declared for the first time that the concept of liberty embodied in the Fourteenth Amendment embraces the religious liberties guaranteed by the First Amendment and renders the legislatures of the states as incompetent as Congress to enact the forbidden laws. Here, three Witnesses were convicted for violating a state statute requiring that, before persons might solicit money for religious or charitable causes, they must first apply to the secretary of the local public welfare council. He was to determine whether the cause was a religious one or bona fide object of charity or philanthropy, and on this basis issue his certificate of authorization. The Court held the statute, as applied to the Witnesses, an unconstitutional deprivation of religious freedom in violation of the Fourteenth Amendment. Justice Roberts, speaking for a unanimous Court, declared: [17]

. . . to condition the solicitation of aid for the perpetuation of religious views or systems upon a license, the grant of which rests in the

---

[14] See Leo Pfeffer, "The Supreme Court as Protector of Civil Rights: Freedom of Religion," *The Annals*, Vol. 275 (May, 1951), p. 76.

[15] For example, *Lovell* v. *Griffin*, 303 U.S. 444 (1938), and *Schneider* v. *Irvington*, 308 U.S. 147 (1939).

[16] 310 U.S. 296.

[17] *Ibid.*, p. 300.

exercise of a determination by state authority as to what is a religious cause, is to lay a forbidden burden upon the exercise of liberty protected by the Constitution.

The Court was careful to point out that nothing said in the opinion "is intended even remotely to imply that under the cloak of religion, persons may, with impunity, commit frauds upon the public." [18] A state may undoubtedly protect its citizens from fraudulent solicitation by requiring a stranger in the community, as a condition of publicly soliciting funds for any purpose, to establish his identity and his authority to act for the cause which he allegedly represents. But the method here adopted by Connecticut to that end violates the liberty safeguarded by the Fourteenth Amendment.

The Court also reversed the conviction of one of the Cantwells on a common law charge of inciting a breach of the peace in the playing of phonograph records which were offensive to his Catholic auditors. The Court held that in the absence of a statute narrowly drawn to define and punish specific conduct as constituting a clear and present danger to a substantial interest of the state, Cantwell's record playing, considered in the light of constitutional guarantees, raised no such clear and present menace to public peace as to render him liable to conviction for the common law offense in question.

From now on, the somewhat erratic course of judicial decision in the field of religious freedom is evidence of the difficulty encountered by the Court in fashioning reliable criteria for the proper balancing of the right to free exercise of religion against the social interest of the community as expressed through the police power.

Since many of the cases pertinent to the subject of this chapter involve a merging of issues of free press with issues of religious freedom, and have therefore been analyzed in the preceding chapter, they will not be further considered here, but the consequences for religious freedom will be summarized later. These cases, it will be remembered, include those involving the requirement of official permits or licenses for the distribution of religious literature, and for the solicitation of funds for religious

[18] *Ibid.*

purposes, as well as those involving the regulation of religious speech in public places.

Perhaps the stormiest controversy stirred up by Jehovah's Witnesses resulted from their defiance of the compulsory flag salute statutes. Within two weeks after the Cantwell decision, the Supreme Court, in the widely criticized Gobitis case,[19] held that freedom of religion was not violated by a state law requiring expulsion from the public schools of pupils who on grounds of religious scruples refused to salute the flag of the United States. Mr. Justice Frankfurter, speaking for an eight to one majority, stated the issue of the case in the following language: [20]

We live by symbols. The flag is the symbol of our national unity, transcending all internal differences, however large, within the framework of the Constitution. . . . The precise issue . . . is whether the legislatures of the various states and the authorities in a thousand counties and school districts of this country are barred from determining the appropriateness of various means to evoke that unifying sentiment without which there can be ultimately no liberties, civil or religious. . . .

Aside from his oratorical tribute to flag salute symbolism, what Justice Frankfurter seems to be saying here is that the flag salute statute raises a political question which must be determined by public opinion and not by the judiciary.

Justice Stone's solitary but vigorous dissent stated clearly his conception of the relationship of the constitutional guarantee of religious liberty and the problem of majority versus minority rights. He pointed out that by this law the state seeks to coerce these children "to express a sentiment which, as they interpret it, they do not entertain, and which violates their deepest religious convictions." [21] In reply to Frankfurter's doctrine of judicial abstention, Justice Stone asserted: [22]

I am not persuaded that we should refrain from passing upon the legislative judgment "as long as the remedial channels of the democratic process remain open and unobstructed." This seems to me no less than

[19] *Minersville School District* v. *Gobitis*, 310 U.S. 586 (1940).
[20] *Ibid.*, 598.
[21] *Ibid.*
[22] *Ibid.*, 603, 604.

the surrender of the constitutional protection of the liberty of small minorities to the popular will. . . . Here we have such a small minority entertaining in good faith a religious belief which is such a departure from the usual course of human conduct that most persons are disposed to regard it with little toleration or concern. In such circumstances careful scrutiny of legislative efforts to secure conformity of belief and opinion by a compulsory affirmation of the desired belief is especially needful if civil rights are to receive any protection.

The increase of mob violence toward the Witnesses after this decision gave melancholy support to Mr. Justice Stone's dissent. Ironically enough, the flag, intended as a symbol of freedom, had become for many persons an instrument of oppression of a religious minority. It was misused to deny the very freedoms it was intended to symbolize.[23]

In *West Virginia State Board of Education* v. *Barnette*,[24] in 1943, the Supreme Court specifically overruled the Gobitis case. Inspired by the Gobitis ruling, the West Virginia State Board of Education (under permissive state law) adopted a resolution requiring all students and teachers to salute and pledge allegiance to the flag as a routine part of the daily school program. Speaking through Justice Jackson, the Court in a six to three decision held that "the action of the local authorities in compelling the flag salute and pledge transcends constitutional limitations on their power and involves the sphere of intellect and spirit which it is the purpose of the First Amendment . . . to reserve from all official control. . . ." Striking with even greater force than had Justice Stone at Frankfurter's judicial self-restraint doctrine in such cases, Jackson declared:

The very purpose of a Bill of Rights was to withdraw certain subjects from the vicissitudes of political controversy, to place them beyond the reach of majorities and officials and to establish them as legal principles to be applied by the courts. One's right to life, liberty, and property, to free speech, a free press, freedom of worship and assembly, and other fundamental rights may not be submitted to vote; they depend on the outcome of no elections.

[23] For a statement of facts relative to this situation, see Victor Rotnem and F. G. Folsome, Jr., "Recent Restrictions upon Religious Liberty," *American Political Science Review*, Vol. 36 (December, 1952), pp. 1161–1163.
[24] 319 U.S. 624 (1943).

Invoking the clear and present danger test, Jackson pointed out that state restriction of these fundamental freedoms may not be judged by the same due process standard as, for example, the regulation of a public utility. "They are susceptible of restriction only to prevent grave and immediate danger to interests which the state may lawfully protect." Further, the history of coercive uniformity shows that those who begin with the elimination of dissent end with the elimination of dissenters. Finally, "If there is any fixed star in our constitutional constellation, it is that no official, high or petty, can prescribe what shall be orthodox in politics, nationalism, religion or other matters of opinion or force citizens to confess by word or act their faith therein."

In *Taylor* v. *Mississippi*,[25] decided on the same day as the Barnette case, the Court added a corollary to the Barnette principle by holding invalid a Mississippi statute which made it unlawful to urge people, on religious grounds, not to salute the flag. The Court reasoned that if the state may not constrain one to violate his conscientious religious tenets by saluting the flag, it may not by the same token punish him for publicly communicating his views on the subject to his fellows and exhorting them to accept those views.

Restrictions on Religious Speech in Public Places

Two later decisions consider state restrictions against speaking on religious subjects in public parks without permits from public authorities. In *Niemotko* v. *Maryland*,[26] members of Jehovah's Witnesses had been found guilty of disorderly conduct because of their attempt to hold a meeting in a town park without a permit. There was actually no evidence of disorderly conduct on the part of the Witnesses. They had already applied for and been refused a permit by local officials, acting not under statutory authorization but in accordance with a local custom under which permits had been issued to other religious and fraternal organizations. In response to their application for permits, the Witnesses were

25 319 U.S. 583 (1943).
26 340 U.S. 268 (1951).

questioned concerning their religious beliefs rather than on matters related to the orderly use of the park. The Supreme Court, in reversing the conviction, concluded that the Witnesses had been denied the use of the park because of the officials' dislike of them or their religious views and that such discrimination was a denial of the equal protection of the laws.

In *Kunz v. New York*,[27] decided on the same day as Niemotko, the conviction of a Baptist minister for conducting religious services in the streets of New York City, without a license from the police commissioner, as required by a city ordinance, was reversed by the Supreme Court. Kunz had been refused a license after a hearing, presumably because he had in the past ridiculed and denounced other religious beliefs in offensive and provocative language and thereby created a condition of strife and threatened violence in violation of the aforementioned ordinance. The Supreme Court reversed the conviction since the ordinance vested an unrestrained discretion in the police commissioner to grant or not to grant a permit with no appropriate standards to guide his action.

Justice Jackson, in dissent, agreed with the New York Court of Appeals "that when, as here, the applicant, claims a constitutional right to incite riots, and a constitutional right to the services of policemen to quell those riots, then a permit need not be issued."

In a still more recent case, the Court invalidated a New York statute because in the judgment of the Court it interfered with the right of a church to choose its own hierarchy of officials and to administer its own property. Such a right has constitutional protection "as a part of the free exercise of religion against state interference." [28]

Cases Lost by Religious Sects

It must not be assumed from the foregoing that the police power of the states has suffered complete defeat at the hands of freedom

---

[27] 340 U.S. 290 (1951).
[28] *Kedroff v. St. Nicholas Cathedral*, 344 U.S. 94 (1952).

of religion. The Witnesses and other religious sects have lost a number of cases. For example, the Court has sustained a state statute forbidding a parade or procession upon a public street without a license, against the contention of the defendants that the procession was a form of worship and interference therewith violated the due process clause of the Fourteenth Amendment. The parade here involved the marching of Jehovah's Witnesses, in groups of fifteen to twenty-five members each, in close single file, along the sidewalks of the business district of a densely populated city. The Court, speaking through Chief Justice Hughes, noted that the authority of a municipality to regulate public highways in order to assure the safety and convenience of the people has never been regarded as inconsistent with civil liberties, but rather as one of the means of safeguarding the good order of the community upon which civil liberties ultimately depend. "Civil liberties, as guaranteed by the Constitution, imply the existence of an organized society maintaining public order without which liberty itself would be lost in the excesses of unrestrained abuses." [29]

The question in a case of this kind is whether the regulation of the use of the streets is exercised in such a manner as not to deny or unwarrantably curtail the important rights of assembly and communication traditionally associated with resort to public places.

The Witnesses suffered another setback in *Chaplinsky* v. *New Hampshire*.[30] Here the Court again unanimously decided that a state statute, which forbade anyone to address "any offensive, derisive or annoying word to any other person who is lawfully in any street or other public place" or to ". . . call him by any offensive or derisive name," had been validly applied to the conduct of a Jehovah's Witness. To a city marshal who had warned him against inciting a public disturbance, Chaplinsky addressed the epithets: "God damned racketeer" and "damned Fascist." This language was defended as an exercise of religious freedom, but Mr. Justice Murphy, himself no mean champion of religious freedom, declared, for the Court, that he "could not conceive that

[29] *Cox* v. *New Hampshire*, 312 U.S. 569 (1941).
[30] 315 U.S. 568 (1942).

cursing a public officer is the exercise of religion in any sense of the term." The prevention and punishment of certain well-defined and narrowly limited categories of speech have always been regarded as outside the sphere of constitutional protection. These include the insulting or "fighting" words, "which by their very utterance inflict injury, or tend to incite immediate breach of the peace." Such words "are no essential part of any exposition of ideas and are of such slight social value as a step to truth that any benefit that may be derived from them is clearly outweighed by the social interest in order and morality."

In 1944, the Court sustained a provision of a Massachusetts child labor statute, making it unlawful for children to sell newspapers or periodicals on the streets or in other public places and for a parent or guardian to permit a child to work in violation of this prohibition. In *Prince* v. *Massachusetts*, the statute was applied against one Sarah Prince, a member of the Witnesses, who allowed her nine-year-old niece to accompany her in the distribution of religious literature on the public streets. Mr. Justice Rutledge held for the Court that the statute as applied here was a valid exercise of the state police power, since "Democratic society depends for its continuance upon the healthy well-rounded growth of young people into full maturity as citizens with all that implies," and "to this end it may take appropriate steps against the crippling effects of child employment." [31] These are noble words, but the question arises whether they pertain to the facts of this case. It may be doubted that the work in which this child was engaged in the company of her aunt constituted a danger to the protected social interest of sufficient seriousness to justify such interference with her religious freedom.

Justice Jackson, in a forceful dissent in which he was joined by Justices Roberts and Frankfurter, maintained that the limits on religious activities "begin to operate whenever activities begin to affect or collide with the liberties of others or of the public. Religious activities which concern only members of the faith . . . ought to be as nearly absolutely free as anything can be." But when a religious group enters the secular market, it is then participating in "Caesar's affairs and may be regulated by the state"

[31] *Prince* v. *Massachusetts*, 321 U.S. 158 (1944).

provided that such regulation is not arbitrary and does not discriminate against anyone because of his religious purpose.[32]

In 1949, the Supreme Court, for want of a substantial federal
question, dismissed a case in which a church group contended that
religious freedom was violated by a zoning ordinance forbidding
the building of churches in certain residential areas.[33]

An interesting and somewhat puzzling case, merging free
speech and freedom of religion, was decided in 1953. In *Poulos
v. New Hampshire*,[34] the Supreme Court of the United States
sustained the conviction of a Jehovah's Witness for holding a
religious meeting in a public park without a license from the city
council as required by ordinance, although the defendant had
been arbitrarily and illegally refused a permit by the council in
response to his efforts to comply with the requirements of the
ordinance. The state supreme court had held that the ordinance
was valid, on the authority of *Cox v. New Hampshire*, but that it
must be administered fairly and without discrimination, and that
in the instant case the council had arbitrarily and illegally denied
the license. However, Poulos should not have violated the ordinance but should have sought relief from illegal refusal through
review by certiorari, as prescribed by state law.

The Supreme Court of the United States, sustaining the conviction, declared through Justice Reed that since the ordinance
must be administered fairly, it was only a routine police measure
and involved no previous restraint on liberty of speech or religion.

This case presents the curious, but not unique, phenomenon
of the Court's formally adhering to libertarian principles but arriving at antilibertarian results. To say that Poulos did not suffer
restraint of religious freedom is to use words without substance.
The Court, in brief, held that one may be constitutionally punished for holding a religious meeting without a license, which has
been arbitrarily and illegally refused by those responsible for ad-

---

[32] For a lucid analysis of Jackson's opinion on this and other First
Amendment freedoms, see Robert J. Steamer, "Mr. Justice Jackson and the
First Amendment," *University of Pittsburgh Law Review*, Vol. 15 (Winter,
1954), pp. 193–221.

[33] *Corporation of the Presiding Bishop of the Church of Jesus Christ of
Latter-Day Saints v. City of Porterville*, 338 U.S. 805 (1949).

[34] 345 U.S. 395 (1953).

ministering the ordinance requiring it. Justice Reed admitted that the delay and expense incident to judicial review of an arbitrary refusal of a license is unfortunate, "but the expense and annoyance of litigation is a price citizens must pay for life in an orderly society." This argument comes perilously close to implying the absurd proposition that freedom of speech and religion are guaranteed only to those who have the patience to wait and the money to pay.

It may well be, as Justice Reed argued, that to allow a person to proceed to hold a public meeting in a city park without prior arrangement is to invite breaches of the peace or create public dangers, but this ignores the fact that Poulos had in good faith sought to make the necessary arrangements and in the face of this was illegally refused a permit. Justice Black, in dissent, mourned this as one of a series of recent decisions "which fail to protect the rights of Americans to speak freely."

RESTRICTIONS ON SUNDAY WORK AND THE FREE EXERCISE OF RELIGION

Although most of the religious cases decided by the Court since 1961 have concerned problems of establishment, three recent cases also raised troublesome questions of free exercise.

The 1961 case of *Braunfeld* v. *Brown* [35] concerned the constitutional validity of the application to a group of Philadelphia merchants of a 1959 Pennsylvania statute forbidding the Sunday sale of certain enumerated commodities. Their retail sale of clothing and home furnishings fell within the proscriptions of the statute. Each was a member of the Orthodox Jewish faith, which required the closing of their stores and abstention from all work from nightfall each Friday to nightfall each Saturday. In a suit for injunctive relief, they contended that the enforcement of the Pennsylvania statute against them would prohibit the free exercise of their religion, because the result of the enforcement

[35] 366 U.S. 599(1961) In *Gallagher* v. *Crown Kosher Super Market of Mass.*, 366 U.S. 617, essentially the same issues were involved.

would be either to compel them to give up their Sabbath observance, a fundamental tenet of their faith, or to suffer serious economic disadvantage if they continued to observe their Sabbath. The enforcement of the statute would also hinder the Orthodox Jewish faith in gaining new adherents.

The Supreme Court, in rejecting these arguments, sought to distinguish this statute from other restrictions on the free exercise of religion which it had struck down. Chief Justice Warren announced the judgment of the Court and delivered an opinion in which Justices Black, Clark, and Whittaker concurred.

This statute, the Chief Justice asserted, does not make criminal the holding of any religious belief or any religious practices; it simply "regulates a secular activity and as applied to appellants operates to make the practice of the religious beliefs more expensive." But this financial sacrifice which these merchants must make in order to observe their religious belief is wholly different from legislation which attempts to make religious practice itself unlawful. This statute imposes only an indirect burden on the exercise of religion, and to strike it down would radically restrict the operating latitude of the legislature. For example, the Chief Justice went on, tax laws which limit the amount which may be deducted for religious contributions impose an indirect burden on the religious observance of those whose religion requires them to contribute a larger amount to their church. It cannot be expected, the Chief Justice argues, that in this religiously cosmopolitan nation, with its hundreds of denominations, the legislators may "enact no law regulating conduct that may result in economic disadvantage to some religious sects and not to others because of the special practices of the various religions." The Chief Justice is careful to admit, however, that not all legislation imposing an indirect burden is unobjectionable. If the purpose or effect of a law is to impede religion or to discriminate invidiously between religions, such a law is invalid even though the burden it imposes may be characterized as indirect. But a general statute designed to advance the state's secular goals is valid "despite its indirect burden on religious observance unless the state may accomplish its purpose by means which do not impose such a burden." [36]

[36] *Ibid.*, p. 607.

The Court finds that there are no alternative means of accomplishing the state's secular goal of bringing about a general day of rest, such as providing exemption for the religious group to which appellants belong. The Court sees two objections to such exemption: first, extreme administrative difficulty in the matter of enforcement, and second, the economic advantage over their competitors to people who rest on a day other than Sunday. The Court fails to mention that more than a majority of the thirty-four states having general Sunday regulations provide exemption of this kind.

Mr. Justice Brennan, in dissent on the free exercise phase of the case, thought that constitutionality could be achieved only by granting exemption to those who in good faith observed as Sabbath some day other than Sunday. He could see no difference between the economic effect of "this state imposed burden on Orthodox Judaism" and "a tax levied upon the sale of religious literature," as in the case of *Follett* v. *Town of McCormack*.[37] In his view the Court "has exalted administrative convenience to a constitutional level high enough to justify making one religion economically disadvantageous."

Whatever the merits of the conflicting arguments of the justices in this case, Justice Brennan is undoubtedly correct in pointing out that the Court departed from the exacting standard of constitutional adjudication which it had in previous cases rather consistently applied as the test of legislation under the First Amendment. Clearly, the free exercise of religion did not enjoy a preferred status in this case.

Mr. Justice Stewart, who indicated substantial agreement with Justice Brennan, simply added that Pennsylvania law "compels an Orthodox Jew to choose between his religious faith and his economic survival" and "grossly violates" his constitutional right to the free exercise of his religion.

In the 1963 case of *Sherbert* v. *Verner*[38] the Court by a seven to two vote held that South Carolina had imposed an unconstitutional burden upon the free exercise of religion by denying unemployment compensation to a Seventh-Day Adventist

[37] 321 U.S. 573 (1944).
[38] 374 U.S. 398 (1963).

because of her refusal to accept work on Saturday, the Sabbath of those of her religious faith. This holding was announced by Mr. Justice Brennan, who had dissented in Braunfeld, and who here declared that the ruling of the South Carolina authorities was invalid because it "forces her [the appellant] to choose between following the precepts of her religion and forfeiting benefits, on the one hand, and abandoning one of the precepts of her religion in order to accept work, on the other hand."

It is difficult to see how this holding can be reconciled with the free exercise holding in the Braunfeld case. Such a task would seem to be especially awkward for Mr. Justice Brennan, who dissented with exceptional vigor in that case. Yet, ironically enough, he sought to accomplish this extraordinary feat by bringing the facts of the Sherbert case within the exceptional situation set forth in Chief Justice Warren's Braunfeld opinion that "if the purpose or effect of a law is to impede the observance of one or all religions or is to discriminate insiduously between religions, that law is constitutionally invalid even though the burden may be characterized as being only indirect." The countervailing factor of Braunfeld—a strong state interest in providing one uniform day of rest for all workers—finds no equivalent in the present case.

Despite this less than plausible attempt at reconciliation of these two cases, Mr. Justice Brennan grounds the conclusion of the Court upon an entirely different standard of judicial construction. Here, as he had insisted in his dissent in Braunfeld, "It is basic that no showing merely of a rational relationship to some colorable state interest would suffice; in this highly sensitive constitutional area only the grossest abuses, endangering paramount interests, give occasion for permissible limitation." [39]

Mr. Justice Stewart, chiding the Court in his concurrence, insists that "to require South Carolina . . . to pay public money to the appellant under the circumstances of this case is . . . clearly to require the state to violate the establishment clause as construed by this Court"—a construction which he regards as "historically unsound and constitutionally wrong." This point raises a serious question as to the possibility of conflict between the two

[39] Quoting *Thomas* v. *Collins*, 323 U.S. 516, 530 (1945).

religious clauses which will be considered later in connection with discussion of establishment cases.

It should also be mentioned that in *Torcaso* v. *Watkins* the Court struck down a religious test for public office. Torcaso was appointed by the Governor of Maryland to the office of notary public; but he was denied a commission because he refused to declare his belief in God, as required by the Maryland constitution. The Court, reversing the state court of appeals, held that the test could not be enforced against Torcaso, because it unconstitutionally invades his freedom of belief and religion.[40]

SUMMARY ANALYSIS OF JUDICIAL CRITERIA OF RELIGIOUS FREEDOM CASES

It would be difficult to draw from the preceding cases, a definite pattern of the constitutional law of religious freedom that would have dependable predictive value. Nevertheless, there are certain criteria of judicial judgment which have been applied in most of the cases. These may be briefly stated: for approximately a dozen years following 1938 the clear and present danger test and the preferred status doctrine were the formulas most frequently used by the Court to rationalize free exercise decisions, but since the early 1950's the use of the clear and present danger test has been largely abandoned in these cases. More recent decisions have been justified on First Amendment and due process grounds without the aid of these intellectual gadgets. Nevertheless, whatever judicial canons are employed by the Court in rationalizing its conclusions and whatever the diversity of opinion with respect to their applicability, it is apparent in all these cases that the justices are weighing the right to religious freedom against the interest of the community threatened by the exercise of the claimed right and are determining which, in the circumstances, is the more important interest.

The preceding pages afford numerous examples of the applica-

[40] 374 U.S. at p. 264.

tion of these criteria. Only a few need be recalled here: The Court in the first Mormon case unanimously determined that the interest of the community in monogamous marriage outweighed the right of the Mormons to practice their religious belief in polygamous marriage and that such a danger to the community could be effectively averted only by forbidden plural marriages. The state's paramount interest in maintaining order and in preventing abuse to innocent persons overrides the right of a Jehovah's Witness to curse and vilify a city official in the public streets. On the other hand, the community's interest in maintaining unlittered streets may not be effected by forbidding the distribution of religious handbills. Nor may the state's interest in safeguarding enjoyment of the privacy of the home override the right of religious proselyters to ring door bells in order to offer the occupants religious pamphlets. Likewise, the state's interest in preventing fraud may not be protected by the granting of unbridled discretion to a public official to withhold the right of soliciting religious contributions from anyone not adjudged by him as representing a bona fide religious cause. Nor may the state's legitimate interest in promoting patriotism be effected by compelling school children to salute the flag in violation of their religious scruples.

In none of these cases, then, did the Court question the right of the state to protect the interest involved; it simply held that infringement of religious liberty was neither a valid nor a necessary means of achieving the desired end.

It should be added, as previously noted, that the members of the Court have not always been in agreement on the applicability of these criteria of judicial judgment. The diversity expresses itself (1) as between different justices in the same cases, (2) in the position of the Court from case to case, and (3) in the position of the same justice in different cases. Illustrative of the first point is the partial dissent from the prevailing position of the Court by Justice Jackson and the apparently complete dissent of Justice Frankfurter. Jackson's position—which, as will be seen, should be termed his later position—was set forth in his dissenting opinion in the Prince case, where he made it clear that he would confine the application of the foregoing criteria of judgment to religious activities that concern only members of the faith. When a religious group goes outside its own ranks and enters the secular market, it is then participating in "Caesar's affairs and may be regulated by the state," subject only to the regular due process limitation of reasonableness.[41]

In Frankfurter's view, no constitutional rights are entitled to a preferred status. Hence, religious freedom is due no greater judicial protection than ordinary commercial interests, and legislation restricting such freedom must be sustained or invalidated on the basis of the presence or absence of rational justification.[42]

The shift in the position of the Court from case to case is sharply illustrated by the two flag salute cases, in the first of which Frankfurter's passion for judicial self-restraint prevailed by eight to one whereas in the second Jackson rested the decision of the Court squarely on the doctrines of clear and present danger and preferred status.

The shift in the position of the same justice from case to case also finds an exemplar in Justice Jackson, who in the second flag salute case took a position which stamped him as one of the most vigorous defenders of the clear and present danger test and related criteria; later, in the Prince case, he apparently had become convinced that the Court went too far in sustaining the religious excesses of Jehovah's Witnesses.

SUMMARY OF HOLDINGS
ON FREE EXERCISE
OF RELIGION

From the cases discussed here, the following rights and limitations seem to have been established: A person may distribute religious literature on the streets and in other public places without prior permission from any public official;[43] he may even circulate

---

[41] 321 U.S. 158 (1944).

[42] See his dissent in *West Virginia State Board of Education* v. *Barnette,* 319 U.S. 624 (1943).

[43] *Lovell* v. *Griffin,* 303 U.S. 444; *Schneider* v. *Irvington,* 308 U.S. 149; *Largent* v. *Texas,* 318 U.S. 418.

religious literature in a privately owned town [44] and in a federally owned housing project [45] without the permission of the owners; he may play phonograph records to any willing listener on the streets for purposes of religious propaganda,[46] and he may ring doorbells in the same cause; [47] he may sell religious literature or solicit funds for a religious cause without a permit or payment of a license tax,[48] and he may do this even if he makes his living entirely from the sale of religious books.[49]

It is unconstitutional for a state or one of its agencies of local government to require pupils in the public schools to salute the flag and to give a pledge of allegiance contrary to the religious scruples of the pupils.[50] Nor can one be punished for publicly urging others not to salute the flag.[51]

Under the naturalization laws, refusal to bear arms in defense of country in wartime is no bar to the grant of citizenship to a conscientious objector willing to perform noncombatant service.[52]

In connection with the holding of religious meetings in public parks, no religious sect may be discriminated against because of its religious beliefs.[53] Nor may a state vest unrestrained discretion in a police officer to grant or not to grant a permit to speak on religious subjects in a public park; furthermore, a minister who has been denied a permit under such conditions may not be punished for preaching without a permit, even though he may have ridiculed and denounced other religious beliefs.[54]

The right of a church to choose its own official hierarchy and to administer its own property is entitled to constitutional protection against state interference.[55]

[44] *Marsh* v. *Alabama,* 326 U.S. 501 (1946).
[45] *Tucker* v. *Texas,* 326 U.S. 517 (1946).
[46] *Cantwell* v. *Connecticut,* 310 U.S. 296 (1940).
[47] *Martin* v. *Struthers,* 319 U.S. 141 (1943).
[48] *Murdock* v. *Pennsylvania,* 319 U.S. 105 (1943).
[49] *Follet* v. *McCormick,* 321 U.S. 573 (1944).
[50] *West Virginia State Board of Education* v. *Barnette,* 319 U.S. 624 (1943), overruling *Minersville School District* v. *Gobitis,* 310 U.S. 586 (1940).
[51] *Taylor* v. *Mississippi,* 319 U.S. 583 (1943).
[52] *Girouard* v. *United States,* 328 U.S. 61 (1946).
[53] *Niemotko* v. *Maryland,* 340 U.S. 268 (1951).
[54] *Kunz* v. *New York,* 340 U.S. 290 (1951).
[55] *Kedroff* v. *St. Nicholas Cathedral,* 344 U.S. 94 (1952).

The following restrictions on the exercise of religion have been upheld by the Court: The practice of polygamy may be forbidden without violation of the constitutional right to freedom of religion.[56] A city ordinance regulating the use of streets for religious parades and processions and imposing a reasonable nondiscriminatory fee for the cost of administration is valid.[57] So also is a state statute forbidding and punishing the addressing of offensive and derisive language to anyone who is lawfully in any street or other public place.[58] Moreover, state child labor laws may validly be applied to those who permit children under their care to sell religious literature on the streets.[59] A state may require male students enrolled in the state university to take a course in military training as one of the conditions of attendance, without exempting conscientious and religious objectors to military training from the requirement.[60] The Court has even sustained state exclusion of a conscientious objector from the practice of law.[61]

A person may be constitutionally punished for holding a religious meeting in a public park without a permit as required by ordinance, even though he has properly sought the permit and been arbitrarily and illegally refused by those responsible for administering the ordinance, if the state provides a judicial remedy for such arbitrary refusal.[62]

Merchants who are members of the Orthodox Jewish faith are not entitled to exemption from a state statute forbidding the Sunday sale of commodities stocked by their stores, even though they are forced to suffer substantial economic loss in order to observe their Sabbath as required by the tenets of their faith; but a state may not deny unemployment compensation to a Seventh-Day Adventist because of his refusal to accept work on Saturday, the Sabbath of his religious faith. Finally, a state may not require an expression of belief in God as a condition of holding public office.

---

[56] *Reynolds* v. *United States,* 98 U.S. 145 (1878).
[57] *Cox* v. *New Hampshire,* 312 U.S. 569 (1941).
[58] *Chaplinsky* v. *New Hampshire* 315 U.S. 568 (1942).
[59] *Prince.* v. *Massachusetts,* 321 U.S. 158 (1944).
[60] *Hamilton* v. *Regents,* 293 U.S. 245 (1934).
[61] In re *Summers,* 325 U.S. 561 (1945).
[62] *Poulos* v. *New Hampshire,* 345 U.S. 395 (1953).

THE ESTABLISHMENT CLAUSE

The rest of this chapter will consider the Court's interpretation of the clause of the First Amendment forbidding Congress to make any "law respecting an establishment of religion," which like the free exercise clause has been held applicable to the states through the due process clause of the Fourteenth Amendment.

Before 1947 the interpretations of this clause had given the Court little difficulty. Unlike free exercise of religion, the establishment clause was almost untested so far as the Supreme Court was concerned. Indeed, there had been only four cases [63] before the Court in more than a century and a half, when in 1947 it was suddenly confronted with the highly sensitive and controversial issue of public aid to private, sectarian schools. The task of the Court today is complicated not only by the absence of applicable judicial precedents, but also by the fact that the intentions of the framers of the establishment clause have been obscured by the passage of time, and that diverse attitudes and traditions have arisen to confuse the accepted meaning of the clause, if such can be said to exist. Even more important is the fact that the modern application of the clause involves situations which were unknown to the framers and could not have been foreseen by them.[64]

It is true, of course, that in 1930 the use of public funds to purchase secular textbooks for pupils in parochial schools in Louisiana was sustained.[65] But here the establishment clause was not considered because the action of Louisiana was contested on the ground that it violated the due process clause of the Fourteenth Amendment by spending tax funds for a private purpose. The Court reasoned that since the tax funds were used for the benefit of the children and not for the sectarian schools, the ap-

[63] *Bradfield* v. *Roberts*, 175 U.S. 291 (1899); *Quick Bear* v. *Leup*, 210 U.S. 50 (1908); *Cochran* v. *Louisiana State Board*, 281 U.S. 370 (1930); Selective Draft Law cases, 245 U.S. 366 (1918).

[64] For a good discussion of these matters, see L. A. Lardner, "How Far Does the Constitution Separate Church and State," *American Political Science Review*, Vol. 45 (March, 1951), pp. 110–132.

[65] *Cochran* v. *Louisiana State Board*, 281 U.S. 370 (1930).

propriation was for a public purpose, and the fact that the schools were operated by members of a particular sect did not alter the character of the appropriation. It is apparent, then, that up to this time virtually nothing had been done by the Supreme Court to fix the boundaries of the establishment clause. Between 1947 and 1952 the Court decided three important cases which contributed little to illuminating the meaning of the establishment clause, if, indeed, they did not further obscure it.

Wall of Separation Doctrine

In *Everson* v. *Board of Education*,[66] the Supreme Court encountered a new problem. The question presented was the validity of a New Jersey statute authorizing the payment from tax-raised funds of the bus fares of Catholic parochial school pupils, as part of a program of paying the cost of transporting all pupils attending "schools other than private schools operated for profit." The holding of the Court sustaining these expenditures for the cost of transporting children to sectarian schools seems clearly inconsistent with its construction of the establishment clause in the same case.

At the outset the Court made it clear for the first time that the establishment clause, as well as the free exercise clause, of the First Amendment is made applicable to the states by the Fourteenth Amendment.

Also for the first time, the Court sought to give meaning to the establishment clause in these words:

The "establishment of religion" clause of the First Amendment means at least this: Neither a state nor the Federal Government can set up a church. Neither can pass laws which aid one religion, aid all religions, or prefer one religion over another. Neither can force nor influence a person to go to or to remain away from church against his will or force him to profess a belief or disbelief in any religion. No person can be punished for entertaining or professing religious beliefs or disbeliefs, for church attendance or non-attendance. No tax in any amount, large or small, can be levied to support any religious activities or institutions, whatever they may be called, or whatever form they may adopt to

[66] 330 U.S. 1 (1947).

teach or practice religion. Neither a state nor the Federal Government can, openly or secretly, participate in the affairs of any religious organization or groups and *vice versa*. In the words of Jefferson, the clause against the establishment of religion by law was intended to erect "a wall of separation between church and state."

Coming then to the specific issue before it, the Court insisted that the New Jersey legislation does no more than provide a general program to help parents get their children, regardless of their religion, safely and expeditiously to and from accredited schools. In short, this is a welfare program in aid of the pupils and not in support of the church schools. These payments, then, were sustained by the Court majority of five only because they were deemed in aid of the children and not in aid of the sectarian schools. This, declared Mr. Justice Black for the majority, "does not breach the wall of separation between church and state."

The majority, however, seems to have overlooked the fact, as Mr. Justice Jackson so forcefully pointed out in dissent, that the beneficiaries of these bus fare payments were selected by an essentially religious test. Before making payments to reimburse parents for pupils' bus fares, the school authorities must ask whether the school attended is a Catholic school, and if it is not, the aid is not afforded.

Moreover, the conclusion of the Court was reached in the face of its unequivocal declaration that "New Jersey cannot consistently with the 'establishment of religion' clause . . . contribute funds to the support of an institution which teaches the tenets and faith of any church." It is difficult to see how the grant of public funds to pay transportation costs of children to and from parochial schools, whose major objective is the teaching of sectarian doctrine, can be squared with this declaration. If the sectarian purposes of the school are aided by payment of bus fares, in that it helps to get children to the school who might not otherwise go there, as the Court majority conceded; if, as is presumed, a direct appropriation to the school would be invalid, is not an indirect appropriation equally invalid? The difference would seem to be in name and method, not in substance.

Furthermore, it might be asked, where does this welfare theory end? If the purchase of textbooks and the payment of bus fares for the pupils of parochial schools are constitutional, what is unconstitutional, other than distinctly sectarian services and supplies? How far can the state go in aiding church schools in the name of promoting the public welfare, with incidental sectarian benefits? May it supply the pupils of those schools with such nonsectarian aids as free lunches, free school clinics, free blackboards, free notebooks, free pencils, and salaries for teachers of nonsectarian subjects? Clearly, the Everson case raises more questions than it answers.

On the other hand, some of the limitations stated by Justice Black as required by the establishment clause of the First Amendment seem to be extreme, as well as inconsistent with the Court's holding in the case. For example, when he says that the First Amendment means at least this: "Neither a state nor the Federal Government . . . can pass laws which aid . . . all religions," some troublesome questions arise. The extension of tax exemption to church property and to gifts made to churches or religious causes is surely aid to religion. Can it be that these practices are invalid? The Court seems to assume that they are not, but the question is an open one.

And Justice Black assures us that all this was done without making the slightest breach in the wall separating church and state. Four of his fellow justices were less complacent about the Court's holdings, as were many outside the Court. Indeed, the most obvious result of the Everson decision was to stir up the very sort of bitter religious controversy which the original supporters of the First Amendment had sought to prevent.

A year after the Everson case, the Court in *McCollum* v. *Champaign Board of Education* [67] invalidated the so-called "released time" program of religious instruction in the schools of Champaign, Illinois. Such plans of religious education had become widespread since their initial adoption around 1914. Under the Champaign plan, public school children, with the written consent of their parents, attended regular weekly classes in religious instruction. The classes were taught by Protestant, Catholic, and Jewish teachers, furnished by a religious council representing the various faiths. They were paid nothing from public funds but

[67] 333 U.S. 203 (1948).

were subject to the approval and supervision of the school super-intendent. Pupils not enrolled in the religious classes were re-quired to continue their secular studies in other classrooms.

The Court held that this released time program fell "squarely under the ban" of the establishment of religion clause of the First Amendment, made applicable to the states by the Fourteenth, as construed in the Everson case. Two principal reasons were given for this holding: First, the program involved "a utilization of the tax-established and tax-supported public school system to aid religious groups to spread their faith." The Constitution forbids both state and federal governments from participation in the affairs of any religious organizations or groups, and vice versa. Second, the state was also aiding sectarian groups by helping to provide pupils for their religious classes through the state's com-pulsory public school machinery.

The decision was greeted with a veritable storm of adverse criticism from interested church groups and from less partisan critics who believed that the Court had taken an extreme, if not an indefensible, position. Justice Black himself observed, in the Clauson case to be considered presently: "Probably few opinions from the Court in recent years have attracted more attention and stirred wider debate." [68]

It is not surprising that church groups attacked the Court's decision, for similar plans of religious instruction were in opera-tion at this time in some 2000 school districts across the nation. But the decision was also denounced by scholars on historical and constitutional grounds. One of the most distinguished of these critics was Professor Edward S. Corwin, who declared that, "The historical record shows beyond peradventure that the core idea of 'an establishment of religion' comprises the idea of preference; and that an act of public authority favorable to religion cannot, without manifest falsification of history, be brought under the ban of that phrase." [69]

It is difficult to see how the Court could reach the conclusion it did in this case without reversing its ruling in the Everson case,

---

[68] *Zorach* v. *Clauson,* 343 U.S. 317 (1952).
[69] "The Supreme Court as National School Board," *Law and Contempo-rary Problems,* Vol. 14 (Winter, 1949), p. 20.

for if there is any difference in the aid afforded the sectarian school in the two cases, it would clearly appear to be greater in the Everson case. In both cases the local government aided religious groups in securing attendance of pupils for religious instruction, but surely the use of schoolrooms for a short while once a week is less of a financial burden on the taxpayers—if, indeed, it is not too infinitesimal to be calculated—then the payment of bus fares. Moreover, the apparent implication of Justice Black's argument, that in no circumstances and to no extent may public schoolrooms be used for religious instruction, would seem to be untenable. The long-accepted doctrine that no person should be taxed to support any religious sect was apparently aimed at the expenditure of public funds for the maintenance of church buildings, ministers' salaries, and other church work. "There was no thought in 1800 of prohibiting the use of microscopic portions of public funds for heating, lighting and maintaining school rooms for short weekly periods of religious instruction of the nature provided in Champaign, Illinois." [70]

Justice Reed, in his lone dissent, relied primarily upon the American tradition of state-church relations. He pointed out that there are many valid public aids to religion, such as tax exemption of church property, the employment of chaplains in both houses of Congress and in the armed forces, and the training of veterans for the ministry at government expense in denominational schools, under the Servicemen's Readjustment Act of 1944. "Devotion to the great principles of religious liberty," he concluded, "should not lead us into a rigid interpretation of the Constitutional guarantee that conflicts with accepted habits of our people." To Justice Reed, the established traditions of church-state relations determined the meaning of the establishment clause rather than what he regarded as dubious textual construction. He even expressed the view that "The phrase 'an establishment of religion,' may have been intended by Congress to be aimed only at a state church." This would seem to be dubious.

Taking Everson and McCollum together, it is apparent that the Court had worked itself into an untenable position. The welfare doctrine which was the basis of the ruling in Everson would

70 Lardner, *op. cit.*, p. 131.

logically justify almost any legislation and consequently deny any prohibitive effect to the establishment clause. On the other hand, the wall of separation doctrine was so applied in McCollum as to carry the implication that the First Amendment forbids all forms of public aid to religion, however general and nondiscriminatory.

Lowering the Wall of Separation

Whether or not it was consciously influenced by the criticism of the McCollum decision, the Court in 1952 reached the opposite conclusion with respect to a New York program in *Zorach* v. *Clauson*.[71] In this case, a majority of six justices (Douglas, Vinson, and Burton, who had voted to invalidate the Champaign plan; Clark and Minton, who had come on the Court after the McCollum decision; and Reed, who had thought the Champaign plan valid) approved the New York state "dismissed-time" program of religious education. Under this plan the children were dismissed from school, on written request of their parents, to attend religious classes in religious centers off school grounds but during school hours. Pupils not dismissed were required to remain in the school classrooms. Teachers were not allowed to announce the program to their students or to comment on attendance, but the churches made weekly reports to the schools, giving the names of pupils who had been released from school, but had not reported for religious instruction.

The Court was here confronted with a dual issue: whether New York "by this system has either prohibited the free exercise of religion" or has made a law "respecting an establishment of religion." Justice Douglas, for the Court majority, quickly disposed of the first. It would, he declared, be obtuse reasoning to inject any issue of "free exercise" of religion into this case, since no one is compelled to take the religious instruction. In sustaining the New York program against the religious establishment claim, Justice Douglas first departed from the absolutist wall of separa-

71 343 U.S. 306 (1952).

tion doctrine applied in McCollum and grounded the Court's decision upon the well-established American tradition of state-church relations. In this connection, he pointed out the difficulty and absurdity of a rigid separation between church and state. The First Amendment does not require that church and state be hostile, suspicious, and unfriendly aliens to each other. If this were so,

Churches could not be required to pay even property taxes. Municipalities would not be permitted to render police or fire protection to religious groups. . . . Prayers in our legislative halls, the appeals to the Almighty in the messages of the Chief Executive; the proclamations making Thanksgiving Day a holiday; "So help me God" in our courtroom oaths—these and all other references to the Almighty that run through our laws, our public rituals, our ceremonies would be flouting the First Amendment.

It would be pushing the concept of separation to these extremes to hold the New York law unconstitutional. Douglas continued: "We are a religious people whose institutions presuppose a Supreme Being," and "When the state encourages religious instruction or cooperates with religious authorities by adjusting the schedule of public events to sectarian needs, it follows the best of our traditions." Nothing in the Constitution requires government to show a callous indifference to religious groups. To do this would be to prefer those who believe in no religion over believers.

Justice Douglas did not stop here. He sought to reconcile this decision with the holding and theory of the McCollum case. The result of this was confusion and contradiction, as the dissenting justices were quick to point out. He thought that McCollum was distinguishable since there the public school classrooms were used for religious instruction, whereas here the public schools merely accommodate their schedules to a program of outside religious instruction. "We follow the McCollum case. But we cannot expand it to cover" the New York program, for "we cannot read into the Bill of Rights such a philosophy of hostility to religion."

Listing the prohibitions of the establishment clause of the First Amendment, Douglas stated:

Government may not finance religious groups nor undertake religious instruction nor blend secular and sectarian education nor use secular institutions to force one or some religion on any person. . . . It may not coerce anyone to attend church, to observe a religious holiday, or to take religious instruction.

It is, however, free to close its doors or suspend its operation for the benefit of those who wish to go to their religious sanctuary for worship or instruction. "No more than that is undertaken here." With respect to the last statement, it should be noted that the schools neither close their doors nor suspend their operations. Pupils who are not dismissed for religious instruction are compelled to continue their regular school activities. This is the crucial fact, which means that here, as in the Champaign plan, the educational system of the state is being adjusted to the promotion of sectarian objectives. Here, as there, the state is manipulating the "class room hours of its compulsory school machinery so as to channel children into sectarian classes."

Dissenting Justices Black, Frankfurter, and Jackson could not detect any substantial difference between this case and that of McCollum. Justice Jackson characterized the attempt to differentiate between the two systems, on the ground that the New York plan provided for religious instruction off the school grounds, as "trivial almost to the point of cynicism, magnifying its non-essential details and disparaging compulsion which was the underlying reason for invalidity."

Justice Frankfurter, like his colleagues Jackson and Black, emphasized the compulsory aspects of the New York dismissed-time plan. "The pith of the case is that formalized religious instruction is substituted for other school activity which those who do not participate in the released-time program are compelled to attend."

These sharp differences among the justices of the Court point up the extreme difficulty of satisfactorily resolving the issues involved in the establishment cases of the last two decades. It is not surprising that these cases did not succeed in fixing clearly the boundaries of religious establishment. In addition to the difficulties emphasized at the outset of this establishment discussion [72] there is also the troublesome problem of the relationship of the

[72] See page 132.

free exercise and establishment clauses. Apparently they may stand in conflict, in which case the Court is confronted with the difficult problem of choice. This point will receive further consideration in connection with the later cases to which we now turn.

The Sunday Closing Law Cases

The principal case concerning the relation of Sunday closing laws to the establishment clause is that of *McGowan* v. *Maryland*,[73] decided in 1961. In this case several merchants were convicted for violation of a section of the Maryland Code which generally prohibited, with certain exceptions, the Sunday sale of merchandise. They contended, among other things, that the statute violated the establishment clause of the First Amendment, made applicable to the states by the Fourteenth Amendment. The crux of their argument was that the purpose of the enforced stoppage of labor on Sunday, the Sabbath day of the predominant Christian sects, was to facilitate and encourage church attendance and to aid the recruitment of church membership by these predominant sects.

After reviewing the history of Sunday closing laws both in England and this country, the Court finds in these laws no violation of the establishment clause. The basic ground of the decision was that, although these laws were originally enacted for religious purposes, they were continued in force for the secular reasons of providing a universal day of rest and of ensuring the health and tranquility of the community. In other words, as Justice Brennan put it in his concurring opinion, government may originally have decreed a uniform Sunday day of rest for the impermissible purpose of aiding religion, but abandoned that purpose and retained the law for the valid purpose of furthering secular ends.

Regarding the position of Sunday closing laws in relation to the First Amendment, the Court concludes: "The Establishment clause does not ban federal or state regulation of conduct whose reason or effect merely happens to coincide or harmonize with the tenets of some or all religions." The general welfare of society,

[73] 366 U.S. 420 (1961).

quite apart from any religious considerations, induces the legislatures to enact such regulations. "Thus, for temporal purposes,
murder is illegal, and the fact that this agrees with the dictates of
the Judeo-Christian religions . . . does not invalidate the regulation. So too with the questions of adultery and polygamy."

Against the argument that there were other ways of achieving the secular purposes of the state and that "the Court should
hold the statute invalid on the ground that the state's power to
regulate conduct in the public interest may only be executed in a
way that does not unduly or unnecessarily infringe upon the
religious provisions of the First Amendment," the Court coun-
tered that "the state's purpose is not merely to provide a one-
day-in-seven work stoppage. In addition to this the state seeks to
set one day apart from all others as a day of rest, repose, recreation
and tranquility." Furthermore, the problems of enforcing a one-
day-in-seven statute would, the Court thought, be vastly more
difficult than those of enforcing a uniform day-of-rest provision.[74]

Moreover, the Court points to the fact that Sunday has come
to have a special significance in this country; it is a day set apart
from all other days as a time of family activity and friendly intercourse. Because of this fact, the Court believes that it would be
unrealistic for enforcement purposes and perhaps detrimental to
the general welfare to require a state to choose [even] a common
day of rest other than that which most people would select of
their own accord. For these reasons the Maryland laws are not
laws respecting an establishment of religion.[75]

School Prayer Cases

The highly sensitive and explosive issue of school prayers and
Bible reading in public schools came before the Court in a series
of three cases decided in 1962 and 1963. The first of these cases,
Engel v. *Vitale*,[76] provoked an emotional outburst which, in the
intensity of its vitriol, probably exceeded that which followed the

[74] *Ibid.*, pp. 450–452.
[75] The case of *Two Guys* v. *McGinley*, decided on the same day, raises
a similar issue.
[76] 370 U.S. 421 (1962).

School Segregation Cases of 1954. An observer from another country, without reading the Court's opinion, might have thought that it had abolished religion and subverted the Constitution. Such was not the case, even though the Court's opinion may be subject to rational criticism.

The facts of the case are briefly these: The State Board of Regents of New York, a governmental agency, composed and recommended a prayer to the local school boards of the state, and the board of education of a local school district, acting in its official capacity under state law, directed the school district's principal to cause a prayer to be said aloud by each class in the presence of a teacher at the begining of each school day. Soon after the practice of reciting the prayer began, the parents of ten pupils brought suit in a New York court, insisting that the use of the official prayer was contrary to the religious beliefs and practices of both themselves and their children and that it violated the establishment clause of the First Amendment made applicable to the state through the due process clause of the Fourteenth Amendment.

After an excursion into the history of church-state relations in both England and America, Justice Black concluded for the Court that the state of New York, by using its public school system to encourage the recitation of the Regents' prayer, had instituted a practice wholly at variance with the establishment clause. The constitutional prohibition against laws respecting an establishment of religion "must at least mean that in this country it is no part of the business of government to compose official prayers for any group of the American people to recite as part of a religious program carried on by government." [77]

No level of government in the United States has the power, declared Justice Black, "to prescribe by law any particular form of prayer which is to be used as an official prayer in carrying on any program of governmentally sponsored religious activity." [78] Since the state prayer program does officially establish "the religious beliefs embodied in the Regents' prayer," it clearly violates the establishment clause. Nor is the prayer saved from the strictures

[77] *Ibid.*, p. 425.
[78] *Ibid.*, p. 430.

of the establishment clause because it is denominationally neutral or that its observance on the part of pupils is voluntary. This clause, unlike the free exercise clause, "does not depend upon any showing of direct governmental compulsion and is violated by the enactment of laws which establish an official religion whether those laws operate directly to coerce nonobserving individuals or not."

This conclusion, Justice Black believes, rests upon the historic conviction of the founders of the Constitution that "a union of government and religion tends to destroy government and to degrade religion" and "that governmentally established religions and religious persecutions go hand in hand." He vigorously denies that this application of the establishment clause indicates "a hostility towards religion or towards prayer. Nothing, of course, could be more wrong. The history of man is inseparable from the history of religion. . . . It is neither sacrilegious nor antireligious to say that each separate government in this country should stay out of the business of writing or sanctioning official prayers and leave that purely religious function to the people themselves and to those the people choose to look to for religious guidance." [79]

Mr. Justice Douglas, in his gratuitous concurring opinion, adds further confusion to the already confused situation with respect to the proper boundaries of the establishment clause. He is unable to say that the authorization of this prayer amounts to the establishment of a religion "in the strictly historic meaning of those words," but the point for decision here is "whether the government can constitutionally finance a religious exercise." He now thinks it cannot and that all the existing exercises financed by government are likewise unconstitutional. "In retrospect" the Everson case seems out of line with the First Amendment.

Mr. Justice Stewart, in dissent, is unable to "see how an 'official religion' is established by letting those who want to say a prayer say it." Furthermore, he is unimpressed by the majority's recital of the history of an established church in sixteenth-century England or in eighteenth-century America. What is relevant, on the contrary, is "the history of the religious traditions of our people, reflected in countless practices of the institutions and

[79] *Ibid.*, p. 446.

officials of our government." [80] He referred to the prayer used in opening the daily session of the Supreme Court and the daily sessions of both houses of the Congress, the presidential invocation of divine guidance, the prayer in the National Anthem, the words "under God" in the Pledge of Allegiance to the Flag, the annual presidential proclamation of a National Day of Prayer, and the motto "In God We Trust" impressed on our coins. The last four of these have had the sanction of congressional action.

Mr. Justice Stewart has a point when he questions the relevance of Mr. Justice Black's selective history, but he seems to gloss over the central point of the majority opinion that the prayer was composed and prescribed by officials of the state. There was really no evidence that any pupils had expressed a wish to join in reciting this prayer, as he suggested.[81]

Some language in the body of the majority opinion as well as the implication of a final footnote (to be considered later) might suggest that the fact that the prayer was officially *composed* as well as officially approved was an important factor in the decision. However, the Schempp and Murray cases emphatically dispelled any such notion. These cases logically extended the principle of the Engel case by holding that no state law or any public authority may require the reading of passages from the Bible or the recitation of the Lord's Prayer in the public schools of the state at the opening of each school day, even if individual pupils may be excused from attending or participating in such exercises.

In the first [82] of these cases, which were considered jointly, the U.S. district court had held invalid a Pennsylvania statute requiring the reading of "at least ten verses from the Holy Bible . . . , without comment, at the opening of each public school on each school day." The Schempp parents and two of their children brought suit to enjoin enforcement of the statute by the school authorities, contending that it was violative of the prohibition against religious establishment under the First and Fourteenth Amendments. The three-judge district court held the law violative of the establishment clause as applied to the states by the due

---

[80] *Ibid.*, pp. 434 , 435.
[81] *Ibid.*, p. 445.
[82] *Abington School District* v. *Schempp*, 374 U.S. 203 (1963).

process clause of the Fourteenth Amendment. The Supreme Court affirmed this decision.

In the Murray case [83] the Board of School Commissioners of Baltimore City in 1905 adopted a rule, pursuant to a provision of the Maryland Code, providing for the "reading, without comment, of a chapter in the Holy Bible and/or the use of the Lord's Prayer." The petitioners in this case, Mrs. Madalyn Murray and her son, were professed atheists. They filed suit in the Maryland court for mandamus to compel rescission and cancellation of the rule. The trial court sustained, and the Court of Appeals of Maryland by a four to three vote affirmed, holding the exercise to be in accordance with the First and Fourteenth Amendments.

Mr. Justice Clark, for the majority, began by emphasizing that religion has been closely identified with our history and government from the days of the founding fathers to the present, but "this is not to say . . . that religion has been so identified with our history and government that religious freedom is not likewise as strongly imbedded in our public and private life." [84] After reviewing the cases the Court reiterated its Engel position that although the establishment and free exercise "clauses may in certain instances overlap, they forbid two quite different kinds of governmental encroachment upon religious freedom." The test of establishment violation is to be found in "the purpose and the primary effect of the enactment." Thus "to withstand the strictures of the establishment clause there must be a secular legislative purpose and a primary effect that neither advances nor inhibits religion." It is the purpose of the free exercise clause to withdraw "from legislative power, state or federal, the exertion of any restraint on the free exercise of religion." Thus it is essential in a free exercise case for one to show the coercive effect of the enactment against him in the practice of his religion.

Applying the establishment clause principles in the present cases, the Court finds that in both states the laws require religious exercises and that these exercises are being conducted in direct violation of the rights of appellants and petitioners.

The Court rejects the argument of school officials that unless

[83] *Murray* v. *Curlett*, 374 U.S. 211 (1963).
[84] *School District* v. *Schempp*, 374 U.S. 212–214.

these religious exercises are permitted a "religion of secularism" will be established. It is agreed that the state may not do this by affirmatively opposing or showing hostility to religion, that it may not prefer "those who believe in no religion over those who do believe." [85] But this decision has no such effect, for the religious exercises are required by the state in violation of the command of the First Amendment "that the Government maintain strict neutrality, neither aiding nor opposing religion."

SUMMARY ANALYSIS

In view of the diversity and confusion issuing from the earlier establishment cases of Everson, McCollum, and Zorach, and the failure of the justices to agree on a clearly reasoned theory of constitutional interpretation, it was virtually certain that additional controversies would press upon the Court. These came in the form of the School Prayer and Bible Reading Cases of 1962 and 1963, and the Sunday Closing Law Cases of 1961. But even now it is doubtful that the boundaries of religious establishment have been any more clearly drawn. [86]

It is difficult to quarrel with the holding of the Court in the Engel case that it is no part of the business of government to prescribe an officially approved prayer for daily recitation in the public schools. It was the degree of the state's involvement in this particular prayer that rendered it vulnerable. The holding as such goes no farther. It does not require the public schools to show hostility or even indifference to religion, or to exclude from their programs a consideration of religion as an important factor in our national history and tradition, so long as it is incidental to some lawful secular purpose such as the expressions of patriotism or the promotion of rest, recreation, and friendly intercourse by setting aside Sunday as a day of rest.

[85] *Zorach v. Clauson*, 343 U.S. 306, 314 (1952).

[86] For a contrary view see William W. Van Alstyne, "Constitutional Separations of Church and State: the Quest for a Coherent Position," 57 *American Political Science Review* 865–882 (December, 1963).

However, despite the soundness of the decision of the constitutional issue, the Court's handling of the case presents certain difficulties and leaves unanswered questions.

First, the distinction drawn in Justice Black's final footnote in Engel between those forms of religious exercise which constitute establishment and those which do not seems to be a very dim line. According to this distinction, school exercises which are primarily religious in character, although they may embody a strong patriotic sentiment, are forbidden as an establishment of religion; whereas those which are primarily patriotic, although they embody a strong religious sentiment, are permissible. In applying this distinction of degree it seems inevitable that some judges will read it one way and some another in similar concrete situations. At any rate, some form of prayer seems to be permissible under this distinction.

Second, the effect of the School Prayer Cases on the distinction drawn in Zorach between released time on the school premises and released time off the premises is not clear. Some language in the Engel opinion suggests that all released time programs are invalid because they involve the manipulation of the school program toward the end of promoting religious exercises and indoctrination, but the Engel opinion is strangely silent on the Zorach and McCollum cases.

Third, the Court has not been able to reach a clear position on the relationship of the free exercise and establishment clauses. In the Prayer Cases, it will be recalled, the Court construed the establishment clause as both overlapping the free exercise clause and as stating a separate and independent limitation. This suggests that they may sometimes be in conflict. This problem seems to have been particularly acute in the Sunday Closing Law Cases. Despite the reasoning of the Court in the Braunfeld case, for example, one finds it difficult to avoid the conclusion that the decision operated to deprive the Jewish merchants of their religious freedom.

In case of conflict the question necessarily is, which shall prevail? Apparently the New York prayer was legally bad because it established the religious convictions expressed in the prayer as the officially approved beliefs of the state, and there was no free exercise conflict, but Professor Paul Freund of the Harvard Law School argues persuasively that the prayer should have been held invalid because of interference with the free exercise of religion. He points out that because of the schoolroom atmosphere and the disposition of school children to conform, the religious exercise was in reality coercive.[87] Even Justice Black agreed that "indirect coercive pressure upon religious minorities" might exist in such a situation. The Zorach opinion took the view that the establishment clause does not set up an absolute separation of church and state, and that the state was not precluded from accommodating its school program to the religious interests and desires of its people. As previously pointed out, this is hardly consistent with the absolutist view expressed in Everson and McCollum, and it suggests that the establishment restriction must sometimes yield to the free exercise of religion. Since Justice Black vigorously dissented in Zorach, it may be assumed that his Engel opinion means to restore the high "wall of separation" and the absolutist principle of no aid to religion first set forth in the Everson opinion.

Yet, even in the absolutist cases the Court, as indicated above, has permitted aid to religion as an incident to a lawful secular end. Despite the absolutist pronouncements of the Everson opinion, the aid to sectarian education was justified as incidental to the valid secular purpose of aiding the safe transportation of pupils to school without discrimination as to religion. Also, in the Sunday Closing Law Cases, the incidental effect of favoring the Christian day of worship did not prevent the state's providing a universal day of rest in order to ensure the health and tranquility of the community. In the Prayer and Bible Reading Cases the religious exercise was regarded as primary and not incidental to a valid secular purpose. It seems, then, that public schools may practice religious exercises if they are incidental to patriotic or other secular purposes.

Professor Philip Kurland of the University of Chicago Law School suggests that this difficulty can be solved by "reading the freedom and separation clauses as stating a single precept: that government cannot utilize religion as a standard for action or in-

[87] See *The New York Times Magazine*, November 13, 1962.

action because these clauses read together as they should be, prohibit classification in terms of religion either to confer a benefit or to impose a burden." [88] He reasons that if the command of the First Amendment is that no inhibitions be placed by the state on the free exercise of religion, it is equally forbidden that the state confer favors upon religious activity; and that it would be impossible to effectuate those commands "unless they are read together as creating a doctrine more akin to the reading of the equal protection clause than to the due process clause." This means that "they must be read to mean that religion may not be used as a basis for classification for purposes of governmental action, whether that action be the conferring of rights or privileges or the imposition of duties or obligations." [89] This proposed switch from a due process doctrinal base to an equal protection base, although plausible, might in practice further complicate an already too complicated situation. At any rate, the Court has shown no disposition to lean in this direction. In the Prayer Cases as noted above, the Court rested its decision solely upon the establishment clause, and it read the clause as stating a separate and independent limitation.

Fourth, the establishment cases are also unclear on the kind and degree of government neutrality that is required by the established clause. It is one thing for government to be neutral between different religious sects. It is quite another thing for it to be neutral as between religion and nonreligion.[90] If neutrality means that government is to be indifferent to religion and regard it as irrelevant to the American way of life, such a conception of neutrality runs counter to an almost unbroken line of tradition of official sympathy for and aid to religion. Does neutrality under the Constitution forbid the granting of tax exemptions to church property? Does it forbid, in governmental ceremonies, a preference for those religious ideas and beliefs held by a preponderant majority of the people and which accord with our national tradition? If

[88] *Religion and the Law* (Chicago, Aldine Publishing Company, 1962), pp. 111–112.

[89] *Ibid.*, p. 18.

[90] The discussion of this point has drawn substantially on Paul G. Kauper, "Prayer, Public Schools and the Supreme Court," 61 *Michigan Law Review* 1031–1068 (April, 1963).

so, again the concept flies in the face of history. It is abundantly clear from this history as well as from current practice that government in the United States has never been absolutely neutral in matters of religion.

The Court has never been called on to determine which of the many governmental religious exercises are valid and which are invalid. Needless to say, distinctions in this area will be difficult. Because of the extreme difficulty of these religious establishment issues the Court perhaps merits sympathy in its failure to formulate a consistent and well-reasoned theory of establishment.

One may wonder, however, why the Court did not exert greater effort to avoid the explosive issue presented in the Prayer Cases—an issue not of transcendent importance. Even Justice Black regarded the prayer in the Engel case as "relatively insignificant." The "standing to sue" defense seemed clearly available to the Court in this case. A decade before, the Court had resorted to this device to avoid consideration of the constitutionality of Bible reading in the schools of New Jersey.[91] The Court majority held that the record failed to show that any ascertainable expense resulted from the Bible reading and hence denied standing to sue.

Mr. Justice Jackson had pointed out in the McCollum case that there were two grounds on which federal courts could intervene against the action of local school authorities. One would be an effort on the part of the school to coerce pupils into submission to some religious ceremony or teaching against their convictions. The other was the imposition of a tax to support a religious activity. Certainly, in the Prayer Cases there was no evidence that the prayer added to school costs. Nor could standing to sue rest on the fact of religious coercion, for Justice Black made no claim that coercion existed. Still, there was somehow standing sufficient to raise an establishment issue.[92]

[91] *Doremus* v. *Board of Education*, 342 U.S. 429 (1952).
[92] On this point see Herman Pritchett, "Prayers and Politics: The Supreme Court, 1961–1962," *American Government Annual 1963, 1964* (Holt, Rinehart, and Winston), p. 32.

6

POLITICAL AND
SOCIAL EQUALITY

The purpose of this chapter is to consider three general aspects of discrimination against political and social equality: first, racial discrimination as restrictive of political freedom; second, geographical discrimination as restrictive of political freedom; and third, racial discrimination as restrictive of the enjoyment of certain social advantages in relation to such matters as transportation, educational opportunities, access to privately owned places of public accommodation, and the acquisition and occupancy of property.

POLITICAL FREEDOM:
SUFFRAGE RESTRICTIONS

Political freedom implies, among other things, the right of general participation in the processes of political decision and control, and as bases for this right the enjoyment of the fundamental rights of free speech, press, assembly, and religion. The latter rights have been considered in the preceding chapters. Here, attention will first be focused on restrictions which have, from time to time, been imposed upon another and more concrete aspect of political freedom, namely, freedom of the suffrage. This, of course, involves consideration of the Fifteenth Amendment, as well as the Fourteenth.

During most of the time since the Fifteenth Amendment established the right of Negroes to vote, by declaring that "The right of citizens of the United States to vote shall not be denied or abridged by the United States or by any State on account of race, color, or previous condition of servitude," members of this race have nevertheless been effectively disfranchised by southern states. The methods of circumvention employed by those states are too familiar to justify recounting in this brief study. Suffice it to say here that, up to 1915, restrictions on Negro suffrage had met with little resistance from the Supreme Court. For example, the literacy test, designed to bar the Negro from the ballot, was sustained by the Court in *Williams* v. *Mississippi* [1] in 1898.

Still, in 1915 the Court in *Guinn* v. *United States* [2] struck down the Oklahoma "grandfather clause" as a violation of the Fifteenth Amendment. This device, similar to those adopted earlier in some half dozen other southern states, provided a loophole for the escape of illiterate whites from a literacy test for voting by exempting from the test those persons and their lineal descendants who were qualified to vote as of January 1, 1866, a date which would not apply to Negroes. Later efforts to circumvent the 1915 decision failed.[3] Nevertheless, these decisions did not dampen the zeal of states bent on disfranchising the Negro. The "white primary" and the poll tax proved to be effective weapons in this enterprise.

The White Primary

The advent of the direct primary election toward the end of the last century and its widespread development in the first two decades of the present century furnished the South, ironically enough, with a new weapon against Negro suffrage. If the Negro

[1] 170 U.S. 213 (1898).
[2] 238 U.S. 347 (1915).
[3] *Lane* v. *Wilson*, 307 U.S. 268 (1939).

could be barred from the Democratic primary, he would, of course, be effectively disfranchised, since in the South the choice made in the Democratic primary determined the outcome in the final election, which merely formalized and legalized the primary.

Inspiration for the first legislative prescription of the white primary apparently came from the inconclusive decision of the Supreme Court in *Newberry v. United States*,[4] in which Mr. Justice McReynolds, speaking for himself and three of his brethren, declared that a primary is no part of election and that the part of the Federal Corrupt Practices Act purporting to limit the expenditures of a senatorial candidate in a primary was unconstitutional.[5]

Soon after this decision, the Texas legislature enacted a law barring Negroes from the polls in any Democratic primary in the state of Texas. The law was invalidated by the Supreme Court in *Nixon v. Herndon*[6] as a violation of the equal protection of the laws clause of the Fourteenth Amendment. The attempt to vest the same power of discrimination in the state central committee of the party failed because the committee received its authority to act from the legislature and hence was an agent of the state.[7] But in *Grovey v. Townsend*,[8] in 1935, the Court upheld the exclusion of a Negro voter from the Democratic primary under the resolution of the state Democratic Convention without benefit of statute. Here, the Court declared that to deny a vote in a primary was a mere refusal of party membership in a private organization, with which "the state need have no concen." The action was not state action.

The great turning point came in 1941 when, in the Classic case, the Court held that Section 4 of Article I of the Constitution authorizes Congress to regulate primaries, as well as general elections, where the primary is by law an integral part of the procedure of choice (of a representative in Congress), or where in fact the primary effectively controls the choice.[9] The Court also held that it was the right of a qualified citizen of the United

4 256 U.S. 232 (1921).
5 Justice McKenna concurred in the judgment on other grounds.
6 273 U.S. 536 (1927).
7 *Nixon v. Condon*, 286 U.S. 73 (1932).
8 295 U.S. 45 (1935).
9 *United States v. Classic*, 313 U.S. 299, 318 (1941).

States to vote in a congressional primary and to have his vote counted as cast.

It should be noted that this case did not settle the question as to whether white people were free to exclude Negroes from primaries at which only state and local officers were chosen, or from primaries for the selection of national officers which were not by state law directly made a part of the state election machinery. There was still *Grovey v. Townsend.*

In 1944 the Court in *Smith* v. *Allwright* [10] outlawed the white primary as violative of the Fifteenth Amendment, and declared that the constitutional right to be free from racial discrimination in voting ". . . is not to be nullified by a state through casting its electoral process in a form which permits a private organization to practice racial discrimination in the election." The Court, after declaring that "It may be taken as a postulate that the right to vote in . . . a primary . . . without discrimination by the state . . . is a right secured by the Constitution," went on to hold that since by state law the primary was made an integral part of the state election machinery, the action of the party in excluding Negroes was action by the state and consequently in violation of the Fifteenth Amendment. Thus the controlling issue here, as in the Grovey case, was whether the Negro had been barred from the primary by *state* action. The Court held that he had, and consequently *Grovey v. Townsend* was overruled.

Although this decision greatly stimulated Negro participation in southern primaries,[11] the resistance to it in most of the affected states was prompt and determined. These efforts at circumvention can be illustrated by the examples of South Carolina and Alabama, from both of which states issued important court decisions.[12]

South Carolina promptly repealed all statutory [13] and constitutional [14] laws relating to primaries, and the Democratic primary

[10] 321 U.S. 649 (1944).

[11] See O. D. Weeks, "The White Primary: 1944–1948," *American Political Science Review*, Vol. 42, No. 3 (June, 1948), pp. 500–510; also Donald S. Strong, "The Rise of Negro Voting in Texas," *ibid.*, pp. 510–512.

[12] For efforts in other southern states, see Weeks, *op. cit.*

[13] Acts and Joint Resolutions, South Carolina, 1944, Sec. 2323.

[14] Constitution of South Carolina, Art. 2, Sec. 10.

was thereafter conducted under rules prescribed by the Democratic party. This bold attempt to circumvent the Allwright decision was struck down by the U.S. district court in *Elmore* v. *Rice*,[15] on July 12, 1947; the decision was sustained by the Court of Appeals of the Fourth Circuit on December 30, 1947, and on April 19, 1948, the Supreme Court of the United States refused to review the latter ruling.[16]

Elmore was denied the right to vote in the Democratic primary under rules promulgated by the Democratic Convention limiting the right to vote in the primary to white persons. Both the district court and the court of appeals ruled that the party and the primary were still serving as instruments of the state in the electoral process despite the repeal of all laws relating to primaries.[17]

It is worth noting that the primary involved in the Allwright case was conducted under the provisions of state law and not merely under party rules, as in this case. Here, the state had *permitted* the party to discriminate against the Negro voter in violation of the Constitution. The appeals court put the question before it sharply in this way:

The question presented for our decision is whether by *permitting* [18] a party to take over a part of its election machinery, a state can avoid the provisions of the Constitution forbidding racial discrimination in elections and can deny to a part of the electorate because of race and color any effective voice in the government of the state. It seems perfectly clear that the question must be answered in the negative.[19] [Hence] no election machinery can be upheld if its purpose or effect is to deny to the Negro on account of his race or color any effective voice in the government of his country or the state or community wherein he lives.[20]

Undeterred, the Democratic party authorities of South Carolina sought to evade the Elmore decision by vesting control of primaries in clubs to which Negroes were not admitted, and by requiring, for voting in the primaries, an oath which was particularly objectionable to Negroes. Among other things, they were to

---

[15] 72 F. Supp. 516 (1947).
[16] *Rice* v. *Elmore*, 165 F. 2d. 387 (1947); 68 S. Ct. 905 (1948).
[17] *Rice* v. *Elmore*, 165 F. 2d. 388.
[18] Italics mine.
[19] *Rice* v. *Elmore*, 165 F. 2d. 389.
[20] *Ibid.*, p. 392.

swear that they believed in the social and educational separation of the races. This effort failed in both the district court [21] and the court of appeals [22] on the strength of the principle enunciated in the Elmore case.

The principle enunciated in the Elmore case was approved and applied by the Supreme Court of the United States in *Terry* v. *Adams* [23] in 1953. Fort Bend County, Texas, had for more than sixty years deprived Negroes of the ballot by setting up an association which included all white voters on the official list of the county and barred Negroes from membership. This organization, known as the Jaybird Democratic Association, claimed to be only a voluntary, private club with no connection whatever with the state political or elective machinery. Its ostensible duty was merely to pick candidates for recommendation to the regular party primary. Expenses were met by assessing the candidates, and no reports or certification of candidates were made to any state or party officials. Here, Justice Black declared that the facts and findings of this case bring it squarely within the reasoning and holding of the Court of Appeals of the Fourth Circuit in the Elmore case, in which the principle was laid down "that no election machinery could be sustained if its purpose or effect was to deny Negroes on account of their race an effective voice in the governmental affairs of their country, state, or community." [24] Indeed, as already pointed out, essentially the same principle had previously been enunciated in *Smith* v. *Allwright*, when the Supreme Court said that the constitutional right to be free from racial discrimination in voting ". . . is not to be nullified by a state through casting its electoral process in a form which permits a private organization to practice racial discrimination in the election." [25]

The preceding cases, taken as a whole, would seem to indicate that no action of any group or organization which controls the choice of public officials and the decision of public issues, and the right of qualified citizens to participate in that choice and decision, is private action. Every attempt at preserving the sub-

---

[21] *Brown* v. *Baskin*, 78 F. Supp. 933 (1948).
[22] *Baskin* v. *Brown*, 174 F. 2d. 391 (1949).
[23] 345 U.S. 461 (1953).
[24] *Rice* v. *Elmore*, 165 F. 2d. 389, 392.
[25] 321 U.S. 644 at 664.

stance of the white primary has ultimately failed in the courts, and it does not seem likely that future subterfuges will succeed except as delaying tactics.

Alabama refused to follow the example of South Carolina and to repeal her primary legislation as a method of circumventing *Smith* v. *Allwright*, apparently because of fear that primary elections could not be properly policed without state regulation. Instead, she sought to limit registration, and consequently voting, to "properly qualified persons." In 1946 the so-called Boswell Amendment to the Constitution of Alabama was adopted, providing that only persons who can "understand and explain" any article of the Constitution of the United States, who are possessed of "good character," and who understand "the duties and obligations of good citizenship under a republican form of government" may qualify as electors.[26]

Under the statutory law the applicant for registration must "understand and explain" the duties and obligations of good citizenship to the reasonable satisfaction of the boards of registrars for the several counties of the state.[27]

It is, of course, not surprising, that a federal district court found that the amendment was intended as a grant of arbitrary power to evade the decision of the Supreme Court in *Smith* v. *Allwright* and to restrict voting on the basis of color, that evidence showed it had in fact been arbitrarily administered for the purpose of excluding Negro applicants from the franchise, whereas white applicants with comparable qualifications were accepted, and that as a rule only Negroes were required to submit to the tests. Thus the amendment, "both in its object and the manner of its administration is unconstitutional because it violates the Fifteenth Amendment." [28] The Supreme Court refused to overrule this decision.[29]

Federal Anti-Poll Tax Legislation

Between 1939 and 1964, when the Twenty-Fourth Amendment became a part of the Constitution, numerous bills designed to

[26] Section 181 of the Constitution of Alabama, as amended (1946).
[27] Title 17, Sec. 21, Code of Alabama, 1940.
[28] *Davis* v. *Schnell*, 81 F. Supp. 872 (1949).
[29] 69 S. Ct. 747 (1949).

prohibit the imposition of a poll tax as a prerequisite to voting in a primary or other election for national officers passed the House of Representatives but failed in the Senate. In the meantime the Twenty-fourth Amendment had been proposed and was approved by the necessary number of states in 1964. This amendment provides that:

The right of citizens of the United States to vote in any primary or other election [for national officers] shall not be denied or abridged by the United States or any state by reasons of failure to pay any poll tax or other tax.

In April 1965, a unanimous Supreme Court in its first interpretation of this amendment held that a Virginia law,[30] requiring voters in federal elections to file a witnessed or notarized certificate of residence at least six months before the date of the election, was a violation of this amendment. The law allowed the voter to pay the state poll tax in lieu of filing the residence certificate.

The precise issue, said the Court, "is whether the State of Virginia may constitutionally confront the federal voter with a requirement that he either pay the customary poll taxes as required for state elections or file a certificate of residence." [31] This, the Court held, contravened the Twenty-fourth Amendment.

Court Upholds Voting Rights Act of 1965

Perhaps more significant than any of the preceding judicial efforts at curbing racial discrimination in voting was the enactment of the Voting Rights Act of 1965 [32] and its sweeping sustention by the Supreme Court in *State of South Carolina* v. *Katzenbach*[33] on March 7, 1966. This act stemmed from recommendations made by President Johnson to the Congress in the spring of 1965, following the voting rights demonstrations and marches at Selma, Alabama. Relatively mild voting rights legislation of 1957, 1960, and 1964

---

[30] There are now only three other states that require a poll tax for voting in state elections—Alabama, Mississippi, and Texas.

[31] *Harman* et al. v. *Lars Forsennius* et al., S. Ct. of U.S., October term, 1964, p. 10.

[32] Public Law 89–110, 89 Cong., S 1564 (August 6, 1965).

[33] 34 L W 4207.

had proved ineffective. Because of the opportunities for delay and evasion afforded the officials involved in the proceedings, the case by case method of handling alleged violations of this legislation was too onerous and time-consuming for effective protection. The Court pointed out that even when favorable decisions were obtained, some states switched to discriminatory devices not covered in the federal decrees or enacted complicated new tests to prolong the disparity between white and Negro registration, or sometimes local registration officials evaded court orders by closing or abolishing their registration offices in order to freeze the voting rolls. The act of 1965, unlike previous legislation, prescribes remedies for voting discrimination which become effective without the need for prior adjudication.

This law was based on the findings of Congress that existing legislation had not been and could not be, effective, and that the unsuccessful remedies of the past "would have to be replaced by sterner and more elaborate measures in order to satisfy the clear commands of the 15th Amendment." Another point which the Court saw emerging from the committee hearings and floor debates on the bill was that "Congress felt itself confronted by an insidious and pervasive evil which had been perpetuated in certain parts of our country through unremitting and ingenious defiance of the Constitution."

The 1965 response to the "insidious and pervasive evil" was the "sterner and more elaborate measures" of the Voting Rights Act of that year. In general the act is characterized by two main features: (1) It makes provision for suspension of a variety of tests and other devices that have been employed to deny citizens the right to vote because of their race or color. (2) It provides for the appointment of federal examiners to help get voters registered in areas where tests and devices have been suspended. The tests or devices covered in the act include those which require a demonstration of ability to read. write, interpret, or understand certain assigned material, proof of good moral character, and proof of qualifications through the testimony of one or more qualified voters who must vouch for the prospective voter. Under the act no person may be denied the right to vote in any election or primary for failure to pass any of these tests, (1) if he lives in a state or political subdivision which maintained such a test or device as a prerequisite to registration or voting as of November 1, 1964; and (2) if less than fifty percent of the total voting age population were registered or actually voted in the 1964 presidential election. Wherever these two factors exist, the state or political subdivision is automatically covered by the 1965 act.

In any area covered by the act the Attorney General may direct the U.S. Civil Service Commission to appoint federal examiners to aid in voter registration, if he believes that such action is necessary to enforce the guarantees of the Fifteenth Amendment, or if he has received twenty meritorious written complaints alleging voter discrimination. The law also contains a finding that the requirement of the payment of a poll tax as a prerequisite to voting has in some areas, the purpose or effect of denying persons the right to vote because of race or color. The Attorney General is directed to institute suits against Alabama, Mississippi, Texas, and Virginia to determine whether their poll taxes violate the Constitution.

In a suit against certain officials of the state of Virginia, the Court, on June 20, 1966, held that the imposition of a poll tax as a condition of voting in state and local elections contravened the equal protection clause as an invidious discrimination on the basis of wealth which, "like race, creed, or color is not germane to one's ability to participate intelligently in the electoral process. . . ." The Court further found that the degree of the discrimination was irrelevant.[34]

A highly controversial section of the act requires the covered states to obtain the Attorney General's approval before making any changes in their voting qualifications or procedures from those in effect on November 1, 1964.

In a suit brought by South Carolina, the Court upheld seven important provisions of the act. The decision rested primarily on the Congressional finding that the law was an appropriate means of executing Congress' authority under the Fifteenth Amendment to forbid racial discrimination in voting. In rejecting the principal contention of South Carolina that voting qualifications were within the powers reserved to the states, and that the power of

[34] *Harper* et al. v. *State Board of Elections*, 86 S. Ct. 1079 (1966).

Congress under the Fifteenth Amendment could reach only discrimination flowing from these qualifications and not the qualifications themselves, the Court declared that "as against the reserved powers of the states Congress may use any rational means to effectuate the constitutional prohibition of racial discrimination in voting." To buttress this conclusion Chief Justice Warren applied to Section 2 of the Fifteenth Amendment, the language applied by John Marshall to Congress' power over interstate commerce: "This power, like all others vested in Congress, is complete in itself, may be exercised to its utmost extent, and acknowledges no limitations, other than prescribed in the Constitution."

Other challenges to the act were decisively rejected, and the Court voiced its feeling of the historic significance of the occasion. "Hopefully," the Chief Justice declared, "millions of non-white Americans will now be able to participate for the first time on an equal basis in the Government under which they live."

Debasement of Vote: County Unit System

An effective variant on the more widespread methods of destroying equality of suffrage in the South has been the county unit system of Georgia, Maryland, and Mississippi. This device does not deprive certain classes of citizens of the suffrage outright, but it has the effect of so diluting their votes as to render them relatively ineffective. Litigation on this scheme has been confined largely to the Georgia system. In that state nomination of candidates for statewide offices and of candidates for the Congress was effected by a county unit vote rather than by popular vote until 1962.

Under this scheme each county was assigned twice as many unit votes as it had representatives in the lower house of the state legislature. The total unit vote of a county went to the candidate receiving a plurality of the popular vote of that county; and to win in the primary a candidate must have had a majority of the unit votes of the state. Under this device a resident of the least populous county had an influence in the nomination of candidates equivalent to ninety-nine residents of the most populous county.

The victims of this system of electoral debasement met only defeat in the federal courts [35] until the spring of 1962 when they gained a partial victory in the federal district court,[36] which was made complete by the Supreme Court on March 18, 1963, in *Gray* v. *Sanders*.[37] Here the Court struck down a revised form of the Georgia county unit system. The revision involved the bracketing of counties into population groups and reduced substantially the disparities of the earlier system.

The district court had held that the amended act had some of the vices of the prior act and therefore denied equal protection to the plaintiffs. It did not, however, hold invalid the unit system as such. It still allowed a unit system to be used in weighing the votes if the system showed no greater disparity against a county than exists against any state in the most recent electoral college allocation, or if the disparity is not in excess of that which exists under the equal proportions formula for representation of the several states in the Congress.[38] Significantly the Supreme Court flatly rejected these analogies. "We think," said the Court, "the analogies to the electoral college, to districting and redistricting, . . . are inapposite." The Court insisted that this was only a voting case. Although Georgia gives every qualified voter one vote in a statewide election, she employs in counting those votes a unit system, which weights the rural vote more heavily than the urban vote. The only weighing of votes permitted by the Constitution, the Court pointed out, is that involved in the allocation of two senators to each state and the use of the electoral college in the choice of the President. In sum, the Court concludes that "once the geographical unit for which a representative is to be chosen is designated, all who participate in the election are to have an equal vote—whatever their race . . . , and wherever their home may be in that geographical unit." [39] Nothing less is required by the equal protection clause of the Fourteenth Amendment.

The Court was careful not to tip its hand on the unsettled issues growing out of *Baker* v. *Carr* and then pending before the

[35] See, for example, *South* v. *Peters*, 339 U.S. 276 (1950).
[36] *Sanders* v. *Gray*, 203 F. Supp. 158 (1962).
[37] 372 U.S. 368 (1963).
[38] 203 F. Supp. 170.
[39] *Gray* v. *Sanders*, *op. cit.*, p. 371.

Court. This case, the Court emphasized, does not involve those issues, nor does it involve the related problem of *Gomillion* v. *Lightfoot*, where gerrymandering was employed to exclude a minority group from voting in municipal elections. Despite the Court's narrow confinement of its holding, it is difficult to see why the reasoning of the Gray case would not apply to the debasement of urban votes in legislative malapportionment. The next term revealed the Court's answer to this question.

Debasement of Vote: Racial Gerrymander

Undoubtedly the boldest use of the gerrymander to debase the votes of Negroes in the South to which reference has just been made was involved in an act of the Alabama legislature passed in 1957, altering the shape of the town of Tuskegee from a square to a twenty-eight-sided figure, thereby excluding from the city all but four or five Negro voters but leaving all white residents undisturbed. The result of the act, of course, was to prevent the excluded Negroes from voting in municipal elections.

The Supreme Court in *Gomillion* v. *Lightfoot* [40] held this act to be a violation of the Fifteenth Amendment, in that the excluded Negroes would be deprived of their right to vote. The opinion by Mr. Justice Frankfurter was neatly contrived to avoid opening up the broad problem of apportionment then pending before the Court in *Baker* v. *Carr*,[41] which rested upon the equal protection clause of the Fourteenth Amendment.

He avoided the broader language of this clause which, of course, has not been limited, in its application, to racial discrimination. This, coupled with Justice Frankfurter's attempt to distinguish Gomillion from *Colegrove* v. *Green* [42] (where the Court refused to take jurisdiction in an apportionment case because it involved a "political question"), seems to give greater constitutional protection against debasement of the value of a vote because of race than because of urban residence.

The crucial point in the distinction of Gomillion and Cole-

[40] 364 U.S. 339 (1960).
[41] 369 U.S. 186 (1962).
[42] 328 U.S. 549 (1946).

grove was the argument that in no case involving the dilution of the value of the vote had the Court sanctioned unequivocal withdrawal of the vote solely from colored citizens. Of course, there was no unequivocal withdrawal of the vote from colored citizens in Gomillion. There was a clear racial discrimination against plaintiffs' right to cast an effective ballot, but they were free to vote in the political unit to which they were assigned. If, then, the debasement of the value of the electoral franchise can be challenged on the ground of racial discrimination, could it also be challenged on the ground of residential discrimination?

Debasement of Vote: Apportionment Cases

This question was dealt with by the Supreme Court in the highly controversial case of *Baker* v. *Carr*.[43] Not since the Segregation Cases of 1954 had a case created so great legal and political maneuvering. But unlike the Segregation Cases, the response here has in general been toward compliance rather than toward defiance.

With the Baker case before the Court, the time was ripe for a thorough reexamination of the doctrine of the "political question" as applied to apportionment cases, and for the statement of a clearly reasoned doctrine of equal protection in relation to apportionment that could serve as a dependable guide to lower courts. As we shall see, the Court confined itself largely to consideration of the question of justiciability of apportionment cases and left the more important and more difficult problem of equal protection in abeyance.

The plaintiffs in the Baker case claimed that the failure of the Tennessee legislature to reapportion its members in accordance with changes in the voting population over the past sixty years as required by the state constitution had debased the value of their votes in violation of the equal protection clause of the Fourteenth Amendment. A three-judge district court, relying on the Colegrove decision, dismissed their claim on the grounds that the court lacked jurisdiction of such a "political question" and

[43] 369 U.S. 186 (1962).

that the complaint failed to state a claim upon which relief could be granted. The Supreme Court held that the dismissal was error.

Although the six opinions in the case cover a total of 165 pages, what the Court actually decided can be stated very briefly, as indeed it was by Justice Stewart in a concurring opinion. The Court simply held: (1) that the federal courts do have jurisdiction in malapportionment cases, (2) that the complaint presented a justiciable controversy, that is, it was capable of adjudication; and (3) that the appellants had standing to bring the suit. It also apparently decided that if the allegations of the appellants were sustained, they had been denied equal protection of the laws. But the Supreme Court did not reach the merits of the case, and the district court to which the case was remanded for trial on the merits of the allegations made was given no guidelines for the disposition of the case.

Justice Brennan, in his opinion for the Court, devoted most of his effort to various distinctions and explanations showing why the district court had been in error in thinking that Colegrove required it to dismiss the suit for want of justiciability. After roaming far and wide through the precedents, he voiced the conclusion that neither Colegrove nor the apportionment cases that followed it held malapportionment claims to be nonjusticiable "political questions." The district court had misinterpreted Colegrove and other decisions of the Court on which it relied. The refusal to award relief in these cases "resulted only from the controlling view of a want of equity." [44] He asserted that the political question doctrine applies properly to "the relationship between the judiciary and the coordinate branches of the Federal Government, and not the federal judiciary's relationship to the states . . ." [45] It is "essentially a function of the separation of powers."

Finally he comes "to the ultimate inquiry whether our precedents as to what constitutes, a nonjusticiable 'political question' bring the case before us under the umbrella of that doctrine." No such precedents are found and the real question before the Court

[44] *Ibid.*, p. 234.
[45] *Ibid.*, p. 210.

is "the consistency of the state action with the federal constitution."

On the more important question as to what standards the district court should apply in determining whether there had been denial of equal protection of the laws and what remedy could be afforded if the court found that the complaining voters had in fact been denied equal protection, the Supreme Court had nothing to say beyond these noncommittal statements: As to standards, "the appellants, in order to succeed in this action," need not "ask the Court to enter upon policy determinations for which judicially manageable standards are lacking. Judicial standards under the Equal Protection Clause are well developed and familiar . . ." There is not the slightest hint as to what these standards are in relation to apportionment. As to remedy, the Court had no reason "to doubt the District Court will be able to fashion relief if violations of constitutional rights are found," indeed, "it is improper now to consider what remedy would be most appropriate if appellants prevail at the trial." [46]

The limitations of space do not permit consideration of the several concurring and dissenting opinions. Suffice it to say here that they reveal a picture of extreme diversity and even confusion. But the Court did definitely settle the question of justiciability in legislative apportionment cases—an issue which was unnecessarily clouded in 1946 by the inconclusive case of *Colegrove* v. *Green*. The Court's handling of the political question doctrine removed some of the vagueness from this indefinable concept and reduced its applicability. Although not reaching the merits of the case, the Court also opened up a new avenue for the extension of the doctrine of state action under the equal protection clause. It invited the lower courts to take jurisdiction of apportionment cases under equal protection and to decide them on their merits. But it vouchsafed no standards by which the lower courts were to determine whether a contested apportionment scheme was or was not in violation of equal protection. Those courts apparently welcomed their new jurisdictional freedom, but their disparate search for substantive standards of decision resulted in extreme diversity and confusion.

[46] *Ibid.*, p. 229.

Through its agreement on June 20, 1963, to review a number of these lower court decisions, the Supreme Court of the United States was presented with the opportunity and the obligation of formulating a clearly reasoned equal protection standard.

The decisions in these cases came on June 15, 1964, and it was in the principal case of *Reynolds* v. *Sims* [47] that the Court finally formulated equal protection standards for the determination of legislative apportionment cases. Two cases intervening Baker and Reynolds, although not directly controlling, revealed the thinking of the Court on the essential issue of equality of voting rights. *Gray* v. *Sanders*,[48] although involving the weighting of votes in statewide elections, as previously pointed out, rather than in state legislative districts, did nevertheless establish the basic principle of equality among voters within a state and held that voters may not be classified on the basis of where they live in a statewide election. Perhaps most prophetic of things to come was Mr. Justice Stewart's statement in his concurring opinion, "Within a given constituency, there can be room for but a single constitutional rule—one voter, one vote." [49]

The later case of *Wesberry* v. *Sanders* [50] also foreshadowed the Court's disposition of the state legislative reapportionment cases. Here the Court, reversing a three-judge district court, held invalid a Georgia statute creating congressional districts, the largest of which contained a population three times that of the smallest. The Court, rejecting the equal protection of the laws plea of petitioners, held that "construed in its historical context, the command of Article I, Section 2, that Representatives be chosen 'by the people of the several states' means that as nearly as is practicable one man's vote in a Congressional election is to be worth as much as another's." [51] Although this case, as just indicated, was unlike the state legislative apportionment case, not based on the equal protection clause, it did declare that the fundamental principle of representative government in the United States is one of equal representation for equal numbers of people,

[47] 377 U.S. 533 (1964).
[48] 372 U.S. 368 (1963).
[49] *Ibid.*, p. 382.
[50] 376 U.S. 1 (1964).
[51] *Ibid.*, pp. 7–8.

"without regard to race, sex, economic status, or place of residence within a State."

Standards for State Legislature Apportionment

On June 15, 1964, the Supreme Court invalidated, as failing to meet the requirements of the equal protection clause of the Fourteenth Amendment, the apportionment of seats in the legislatures of Alabama,[52] Colorado,[53] Delaware,[54] Maryland,[55] New York,[56] and Virginia.[57] Only the first two of these cases will be considered here, for the principles enunciated in these are applicable to all the others.[58]

In considering first the principal case of *Reynolds* v. *Sims* it is important to note at the outset the central constitutional point of view of the Court in its approach to the problem of determining the validity of state legislative apportionment. Said the Court: "A predominant consideration in determining whether a state's legislative apportionment scheme constitutes an invidious discrimination violative of rights asserted under the Equal Protection Clause is that the rights allegedly impaired are individual and personal in nature." [59]

The Court, then, approaches the problem of legislative apportionment not merely as a matter of institutional arrangement or of governmental power relationships, but rather from the point of view of the constitutional right of a qualified voter to an effective voice in his government. To the extent that malapportionment reduces the effectiveness of an individual's vote in one voting district as compared with that of an individual in another district within the same governmental area, it becomes involved in the constitutional right to vote. From this point of view the talk about

[52] *Reynolds* v. *Sims*, 377 U.S. 533 (1964).
[53] *Lucas* v. *Colorado General Assembly*, 377 U.S. 713 (1964).
[54] *Roman* v. *Sincock*, 377 U.S. 695 (1964).
[55] *Maryland Committee* v. *Tawes*, 377 U.S. 656 (1964).
[56] *WMCA, Inc.* v. *Lomenzo*, 377 U.S. 633 (1964).
[57] *Davis* v. *Mann*, 377 U.S. 678 (1964).
[58] In a series of *per curiam* decisions one week later the Court invalidated the apportionment of seats in eight other states.
[59] 377 U.S. 533 (1964).

entering "political thickets" and "mathematical quagmires" is irrelevant; for the denial of a constitutionally protected personal
right demands judicial protection.

Relating this concept to the broad principles of representative
government and majority rule, the Court held "that as a basic
constitutional standard, the Equal Protection Clause requires that
the seats in both houses of a bicameral state legislature must be
apportioned on a population basis. Simply stated, an individual's
right to vote for state legislators is unconstitutionally impaired
when its weight is in a substantial fashion diluted when compared
with votes of citizens living in other parts of the state." [60] Thus,
"the Equal Protection Clause demands no less than substantially
equal state legislative representation for all citizens of all places
as well as of all races."

It is, of course, clear that the linkage of equality of representation and the right to vote without geographical discrimination
springs from the fact that the only way that the voice of the voter
can be effectively registered is through the voice of his representative. As Professor B. F. Wright puts it, "Equality of representation
is a complementary right of the right to vote and to have that vote
counted as cast." [61]

The basic and unchanging principle of representative government posited by the Court is that "the weight of a citizen's
vote cannot be made to depend on where he lives."

Again the Court found the federal analogy argument inapposite and irrelevant to state legislative districting plans. Reliance
on this alleged analogy is little more than rationalization offered
in defense of existing malapportionments. The federal analogy is,
of course, historically and theoretically erroneous. The states have
equal representation in the Senate because this plan was adopted
as part of a historic compromise in formulation of the federal
union. Moreover, the coordinate relationship of the states and
the federal government in this union is entirely different from that
between the states and local governmental units. These latter, it
is well known, are legally the creatures of the states and subject

[60] *Ibid.*, 568.
[61] See his "The Right of Majorities and Minorities in the 1961 Term of
the Supreme Court," 57 *American Political Science Review* 104.

to their complete control. Such a federal plan cannot be permitted under the equal protection clause because it would result in submergence of the equal population principle in at least one house of a state legislature. This, of course, could result in government by deadlock, and the individual citizen's ability to exercise an effective voice in his government might be "as effectively thwarted as if neither house were apportioned on a population basis."

Although the one-person-one-vote standard may on its face seem very rigid, the Court is careful to point out that the standard is not an unreasonably rigid one. It realizes that it "is a practical impossibility to arrange legislative districts so that each one has an identical number of residents, or citizens, or voters. Mathematical exactness or precision is hardly a workable constitutional requirement." But the predominant basis of representation must be population and a state must "make an honest and good faith effort to construct districts, in both houses of its legislature, as nearly of equal population as is practicable." Such minor deviations from the basic population standard may be made "as may occur in recognizing certain factors that are free from any taint of arbitrariness or discrimination." For example, deviation may be justified in the apportionment of seats in one or both houses of a state legislature in order to use political subdivisions as bases for electoral districts. Recognition of this factor in districting may be justified on these grounds: (1) districting without regard to political subdivisions could, in some circumstances, be "little more than an open invitation to partisan gerrymandering"; (2) local governmental units are frequently charged with certain responsibilities in connection with the operation of state government; (3) much of a state legislature's activity is concerned with the enactment of local legislation, "directed only to the concerns of particular political subdivisions."

In addition, deviations resulting from shifting population distribution between reasonable periodic reapportionments are necessarily permissible. Constitutional requirements are apparently satisfied if a state reapportions its legislative seats at least every ten years.

Considerations of history, of balancing urban-rural interests or other group interests, or of area will not alone justify deviation from the population principle. "Citizens, not history or economic interests, cast votes . . . people, not land or trees or pastures, vote."

Finally, in the case of *Lucas* v. *Forty-Fourth General Assembly*,[62] the Court held that the availability of a political remedy such as the initiative and referendum "has no constitutional significance if the plan does not meet Equal Protection requirements." In this case, where the majority of the votes in every county in Colorado had approved a constitutional amendment providing for population based representation in one house only in preference to an alternative proposal that would have reapportioned both houses on a population basis, the Court declared that "an individual's constitutionally protected right to cast an equally weighted vote cannot be denied even by a vote of a majority of a state's electorate." This is, of course, consistent with the basis of the Court's decision in Reynolds that the right to cast an undiluted vote is a fundamental personal and individual right protected by the equal protection clause.

If this seems difficult to reconcile with what the Chief Justice said about the logical necessity, under representative government, "that a majority of the people of a state . . . elect a majority of that state's legislators," [63] it should be noted that the majority vote in the Colorado referendum was of a fundamentally different nature from the majority vote in the choice of a state legislature. The majority vote in the referendum would have denied the minority voters their right to cast an equally weighted vote in the choice of state legislators. What makes a majority vote valid is the observance of the principle that the right of each individual voter to participate in such a vote on a basis of substantial equality with other voters is not itself subject to a vote.

The significance of the apportionment cases of June 15, 1964, is that the right to substantial equality of representation has been brought under the coverage of the equal protection clause of the Fourteenth Amendment as a fundamental personal right to cast an effective vote and to have that vote counted as cast. Thus the

---

62 377 U.S. 713 (1964).
63 *Reynolds* v. *Sims*, 377 U.S. 533, 538 (1964).

right to vote for legislative representatives has been raised to the constitutional level of freedom of speech, press, religion, and assembly.

This far-reaching achievement is but the logical extension of the development of equal protection doctrine during the past quarter century with respect to fundamental civil rights. This development has been particularly noteworthy in the racial cases, including both the electoral and the school cases.

RACIAL DISCRIMINATION AND EQUAL PROTECTION OF THE LAWS

Many Supreme Court cases since 1937 have involved the issue of racial discrimination. Only a few of these, deemed most significant as charting doctrinal trends, can be considered here. It may be noted, however, that these cases, taken as a whole, reflect a consistent, though sometimes cautious, tendency on the part of the Court during this period so to interpret the Fourteenth Amendment and other pertinent provisions of the Constitution as to insure genuine equality of public treatment to racial minorities.

Doctrinal progress in this direction can be illustrated by a brief review of cases concerning segregation with respect to: (1) the acquisition and occupancy of real property; (2) access to public transportation facilities; (3) the right to equal educational opportunity; and (4) access to other privately owned public facilities.

Segregation in Residential Areas

Three cases,[64] all decided since the beginning of 1948, have gone far to free the colored race from earlier restrictions with respect to the acquisition, occupancy, and conveyance of real prop-

[64] *Shelley* v. *Kraemer*, 334 U.S. 1 (1948); *Hurd* v. *Hodge*, 334 U.S. 24 (1948); *Barrows* v. *Jackson*, 346 U.S. 249 (1953).

erty. This emancipation has come about largely through an expansion of the concept of state action on the part of the Supreme
Court. It had been held in the Civil Rights Cases,[65] as early as
1883, that the Fourteenth Amendment does not forbid private
discrimination against the Negro. This doctrine was, of course,
applicable in decisions holding that private property owners may
covenant with one another not to sell or lease their property to
Negroes. These "restrictive covenants," as they were called, became
more important after the Supreme Court ruled in *Buchanan* v.
Warley [66] in 1917 that an ordinance of Louisville, Kentucky, setting
up exclusive residential areas based on color, was in violation of
the Fourteenth Amendment. Such segregation of races in residential areas could still be effected through private covenants if
violation of the covenants could be enforced in the courts. In
1926 private covenants forbidding the transfer of land to, or its use
by, Negroes for a period of years was unanimously sustained in
Corrigan v. *Buckley* [67] on the ground that the discrimination was
not effected by state action.

The Supreme Court avoided meeting this issue in subsequent
cases for more than two decades.[68] In 1948, however, the Court
held that racially restrictive covenants may not be enforced in
equity by state courts against Negro purchasers.[69] Although such
covenants are valid as between private persons, enforcement by
the state courts constitutes a denial of the equal protection of
the laws. The fact that the state uses its courts to give effect to the
discriminatory private contract makes the state a party to the
action. In *Hurd* v. *Hodge*,[70] decided the same day, restrictive covenants in the District of Columbia were held equally unenforce-
able in federal equity courts. Here the Court sidestepped the
constitutional issue and held that restrictive covenants are prohibited by the section of the Civil Rights Act of 1866, which
provides that "all citizens of the United States shall have the

[65] 109 U.S. 3 (1883).
[66] 245 U.S. 60 (1917).
[67] 271 U.S. 323 (1926).
[68] *Hansberry* v. *Lee*, 311 U.S. 32 (1940); *Mays* v. *Burgess* 147 F. 2d. 869
(App. D.C. 1944; cert. denied, 325 U.S. 868 (1945).
[69] *Shelley* v. *Kraemer*, 334 U.S. 1 (1948).
[70] 334 U.S. 24 (1948).

same right, in every state and territory, as is enjoyed by white citizens thereof to inherit, purchase, lease, sell, hold and convey real and personal property. . . ."

In the later case of *Barrows* v. *Jackson*,[71] the Court went further and ruled by a six to one vote that a state court may not, for the same reason as set forth in the Shelley case, take jurisdiction of a damage suit at law for breach of the restrictive covenant brought by one white covenanter against another. For state courts to entertain such damage suits amounts to state encouragement of the use of restrictive covenants, said Mr. Justice Minton, and thus coerces the property owner to continue to use his property in a discriminatory manner. It is, therefore, the state's choice that he either observe the covenant or suffer damages. These cases would seem to invalidate any state assistance to private efforts to enforce racial discrimination with respect to the use or conveyance of property. Nevertheless, the Supreme Court in 1950 refused to review a decision of the New York Court of Appeals, holding that a private housing corporation could exclude Negroes from a housing project constructed with the assistance of the state's power of eminent domain and city tax exemption for twenty-five years.[72]

It appears from a more recent case [73] that where the state court merely refused to interfere with discrimination arising from a private agreement, the action of the court is not state action as in Shelley and Barrows where the agreement had been ineffective without judicial intervention. In these cases the action of the court had the effect of forcing discrimination on parties willing to deal on a nondiscriminatory basis.

Segregation in Transportation Facilities

Cases involving segregation in public transportation facilities have been decided under such diverse constitutional provisions as the commerce and equal protection clauses. Under both provisions the Supreme Court has followed a tortuous and confusing course

[71] 346 U.S. 249 (1953).
[72] *Daisy* v. *Stuyvesant*, 299 N.Y. 512 (1949); 339 U.S. 981 (1950).
[73] *Black* v. *Cutlers Laboratories*, 351 U.S. 292 (1956); see also *Rice* v. *Sioux City Park*, 349 U.S. 70 (1955).

in the determination of the difficult questions which have come before it. In the first Jim Crow case,[74] the Court in 1878 held invalid, as a burden on interstate commerce, a Louisiana reconstruction statute forbidding steamboats on the Mississippi River from segregating passengers according to race. A Negro woman was refused accommodations in the white cabins on a Mississippi steamer traveling from New Orleans to Vicksburg, Mississippi. This, the Court said, was a subject requiring uniformity of regulation which only Congress could adopt, and in the absence of congressional regulation the carrier was free to enforce such regulations for the arrangements of his passengers as he might deem "most for the interest of all concerned."

Some years later, however, the Court sustained laws requiring segregation within a state on the ground that they regulated only intrastate commerce and hence imposed no burden on interstate commerce.[75]

In *Plessy* v. *Ferguson* [76] in 1896, the equal protection clause of the Fourteenth Amendment likewise failed as a bulwark against Jim Crow legislation. Here a Louisiana statute providing separate but equal accommodations for white and colored persons on railroads in the state was held not to deny equal protection of the laws. On the contrary, it was a valid exercise of the state police power to preserve public peace and good order.

Justice Brown rested the conclusions of the Court largely on the observation that the underlying fallacy in the argument of the Negro plaintiff consisted in

. . . the assumption that the enforced separation of the two races stamps the colored race with a badge of inferiority. If this be so, it is not by reason of anything found in the act, but solely because the colored race chooses to put that construction upon it. [Justice Harlan declared in dissent that] there can be no doubt but that segregation has been enforced as a means of subordinating the Negro. . . . [and] That the thin disguise of "equal" accommodation . . . will not mislead anyone nor atone for the wrong this day done. . . .

Thus segregation with respect to transportation facilities became constitutionally reconcilable with equality, and the formula

---

[74] *Hall* v. *De Cuir*, 95 U.S. 485 (1878).
[75] *Louisville, N. O. & T. R. Co.* v. *Mississippi*, 133 U.S. 587 (1890).
[76] 163 U.S. 537 (1896).

of "separate but equal" operated for more than a half-century to perpetuate what later came to be regarded as a gap between the theory and practice of equality of the races before the law. To be sure, the separate accommodations must be equal, but the Court until the 1930's, was extremely lenient in its construction of the requirements of equality. This was especially true with respect to equality of educational opportunity, as will be seen shortly.

After the Plessy decision, the opponents of segregation again turned to the commerce clause, since the De Cuir case had not actually been overruled. But it was not until half a century after Plessy that the commerce clause was successfully invoked against segregation in public transportation. However, there had been a tendency in some earlier cases to interpret the requirements of equality more rigidly. For example, in *McCabe* v. *Atchison* [77] in 1914, an Oklahoma statute which permitted carriers to provide sleeping and dining cars for white persons only was held invalid, despite the legislative recognition that there would be little demand for them by colored people.

Finally, in *Mitchell* v. *United States*,[78] decided in 1941, the Court construed the Interstate Commerce Act to require equal accommodation for Negroes. A. W. Mitchell, a Negro congressman from Chicago, traveled from Chicago to Hot Springs, Arkansas, on a ticket which entitled him to Pullman accommodations. When the train crossed the Arkansas border, he was ejected from the Pullman car and forced to ride in a day coach reserved for colored passengers. The railroad purported to provide Negroes with separate but equal facilities required by the Arkansas statute, by permitting Negroes who wished Pullman accommodations to buy drawing room space at ordinary Pullman rates. No such space was available on this occasion. It was not disputed that there was little demand for Pullman space by Negroes. Mitchell filed a complaint with the Interstate Commerce Commission, claiming discriminatory treatment in violation of the Interstate Commerce Act. The commission dismissed his complaint, but the Supreme Court, speaking through Chief Justice Hughes, unanimously held that Mitchell was entitled to relief under the federal statute which forbids discriminatory treatment by railroads on account of race.

[77] 235 U.S. 151 (1914).
[78] 313 U.S. 80 (1941).

The test of equality was not met, the Court pointed out, since Negroes with first class tickets were given accommodations equal to those afforded white persons traveling on second class tickets. Allowing Negroes to buy drawing room space, if available, similarly did not meet the test, nor is inequality to be justified by the small number of Negroes desiring Pullman accommodations. It is the individual who is entitled to the equal protection of the law.

It is clear, of course, that neither of the two preceding cases challenged the constitutionality of segregation in interstate commerce. They do, however, reveal a new determination on the part of the Court that the constitutional requirement of equality shall be meaningful. Then, in 1946, the Court in *Morgan* v. *Virginia* [79] reverted to the De Cuir doctrine and held invalid a Virginia statute requiring segregation on all buses in interstate as well as intrastate commerce. The case involved the prosecution of a Negro woman who refused to move to the back of the bus on the request of the driver, when traveling from Virginia to Baltimore. Reversing the state supreme court of appeals which had affirmed the passenger's conviction, the Supreme Court of the United States held the segregation law to be a burden on interstate commerce in matters where uniformity is necessary. As indicated, the Court here followed *Hall* v. *De Cuir*, and in doing so opened the way, as Mr. Justice Burton suggested in dissent, for other suits in eighteen states where segregation was prohibited. So, in *Bob-Lo Excursion Co.* v. *Michigan*,[80] the Court found the commerce clause being invoked to protect discrimination. In this case the Michigan Civil Rights Act was invoked against an amusement park company, which operated a boat between Detroit and an island on the Canadian side of the Detroit River and which refused to transport a Negro girl to the island in company with white girls. The defense was that the state law could not be validly applied to foreign commerce. The majority of the Court held that, although the commerce was technically foreign, the Canadian island was so close to Detroit as to be an amusement adjunct of the Michigan city. De Cuir and Morgan did not involve such "locally insulated" situations. The judicial drive against segregation in transportation was continued in the 1950 case of *Hender-*

[79] 328 U.S. 373 (1946).
[80] 333 U.S. 28 (1948).

son v. *United States*,[81] but again the Court sidestepped the constitutional issue of whether segregation as such denied equality. The Court found that the practice of the Southern Railway Co. in assigning one table in the dining car exclusively to Negroes, separated by a curtain from ten other tables reserved for whites, violated the provisions of the amended Interstate Commerce Act, which made it "unlawful for any railway engaged in interstate commerce to subject any particular person . . . to any undue or unreasonable prejudice or disadvantage in any respect whatever." [82] The Court rejected the argument that the segregation was rendered reasonable by the possibility that white passengers could be subjected to the same disadvantage as Negroes.

Despite the Court's insistence upon a more genuine equality in these later transportation cases, it carefully avoided making any assault upon the citadel of "separate but equal." This historic feat was reserved for the field of education.

It may be stated at this point that, after the segregation case of *Brown* v. *Board of Education*,[83] which will be discussed presently, the Court held, in a series of *per curiam* opinions,[84] segregation on intrastate buses, on public golf courses, public beaches, parks, and playgrounds to be a denial of the equal protection of the laws clause of the Fourteenth Amendment. In all these cases the Court simply cited *Brown* v. *Board of Education*.

Segregation in Education

The "separate but equal" doctrine which has been at the heart of the discussion of the problem of the desegregation of public schools since *Brown* v. *Board of Education* was first employed by the Supreme Court in the transportation case of *Plessy* v. *Ferguson* [85] in 1896, and, through that case, came to serve as the legal basis for the practice of segregation in education. Space does not permit further analysis of the Plessy case here. Suffice it to say

[81] 339 U.S. 816 (1950).
[82] 54 Stat. 902, 49 U.S.C. § 3(1), 1946.
[83] 349 U.S. 294 (1944).
[84] *Owen* et al. v. *Browder* et al., 352 U.S. 903; *Mayor and City Council of Baltimore* v. *Dawson*, 350 U.S. 877; *Holmes* v. *City of Atlanta*, 350 U.S. 879.
[85] 163 U.S. 537 (1896).

that it would be difficult to gainsay the conclusion of Robert J. Harris that "The opinion of the Court in *Plessy* v. *Ferguson* is a compound of bad logic, bad history, bad sociology, and bad constitutional law." [86]

However, the Plessy doctrine was destined to stand as the rationale of compulsory racial segregation for six decades. Still until 1954, the fact of segregation was never squarely challenged before the Supreme Court as a denial of equal protection of the laws. Instead, the complaint had generally been against inequality of the separate facilities.[87]

With the Gaines case [88] in 1938, the Court began to take seriously the "equal" part of the formula. It accepted the "separate but equal" formula, but for the first time held racial discrimination in education unconstitutional. It held that Missouri had denied equal protection of the laws to Gaines, a Negro, by refusing him admission to the University of Missouri Law School, and offering instead to pay his tuition fees in a law school of a non-segregated state. Equal protection can be afforded only within the jurisdiction of the state.

Although this case apparently recognized the legal validity of the "separate but equal" doctrine, its significance lies in the fact that its strict interpretation of the formula marks the beginning of the end of legally enforced segregation. From now on the Court consistently enforced a much more rigid test of equality. It insisted on reviewing more critically the facts of the cases brought before it to ascertain whether equality was in truth afforded.

The big surge towards repudiation of the "separate but equal" formula came in 1950, when the Court in two vitally significant cases unanimously condemned racial segregation in the professional and graduate schools of two state universities. In the first of these cases, *Sweatt* v. *Painter*,[89] the Court held that the barring

[86] For support of conclusion see his *The Quest for Equality* (Louisiana State University Press, 1960), Chapter 4.

[87] See *Cumming* v. *County Board*, 175 U.S. 528 (1899); *Berea College* v. *Kentucky*, 211 U.S. 45 (1908); *Gong Lum* v. *Rice*, 275 U.S. 98 (1927).

[88] *Missouri ex rel. Gaines* v. *Canada*, 305 U.S. 337 (1938).

[89] 339 U.S. 629 (1950).

of a Negro applicant from the University of Texas Law School had deprived him of the equal protection of the laws, even though Texas had provided a separate law school for Negroes within the state. In effect, the Court found that a segregated law school for Negroes could not provide them equal educational opportunities. In reaching such a conclusion the Court relied heavily on "those qualities which are incapable of objective measurement but which make for greatness in a law school." Chief Justice Vinson contrasted the two law schools with respect to such matters as the reputation of the faculties, the size of the student body and libraries, the influence and prestige of the large body of alumni of the university law school as against the single alumnus of the Negro law school, the experience of the administration, and the traditions and prestige of the university law school in general. The Court also pointed to the practical disadvantages incident to the state's exclusion from the Negro law school of eighty-five percent of the population of the state—a group which includes most of the lawyers, judges, jurors, witnesses, and other officials with whom Negro lawyers would necessarily have to deal in the practice of their profession.

The Sweatt ruling was reinforced in the case of *McLaurin v. Oklahoma State Regents*,[90] where the Court held that enforced segregation of the activities of a Negro graduate student who had been admitted to the state university under court order was a denial of equal protection in that it handicapped him in the effective pursuit of his graduate studies.

Here the Court leaned even more heavily than in Sweatt upon psychological and other intangible factors; but in both cases the Court explicitly refused either to affirm or to reexamine the doctrine of *Plessy v. Ferguson*. In effect, it rejected segregation in graduate and professional institutions without repudiating or overruling the "separate but equal" doctrine. However, it raised the standard of equality to such a level as to make it extremely difficult for any scheme of racial segregation in education to meet the test of constitutionality. Thus the way was paved for the historic school segregation decision of May, 1954.

[90] 339 U.S. 637 (1950).

The School Segregation Cases

When the Supreme Court convened in the fall of 1952, five cases in which racial segregation of children in public schools was squarely challenged as unconstitutional awaited its consideration. These cases were twice argued with elaborate briefs, and the decision of the Court was not reached until May 17, 1954. Four cases arising from the states of South Carolina, Virginia, Delaware, and Kansas were considered in a consolidated opinion under the style of *Brown* v. *Board of Education of Topeka*.[91]

Chief Justice Warren, again emphasizing the intangible factors of Sweatt and McLaurin, declared for the unanimous Court that such considerations apply with added force to children in grade and high schools. To separate children of the minority group from others of similar age and qualifications solely because of their race creates a feeling of inferiority as to their status in the community, and this sense of inferiority affects the motivation of the child to learn. The Court, therefore, concluded that the doctrine of "separate but equal" has no place in the field of public education, that "separate educational facilities are inherently unequal," and that the plaintiffs here involved "have been deprived of the equal protection of the laws guaranteed by the Fourteenth Amendment." [92]

In reaching this conclusion the Court considered "public education in the light of its full development and its present place in American life throughout the Nation." It was not possible to turn the clock back to the time of the adoption of the Fourteenth Amendment or even to *Plessy* v. *Ferguson* in 1896.

Implementation of Court's Decision: Criteria of Implementation

The Supreme Court in its implementing decision a year later declared that "Full implementation of these constitutional prin-

[91] 347 U.S. 483 (1954). The fifth case (*Bolling* v. *Sharpe*, 347 U.S. 497), relating to the District of Columbia, was decided under the due process clause of the Fifth Amendment.

[92] *Ibid.*, 495.

ciples may require the solution of varied local school problems.[93] It placed "primary responsibility for elucidating, assessing, and solving these problems" on local school boards and assigned to the federal district courts the task of deciding "whether the action of the school authorities constitutes good faith implementation of the governing constitutional principles." The lower courts were directed to require that the school authorities "make a prompt and reasonable start toward full compliance" with the Court's ruling, and to use such procedures as will accomplish the objective of desegregated schools "with all deliberate speed."

In effecting a gradual transition from segregated to nonsegregated schools the courts "may consider problems related to the physical condition of the school plant, the school transportation system, personnel, revision of school districts and attendance areas into compact units to achieve a system of determining admission to the public schools on a nonracial basis, and revision of local laws and regulations which may be necessary in solving the foregoing problems." The burden of proof that any delay is necessary rests with the school board.

Although there is every indication in these prescriptions that reasonable time should be afforded for adjustment of difficult local situations, it is clear from the language of the Court that all of these procedures must look toward full compliance with its ruling at the earliest practicable date. The opinion of the Court recognizes diversity of local conditions and does not contemplate uniform compliance as of a given date. But it demands a prompt and reasonable start toward good faith compliance, and it clearly does not sanction indefinite delay in full compliance.

Methods of Resistance to the Court's Ruling

Although the foregoing standards seemed reasonable and suited to the conditions of the day in the South, their very reasonableness in affording time to assess problems and to plan methods of adjustment to the Court's far-reaching decision seemed to inspire the political leadership of some of the affected states to launch

[93] *Brown* v. *Board of Education,* 349 U.S. 294, 298 (1955).

the most callous and unconscionable campaigns of frustration, evasion, circumvention, defiance, and distortion of the law that twentieth-century America has known. Ironically, all this was accompanied by loud protestations of "reliance on the Constitution as the fundamental law of the land." Space will not permit consideration here of all the complex developments of the past ten years in connection with the slow progress of, and resistance to, the desegregation movement. Instead, the principal devices of resistance employed will be mentioned and brief comments will be made on one or two that posed serious threats to public education.

The difficulties of the district courts in deciding the validity of school board plans with all of the normal delays in legal procedure such as dilatory pleas, motions, and objections, would have been enough to cause years of delay in the implementation of the Court's mandate. But, in addition, the courts were faced with an ever-mounting volume of state legislative obstructions intended to prevent, if possible, and if not, to delay, desegregation of the public schools. These legislative roadblocks included resolutions concerning the long-discredited doctrine of interposition, statutes relating to pupil placement and transfer, school closing laws, cutoff of appropriations to segregated schools, repeal of compulsory school attendance laws, tuition grants to "private" schools, and laws providing for segregation by choice.[94] In addition, there have been laws and other legislative action designed to harass those who promote or advocate desegregation. These include compulsory production of NAACP membership lists before legislative investigating committees, and its punishment for the crime of barratry (i.e., the soliciting, inciting, or fomenting of litigation), and statutes providing for the removal of teachers who belong to organizations which, or who personally, advocate the desegregation of the races.[95] Although most of these devices have been invalidated by the Court, some have continued to block the progress of desegregation, and some have posed a real threat to public education.

Perhaps the school closing laws and the tuition grants to so-

94 See 2 Race Rel. L. Rep. 889–891.
95 *Ibid.*, 892–894.

called private schools posed the most serious threat to public education. On January 19, 1959, Virginia's school closing and fund-withholding laws were simultaneously held unconstitutional by a three-judge federal district court and the Supreme Court of Appeals of Virginia as violative of the equal protection clause of the Fourteenth Amendment and of the constitution of Virginia respectively. The federal court declared that "no one public school or grade in Virginia may be closed to avoid the effect of the law of the land as interpreted by the Supreme Court, while the State permits other public schools or grades to remain open at the expense of the tax payers." [96]

Likewise, tuition grants to private schools in Prince Edward County, Virginia, where public schools had been abandoned, were held unconstitutional. The federal district court held that it was a denial of equal protection for the county to provide tuition grants to students in private schools as long as its public schools were closed.[97]

In April 1959, the General Assembly of Virginia abandoned "massive resistance" to desegregation and set up instead a so-called "freedom of choice" program. In June, 1959, the Court of Appeals of the Fourth Circuit directed the federal district court to require the county school board to take "immediate steps" toward admitting students, without regard to race, to the white high school "in the term beginning September 1959," and to require the board to make plans for admission to elementary schools without regard to race.[98]

But the board of supervisors of the county in pursuance of its resolution of 1956 never to operate public schools "wherein white and colored children are taught together," refused to levy any school taxes for the 1959–60 session, on the excuse that they were "confronted with a court decree which requires the admission of white and colored children to all the schools of the county without regard to race or color." The result was that the county's pub-

[96] *James* v. *Almond*, 170 F. Supp. 331; *Harrison* v. *Day*, 200 Va. 439 (1959).
[97] See Book 2, U.S. Comm. on Civil Rights (1961), p. 215; *Allen* v. *Prince Edward School Board*, Civ. No. 1333, E.D.Va., 1960.
[98] *Allen* v. *County School Board of Prince Edward County*, 266 F. 2d. 507, 511 (1959).

lic schools did not open in the fall of 1959 and remained closed for five years.

A private group under the style of the Prince Edward School Foundation, was formed in 1959 to operate private schools for white children in the county. This group built its own plant and operated for one session on private contributions, but from 1960 on its major source of financial support for its schools was in the form of tuition grants and tax credits authorized by the General Assembly of Virginia and the board of supervisors of the county, and paid to children attending Foundation schools.

After further legal stallings, the Supreme Court of the United States finally held the Prince Edward scheme of private education unconstitutional on May 25, 1964, and ordered the public schools reopened. The Court found that the Foundation plan was created to perpetuate racial segregation by closing the public schools and operating only segregated schools supported by state and county funds. Thus the plan operated to deny Negro children equal protection of the laws.[99]

If the state is to permit the county to abandon public schools while they are being operated in all other counties, it must find a constitutional purpose for doing so, and "grounds of race and opposition to desegregation do not qualify as constitutional." The Court found that the record in the case permitted only one conclusion: that the scheme of closing public schools and the operation of "private" schools in their place with state and county support had but one purpose and that was to insure "that white and colored children in Prince Edward County would not under any circumstances, go to the same school." [100]

It was clear to the Court that Virginia law treated the school children of Prince Edward differently from the way it treated the school children of all other Virginia counties. If they go to school in the county, they "must go to racially segregated schools which, although designated as private, are beneficiaries of county and state support." The patience of the Court had finally worn thin. "The issues imperatively call for decision now. . . . There has

[99] *Griffin* v. *County School Board of Prince Edward County,* 377 U.S. 218, 222 (1964).
[100] *Ibid.,* p. 231.

been entirely too much deliberation and not enough speed. . . . Relief needs to be quick and effective."

Nevertheless, the order to reopen the public schools did not yet eliminate segregation in publicly supported schools in Prince Edward County. The issue of whether tuition grants could be paid to the parents of pupils attending the white Foundation school after the reopening of the public schools was not determined by the Supreme Court. This was left to the Court of Appeals of the Fourth Circuit.

Public schools in Prince Edward reopened in the fall of 1964, but all except a few of the white pupils stayed on in the Foundation school under substantial support from tuition grants. The determination of the Prince Edward authorities to leave no stone unturned in order to evade and frustrate the law is illustrated by the following action: In response to a court order to appropriate by June 25, 1964 "such county funds as are reasonably necessary for the opening and maintenance of the public schools . . . on a nondiscriminatory basis," the board of supervisors on June 23, 1964, appropriated $189,000 to reopen and maintain the public schools which were expected to accommodate some 1,600 Negro children. At the same meeting, the supervisors allotted $375,000 for the 1964–65 tuition grants for an approximately equal number of white pupils expected to attend the "private" schools.

This was the scheme which was contested before the Court of Appeals of the Fourth Circuit in December, 1964.[101] The suit also included Surry County, which had closed its white schools after a desegregation order but kept open the school for Negroes. Chief Judge Soboloff's opinion, it would seem, has decisively disposed of the tuition grant issue. The program attacked by the plaintiffs in this case was simply one more effort on the part of Prince Edward and Surry Counties to continue to offer their school population education at public expense on a racially segregated basis in direct contravention of the Bown decisions. Whether the grants are made directly to Foundation schools or indirectly through pupil subventions for use as tuition fees is of no constitutional significance. The circumstances of the cases show "a transparent evasion of the Fourteenth Amendment. . . . The involvement of

[101] *Griffin* v. *Board*, 339 F. 2d. (1964).

public officials and public funds so essentially characterizes the enterprise in each of the counties that the Foundation schools must be regarded as public facilities in which discrimination on racial lines is constitutionally impermissible." [102]

The transparent claim that tuition grants protected the right of the white pupils to choose their associates was rejected by Judge Sobeloff with sharp dispatch: "There is a right of association which the Constitution respects and protects. However, to invoke the right in the manner of Prince Edward and Surry is merely to assert euphemistically a right to enforce involuntary segregation of the races in public facilities." [103] This is, of course, precisely the claim which the Supreme Court has rejected in *Brown* v. *Board* and numerous other decisions. At last it should be clear that people have no constitutional right to associate in publicly maintained facilities on a racially segregated basis.

The extreme measures to which the Prince Edward authorities resorted, with such extraordinary determination and persistence in order to perpetuate racially segregated public education in the teeth of the Brown decisions, are eloquently and forcefully summarized in this brief passage from Judge Sobeloff's opinion:

Prince Edward County's hard and bitter resistance included, . . . the extreme step of shutting down all public schools for five years. Only under direction of the Supreme Court has it reopened them, and then only on its own terms—terms calculated still to preserve the segregation of the races. Thus after thirteen years of struggle in the courts and after five years of total educational deprivation, Negro children returned this fall to the same segregated schools to which they or their brothers and sisters were assigned in 1951 when legal proceedings were first initiated to end public school segregation.[104]

It is inconceivable that the Supreme Court will reverse this holding of the court of appeals. Thus all so-called private segregated schools receiving substantial public support in the form of tuition grants, tax rebates, or other schemes of public support, would seem to be doomed.

[102] *Ibid.*, p. 492.
[103] *Ibid.*, pp. 492–493.
[104] *Ibid.*, p. 492.

Racial Discrimination and Privately Owned
Public Facilities: State Action

In the Civil Rights Cases [105] of 1883, the Supreme Court ruled that racial discrimination by theaters, inns, and private common carriers was not covered by the equal protection clause of the Fourteenth Amendment. It applied only to discrimination by the state, not to private invasion of individual rights. This sharp distinction between public and private action is by no means so clear in the complexities of the 1960's.

Since 1961, the Supreme Court has been exploring a new area of segregation involving a new application of the concept of state action. The central problem of the Court in these state action cases has been the determination of the nature and degree of governmental involvement necessary to justify the attribution of discriminatory action of private parties to the state.

In 1961, the Supreme Court held that a privately operated restaurant leased from a city could not constitutionally refuse service to Negroes. The Court concluded that the reciprocal advantages of the leasing agreement were sufficient to achieve "that degree of state participation and involvement in discriminatory action which it was the design of the Fourteenth Amendment to condemn." [106]

On May 20, 1963, the Court advanced much farther along the line of an expanding concept of state action. This step was taken in five cases arising from the states of North and South Carolina, Alabama, and Louisiana, which involved sit-in demonstrations against segregation at lunch counters in privately owned stores in five cities. It was held in all five cases [107] that since the cities concerned had made racial segregation a public policy either by ordinance or by official declaration of their agents, they had become parties to such segregation in violation of the equal protection clause of the Fourteenth Amendment.

[105] 109 U.S. 3 (1883).
[106] *Burton* v. *Wilmington Parking Authority,* 365 U.S. 715, 714 (1961).
[107] *Peterson* v. *City of Greenville,* 373 U.S. (1963) (May 20, 1963); *Lombard* v. *State of Louisiana,* 373 U.S. 276; *Shuttlesworth* v. *City of Birmingham,* 67 S. Ct. 1–4 (May 20, 1963); *Gober* v. *City of Birmingham,* 66 S. Ct. (May 20, 1963); *Avent* v. *North Carolina,* 11 S. Ct. (May 20, 1963).

The essence of the Court's reasoning is set forth in the Peterson (Greenville, South Carolina) and Lombard (New Orleans) cases. In the former case ten Negro boys and girls were convicted under South Carolina's trespass law for refusing to leave a Kress store lunch counter in Greenville after the manager had announced that the counter was closed. It is important to note that the Negro sit-ins were not prosecuted under Greenville's segregation ordinance. It was the use of the trespass law to enforce the policy of segregation as declared by the ordinance that involved the state in racial discrimination in violation of equal protection. The convictions under the trespass law "had the effect, . . . of enforcing the ordinance passed by the City of Greenville, the agency of the state."

The most difficult of the cases was that of *Lombard* v. *Louisiana*,[108] because New Orleans had no segregation ordinance. When the sit-in demonstrations began, however, the superintendent of police and the mayor severely criticized them, and the mayor issued a statement that the demonstrations would not be permitted. Those official statements, said Chief Justice Warren, were equivalent to a declaration that the city as such "would not permit Negroes to seek desegregated service in restaurants. Consequently, the city must be treated exactly as if it had an ordinance prohibiting such conduct." So here, as in Peterson, the Chief Justice concluded, the convictions are linked to the command of the state for segregated service at the restaurant and cannot stand.

The Chief Justice freely conceded that under the Court's prior decisions "Private conduct abridging individual rights does no violence to the Equal Protection Clause unless to some significant extent the state in any of its manifestations has been found to have become involved in it." [109] Does this mean that a restaurant owner in a city without a segregation ordinance or other official declaration of such a policy is free to refuse service to Negroes? If so, the Court's decision leads to anomalous results.

These cases did not reach the central issue, whether it would be unconstitutional, as the sit-in demonstrators argued, for a

[108] 373 U.S. 267 (1963).|
[109] *Peterson* v. *City of Greenville, op. cit.* quoting J. Clark in *Burton* v. *Wilmington*, 365 U.S. 715, 722.

government to use its power of arrest under its trespass laws to enforce a policy of private discrimination by a restaurant or a store that solicits public patronage. There was reason to believe that the Court would have to face up to this difficult question in its 1963–64 term. The sit-in cases which reached the Court in this term involved situations where there were no segregation laws, and where the state and local officials were presumably neutral. So that here refusal of a restaurant or store manager to serve Negroes resulted from the free exercise of his own will. Under the doctrine of the restrictive covenant cases, would police enforcement of a person's undirected private choice be sufficient to make his action state action? Or could the Court find new vitality in the dissenting opinion of Mr. Justice Harlan in the Civil Rights Cases of 1883, in which he took the position that discrimination by such privately owned public facilities as railroads, inns, and theaters, operating under the authority of state law, is state action.

The decisions of the Court in the 1964 sit-in cases still did not reach the central question; they were all decided in a manner that avoided it, while at the same time reversing the sit-in convictions.

In *Griffin* v. *Maryland*,[110] state action was found because the private police officer who caused the arrest was deputized as a deputy sheriff. The issue in this case was the constitutional validity of the conviction of five Negro youths who had entered privately owned Glen Echo Amusement Park in Montgomery County, Maryland, and boarded a carousel for which they had valid tickets. They were arrested by Mr. Collins, a private detective, who acted on the instruction of the park management, but he had been deputized by the local sheriff and purported to exercise the authority issuing from this status. The Supreme Court reversed the convictions on the ground that the discrimination involved state action. Collins was responsible for the administration of the policy of segregation in a privately owned amusement park. His job, among other things, was to persuade those Negroes who entered the park to leave, and then to arrest those who refused. These functions combined with his status as a deputy sheriff were sufficient to make his action state action.

[110] 378 U.S. 130 (1964).

In *Robinson* v. *Florida*,[111] the Court reversed a trespass conviction of sit-in demonstrators who had sought service in a department store restaurant because the state had become involved through a regulation of the board of health requiring separate toilet facilities for each race in restaurants "whether employed or served in the establishment." While these Florida regulations do not directly and expressly forbid restaurants to serve both white and colored people together, declared Mr. Justice Black, "they certainly embody a state policy putting burdens upon any restaurant which serves both races, burdens bound to discourage the serving of the two races together." Thus, it would seem, the equal protection clause forbids a state to exert an influence encouraging private discrimination.

In two other 1964 cases, the Court ignored the equal protection claims of the sit-in demonstrators and reversed trespass and breach of peace convictions on rather technical due process grounds.[112]

In *Bell* v. *Maryland*, twelve Negro students, who had been convicted under the state's criminal trespass laws for engaging in a restaurant sit-in, appealed their convictions unsuccessfully through the various state courts on both due process and equal protection grounds. As the case reached the Supreme Court of the United States it promised to be the most important of the 1964 sit-in cases. Here was present none of the factors which enabled the Court in the other cases to by-pass the main issue. Indeed, six of the justices revealed their position on the central constitutional issue in three opinions—two concurring and one dissenting. Justices Douglas and Goldberg and the Chief Justice thought the judgment of conviction should be reversed as violation of the Fourteenth Amendment. Justices Black, Harlan, and White failed to see sufficient state involvement to justify reversal.

But Mr. Justice Brennan's opinion for the Court (in which Goldberg, Douglas, and Warren also joined) did not reach the questions that had been argued under the equal protection and due process clauses of the Fourteenth Amendment. Instead, the

[111] 378 U.S. 153 (1964).
[112] See *Bouie* v. *City of Columbia*, 378 U.S. 347 (1964), and *Barr* v. *City of Columbia*, 378 U.S. 146 (1964).

Court reversed the trespass conviction and remanded the case to the Court of Appeals of Maryland to consider with a view to the conviction's being vacated in the light of a recent change in Maryland law regarding public accommodations. In the opinion of the Court, avoidance of the issue was based on the fact that after the convictions were affirmed by the highest state court, but before the case had reached final disposition in the Supreme Court, the legislature had passed a law prohibiting restaurant owners from denying service to anyone because of his race. Baltimore had previously passed an ordinance to the same effect.

Because of this situation Mr. Justice Brennan argued that the Court of Appeals of Maryland might reverse the convictions or order the indictments dismissed by the application of "the universal common law rule that when the legislature repeals a criminal statute or otherwise removes the state's condemnation from conduct that was formerly deemed criminal, this action requires the dismissal of a pending criminal procedure charging such conduct." Thus the Court construed the Maryland law to mean that a conviction confirmed by the highest court of the state could be challenged on the ground that it was contrary to a subsequently enacted public accommodations law. Rarely has the Court resorted to such extreme and complicated interpretation in order to avoid facing up to a central constitutional issue.

The Civil Rights Act of 1964

With the enactment by Congress of the Civil Rights Act of 1964, which is probably the most important civil rights legislation ever enacted by the Congress, the Court may have been spared the task of ever coming to grips with the main issue of the sit-in cases. In addition to the public accommodations title to be considered in connection with Court litigation, the act contains provisions designed to eliminate discrimination on the basis of race, color, religion or national origin with respect to voting, the enjoyment of education opportunity, federal financial assistance through grants, loans or contracts; and employment opportunities.

On December 14, 1964, the Court sustained under the com-

merce clause the highly controversial public accommodations provisions of this act, and on the same day vacated other sit-in
convictions and ordered the prosecutions dismissed.

The constitutionality of Title II of the act was attacked in
two cases—one involving a motel and the other a restaurant.
Section 201 (A) of Title II of the act provides that: "All persons
shall be entitled to the full and equal enjoyment of the goods,
services, facilities, privileges, advantages, and accommodations of
any place of public accommodation as defined in this section,
without discrimination or segregation on the ground of race, color,
religion, or national origin." Another section includes motels and
restaurants in the definition of public accommodations within the
meaning of Section 201 (A) "if its operations affects commerce
(and it does affect commerce if it serves or offers to serve interstate travelers. Or if discrimination or segregation by it is supported by state action." Still another section provides, among other
things, that "any inn, hotel, motel, or other establishment which
provides lodging to transient guests" affects commerce *per se.*

As the preceding quotations suggest, the act was based on
both the commerce clause of the Constitution and on section 5
and the equal protection clause of the Fourteenth Amendment.
In the case of *Heart of Atlanta Motel* v. *United States,*[113] an
establishment catering to interstate travelers brought a declaratory
judgment action attacking the constitutionality of Title II of the
Civil Rights Act and sought an injunction against the enforcement of the act. It was admitted by the motel that its operation
brought it within the provisions of Section 201 (A) of the act,
that it refused to provide lodging for transient Negroes because of
their race or color, and that it intended to continue that policy
unless restrained. Thus the only question before the Court was
the constitutionality of the Civil Rights Act of 1964 as applied to
the facts.

The Court chose to base its decision on the commerce clause
rather than the equal protection clause, and in doing so, further extended the commerce power into the civil rights area. In
holding the public accommodations provisions of the Civil Rights
Act valid under the commerce clause, the Court explicitly based

[113] 379 U.S. 241 (1964).

its decision on principles first formulated by Chief Justice Marshall in *Gibbons* v. *Ogden* (1824) as they apply to the present state of commerce. Mr. Justice Clark's opinion for the Court is replete with quotations and citations from Marshall's great opinion and other leading commerce cases. The Court finds that racial discrimination in hotels and motels whose business affects interstate commerce imposes burdens upon that commerce which Congress has the power to remove. The determinative test of the exercise of power by the Congress under the commerce clause is simply "whether the activity sought to be regulated is [quoting Marshall] 'commerce which concerns more than one state' and has a real and substantial relation to the national interest." In view of the dramatic changes in the condition of commerce and transportation, the Court was required, said Justice Clark, to apply the Marshall principles to the present state of commerce.[114] This the Court did not find difficult, for voluminous testimony before Senate and House committees "presented overwhelming evidence that discrimination by hotels and motels impedes interstate travel." For example, there was evidence that the uncertainty caused by racial discrimination "had the effect of discouraging travel on the part of a substantial portion of the Negro community."

The nature and locale of the source from which the impediment to commerce springs is not the test of Congress' power to remove the impediment but the effect which it has on interstate commerce. Thus Congress, in enacting the public accommodations provisions of the Civil Rights Act, was not restricted by the fact that the particular obstructions with which it was dealing in this act constituted a moral and social wrong. Nor did it matter that the business as such was local. Congress could prohibit racial discrimination by motels serving interstate travelers, however local their operations might appear. As Mr. Justice Clark put it, "If it is interstate commerce that feels the pinch, it does not matter how local the operation which applies the squeeze."

In the companion case of *Katzenbach* v. *Ollie McClung*, the Court held, again by Mr. Justice Clark, that Congress had ample basis upon which to find that racial discrimination at restaurants which received from other states a substantial portion of food

[114] *Ibid.,* p. 354.

served, had a direct and adverse effect on interstate commerce. Again as in Heart of Atlanta Motel, however local the activity at the restaurant, or whatever its nature, Congress could still reach it, if it exerted a substantial economic effect on interstate commerce. Again the Court found the evidence overwhelming: ". . . confronted as we are, with the facts laid before the Congress, we must conclude that it had a rational basis for finding that racial discrimination in restaurants had a direct and adverse effect on the free flow of interstate commerce." [115]

A clear-cut decision might have been made on the main issue of the sit-in cases—namely the extent to which states may support a private choice which the state cannot itself constitutionally make—had not the 1964 Civil Rights Act intervened. On the day that the Court decided the Bell case, it granted certiorari in two additional sit-in cases [116] which seemed to present the issue more sharply than any of the previous cases. Both cases involved recent acts that specifically punished a refusal to leave an establishment after a request to do so, whereas earlier statutes had simply made it a crime to enter after notice.[117]

But the cases were never decided on their merits. Convictions for sit-in demonstrations in luncheon facilities of retail stores had been affirmed by the courts of last resort in South Carolina and Arkansas. The Supreme Court of the United States held [118] that under the Civil Rights Act of 1964 the convictions were required to be vacated and the prosecutions dismissed. The reason is this: the act forbids discrimination in places of public accommodation and removes peaceful attempts to be served on an equal basis from the category of punishable activities. The fact that the conduct in these cases occurred prior to enactment of the act makes no difference; the still pending convictions are abated by its passage.

Now there is, of course, no reference in the act to any such

[115] Ibid., p. 384.
[116] Hamm v. City of Rockhill, 377 U.S. 988, 1964, and Lupper v. Arkansas, 377 U.S. 989 (1964).
[117] M. G. Paulsen, "The Sit-In Cases of 1964: But Answer Came There None," from the Supreme Court Review 1964, p. 169.
[118] Hamm v. Rockhill, Lupper v. State of Arkansas, 379 U.S. 306 (1964).

abatement of pending prosecutions. Still, the Court finds no retro-active intrusion into state criminal law. Rather, the case involves the application of a long-standing federal rule. The Court reasons that since the Civil Rights Act substitutes a right for a crime, any state statute, or its application to the contrary, must by virtue of the supremacy clause give way under the normal abatement rule covering pending convictions arising out of a preenactment activity.

Since it is agreed that provisions of the act would abate all federal prosecutions, it follows that the same rule must prevail with respect to state prosecutions under the supremacy clause which requires that a contrary state act must give way. The act, in effect, prohibits the application of state laws in a way that would deprive any person of the rights granted under the act, and the "present convictions and the command of the Civil Rights Act of 1964 are clearly in direct conflict."

Despite this reasoning, the Court, in facing the final question as to "whether Congress exercised its power in the act to abate the prosecutions here," resorted to a very practical argument. Said Mr. Justice Clark: "If we held that it [Congress] did not, we would then have to pass on the constitutional question of whether the Fourteenth Amendment, without benefit of the Civil Rights Act, operates of its own force to bar criminal trespass convictions, where, as here, they are used to enforce a pattern of racial dis-crimination." Since this point is not free from doubt in view of the division of the justices, and since "as we have found Congress has ample power to extend the statute to pending convictions, we avoid that question by favoring an interpretation of the statute which renders a constitutional decision unnecessary." [119] In short, Congress has exercised its constitutional power in the act and "there is no public interest to be served in the further prosecution of the petitioners." The result of this holding is, in effect, the abatement of all pending prosecutions for peaceful sit-in demon-strations.

It is odd that the Court should have found it easier to up-hold the public accommodations provisions of the Civil Rights

[119] *Hamm* v. *Rockhill, Lupper* v. *State of Arkansas,* 379 U.S. 306 (1964).

Act under the commerce clause than under the equal protection clause. The latter was especially designed to protect the Negro from discrimination because of his race, and the former certainly was not. Nevertheless, the commerce clause has sometimes served as a more effective weapon against racial segregation than the equal protection clause. Odd as the Court's latest venture may seem, it is solidly grounded on 140 years of precedent.

Judicial Sharpening of Principles of Implementation

Judicial advancement in the implementation of the constitutional principles of racial desegregation enunciated in the second Brown decision is perhaps as significant as the previously considered extension of the doctrine of state action.

There had been an almost complete withdrawal of the Supreme Court from the battle of implementing this decision until the early 1960's. Although the Court in the Little Rock case [120] of 1958 sought to clarify and amplify both the constitutional principle of state action enunciated in the school segregation cases and its instructions concerning implementation; neither the sharper articulation of the principle of state action nor the clarification of the obligations of implementation by the Court was sufficient to reduce significantly the conflict and delay in the march toward the goal of eliminating racial segregation. Both Congress and the President were largely inactive in the implementation of the Brown case until a persistent program of civil disobedience in the streets and the crises of violence and bloodshed in Oxford, Mississippi, in 1962, and Birmingham, Alabama, in 1963, forced President Kennedy not only to use federal power (as President Eisenhower had earlier done in Little Rock, Arkansas) to quell resistance, but also to propose legislation which later evolved into the Civil Rights Act of 1964.

The mounting racial tension seemed to spark the Court to a new determination and a new sense of urgency in the vindication of the constitutional right against racial segregation by the states. On May 27, 1963, the Court, with Justice Goldberg as spokesman,

[120] *Cooper* v. *Aaron,* 358 U.S. 1, 7 (1958).

unanimously refused to countenance further delay in the desegregation of the public parks and other recreational facilities of the city of Memphis—a delay which the lower court had sanctioned on the basis of the second Brown decision. This, in itself, was no occasion for surprise. The significance of the case lies in the Court's illumination of the precepts of the second Brown decision, and its insistence on prompt compliance with the constitutional principles enunciated in the first Brown case.

After pointing out that the desegregation of parks and other recreation facilities does not present the same kinds of difficulties inherent in the elimination of racial segregation in schools, the Court declared that even the delay permitted by the second Brown decision was an exceptional "adaptation of the usual principle that any deprivation of constitutional rights calls for prompt rectification." The Court went on to emphasize that "The basic guarantees of our constitution are warrants for the here and now and, unless there is an overwhelmingly compelling reason, they are to be promptly fulfilled." [121] Thus the "narrowly drawn" Brown decision "is not to be unnecessarily expanded in application."

Moreover, the Court in what may turn out to be a highly significant dictum said: "Given the extended time which has elapsed, it is far from clear that the mandate of the second Brown decision requiring that desegregation proceed with all deliberate speed would today be fully satisfied by types of plans or programs for desegregation of public school facilities which eight years ago might have been deemed sufficient." If, then, in 1955, the public interest in certain areas and in certain circumstances justified an exception to the traditional principle of prompt and complete vindication of personal constitutional rights, the time for such exception is now past. At least delay in the future will require the demonstration of "overwhelmingly compelling" reasons.

The Court's determination to speed up the pace of desegregation found further expression just one week after the Memphis case in connection with its rejection of two public school transfer plans in Knoxville and Davidson County, Tennessee. The Court thought they had the effect of perpetuating segregation. Justice Clark for the unanimous Court, pointed out that the time

[121] *Watson* v. *City of Memphis*, 373 U.S. 526 (1963).

formulas of "good faith compliance at the earliest practicable date" and "all deliberate speed" were designed to meet the local difficulties of the period of transition. Now, after eight years, said the justice, "the context in which we must interpret and apply this language to plans for desegregation has been significantly altered." [122]

SUMMARY ANALYSIS

There can be little question that the most substantial contribution of the Supreme Court to the constitutional law of civil liberties since 1937 has been with respect to the political and social equality of the Negro. A significant landmark in the history of the South was the decision of the Court in *Smith* v. *Allwright*, by which the white primary was outlawed in state as well as national elections. This case, together with those which followed it for a decade, wrought a mild revolution in the political freedom of the Negro. The most ingenious devices for circumventing the Court's ruling against the white primary were struck down by the federal courts.

The controlling issue in all these cases, as in other race discrimination cases, was whether the action taken against the Negro was state action. In the principal case the Court declared that the constitutional right to be free from racial discrimination in voting cannot be nullified indirectly by a state, through casting its electoral process in a form permitting a private organization to practice racial discrimination in an election. The principle of the cases is that no election machinery can be sustained if its purpose or effect is to deny to the Negro, because of his race, an effective voice in the selection of his public officials or in the governmental affairs of his community or nation. Thus a state cannot escape the responsibility for unconstitutional discrimination by delegating power to accomplish this purpose to a private organization or by taking any action which permits a private organization to accomplish such a purpose. The state may not become actively identified with nor materially aid a private scheme of racial discrimination.

[122] *Goss* v. *Board of Education*, 373 U.S. 683 (1963).

Other subterfuges, such as grandfather clauses and restrictive registration requirements, have likewise been struck down by the Court as violative of the Fifteenth Amendment in purpose and effect. The suffrage cases as a whole seem to leave no legal loophole through which Negroes may be deprived of the ballot because of their race.

The Twenty-fourth Amendment, which became a part of the Constitution in 1964, has abolished the poll tax requirement in federal elections. In its first interpretation of this amendment in April, 1965, the Court struck down an attempt on the part of the Virginia legislature to circumvent it, by requiring the voter to file at least six months before the election a witnessed or notarized certificate of residence unless he paid the poll tax as required for state elections.

The poll tax as a prerequisite for voting in state elections has also been struck down as invidious discrimination between the indigent and the affluent, and consequently violative of equal protection of the laws.

The principle of equal protection and the doctrine of state action applied in the White Primary Cases were later extended to the dilution and debasement of the vote through the county unit system and the malapportionment of representatives in the legislatures.

Baker v. *Carr* established the jurisdiction of federal courts in apportionment cases, and *Reynolds* v. *Sims* formulated equal protection standards for the determination of apportionment cases. In approaching this problem, the Court started from the premise that the rights denied through inequality of representation are individual and personal in nature. The problem of legislative apportionment is not merely a matter of institutional arrangement, but it involves also the right of a qualified voter to an effective voice in his government. To the extent that unequal representation reduces the effectiveness of an individual's vote in one legislative district as compared with that of an individual in another district within the state, it becomes involved in the constitutional right to vote. For this reason, the Court held that as a basic constitutional principle, equal protection requires that the seats in both houses of a bicameral state legislature must be apportioned on a population basis and that "the weight of a citizen's vote cannot be made to depend on where he lives." Thus was established the one-man-one-vote standard.

Judicial condemnation of racial discrimination with respect to the enjoyment of such social advantages as the occupancy and conveyance of real estate, access to privately owned places of public accommodation, the use of public transportation facilities, and educational opportunity has been no less impressive than that concerning political discrimination.

The most significant as well as the most controversial case in the whole realm of racial discrimination was, of course, the school segregation case of *Brown v. Board of Education*. Here the Court ordered removal of the public stigma of inferior status because of race and set afoot the most turbulent and prolonged domestic controversy in this century. The leeway allowed by the Court for orderly compliance with its order prompted, in some quarters, widespread efforts looking toward indefinite evasion and defiance of the Court's order.

A blow against private racial discrimination was struck by the Court—first in the restrictive covenant cases in which it was held that state courts may not enforce private contracts involving racial discrimination; and later in the series of sit-in cases in which it was held that private discrimination, in which the states become involved through the enactment or declaration of a public policy of discrimination, violates equal protection of the laws.

In 1964 Congress stepped into the picture and forbade discrimination in privately owned places of public accommodation under the commerce clause as well as that of equal protection. On December 14, 1964, the Court sustained under the commerce clause the highly controversial public accommodations provisions of the Civil Rights Act of 1964.

An important influence in bringing this act and subsequent programs, along with the Voting Rights Act of 1965, into being was the so-called Civil Rights Movement. Because of their impatience with the slowness of judicial processes and a growing sense of injustice, Negroes, along with many of their white supporters, left the courtroom and went into the streets to demonstrate in protest; this was a strong factor in bringing the legislative and executive branches of the government into the civil rights picture.

Equally significant in this involvement has been the growing determination on the part of the Court to accelerate the pace of desegregation in the public schools. The Court is now committed to the principle that the basic guarantees of the Constitution are to be promptly fulfilled unless there are overwhelmingly compelling reasons to the contrary.

7

THE COLD WAR
AND INTERNAL SECURITY: I

When we come to know and understand our basic liberties, we recognize that they are not eternal and absolute truths, which must exist in equal degree in any and all circumstances. Even in ordinary times, they are necessarily limited by the equal rights of others and the general interests of the community. In time of war or threat of war, the demands of national safety place exceptionally serious strains on our civil liberties. If we needed any schooling to help us realize this, the two world wars of this century have taught it to us. We have learned that the exigencies of warfare make it necessary to prevent people from saying and doing many things which would be regarded as harmless, if not proper, in time of peace. As Mr. Justice Holmes remarked in the aforementioned Schenck case, "When a nation is at war many things that might be said in time of peace are such a hindrance to its effort that their utterance will not be endured so long as men fight and that no Court could regard them as protected by any constitutional right."

BASIC FREEDOMS

Yet, with the glaring exception of the Korematsu case [1] (which sustained, on the ground of military necessity, a military order

[1] *Korematsu v. United States*, 323 U.S. 214 (1944).

under which 70,000 native-born Japanese-Americans were forced to leave their homes and occupations on the West Coast and spend the duration of the war in "war relocation centers" in the desert areas of the Far West), the Court's decisions during World War II were generally favorable to the liberties of the individual. This attitude is illustrated by the decision in *Hartzel* v. *United States*,[2] also decided during the war. Like Schenck in 1919, Hartzel was convicted for violating the Espionage Act of 1917, and his offense was not substantially different from that of his earlier counterpart. However, the Court held the government to stricter standards of proof; it held that Hartzel's pamphlets opposing our war with Germany and defending German policies did not constitute a clear and present danger to our national security and, therefore, reversed his conviction.

With the emergence of the situation between the United States and the Kremlin, designated as the "cold war," about 1946, the judicial attitude of the Court changed in respect of basic liberties vis-à-vis subversion. The decade that followed was marked by suspicion, uncertainty, secrecy, fear, and hysteria on the part of a large segment of the American people. As a result of these disabling emotions and the incapacities they generated, our basic civil liberties faced threats and suffered setbacks probably as serious as at any time in our history. The fear, of course, was not altogether groundless. The external physical threat of nuclear war, with the possibility of total destruction, was made more clearly manifest by Communist infiltration into the industry and government of countries not under the control of the Kremlin. In addition, but with perhaps less reason, we have been fearful of the growth of Communism in the United States.

Some of the attitudes toward these dangers and the methods of combating them in turn created other dangers and threats to the security of our basic civil liberties. Thus we faced a conflict "between physical security and the intangibles of our democratic principles the preservation of which are equally necessary to the safety of our nation." [3]

[2] 322 U.S. 680 (1944).
[3] Eleanor Bontecou, "Does the Loyalty Program Threaten Civil Rights?" *The Annals*, Vol. 275 (May, 1951), p. 118.

Certainly no thoughtful citizen would deny that military and industrial information and equipment must be protected from espionage and sabotage and that persons in our midst who are committed to furthering the revolutionary objectives of a foreign power should be barred from positions of influence and power in the government. It is, however, equally important that, in the process, our basic liberties not be destroyed or seriously impaired. Otherwise a program for the control of subversion will become self-defeating. The highest purpose of national security is to preserve individual freedom.

Of course, the initiative in the control of subversion is taken by the legislative and executive branches of the government. Our concern here is with the Court's response to these programs. For this purpose, we limit the discussion to the Court's response to (1) federal antisubversive legislation, (2) the loyalty and security programs, (3) the application of subversive control programs to aliens and naturalized citizens, and (4) the legislative investigatory power. The first of these will be discussed in the next chapter.

THE COURT'S RESPONSE TO ANTISUBVERSION PROGRAMS

Executive Loyalty and Security Programs

On the national level, one answer to the problem of Communist subversion was the institution of an elaborate system for the investigation and screening of public employees. As Justice Jackson observed, "The Government is using its power as never before to pry into their lives and thoughts upon the slightest suspicion of less than complete trustworthiness." [4] The President's Loyalty Order of March 21, 1947, set up an elaborate scheme to rid the executive branch of the government of disloyal employees. It required an investigation into the loyalty not only of every person entering the government, but also of those already in the govern-

---

[4] Dissenting opinion in *Frazier* v. *United States*, 335 U.S. 497 (1948).

ment. The order fixed a standard for determining the loyalty of employees and provided procedures by which employees, charged with disloyalty and recommended for dismissal by the Loyalty Board of their respective departments or agencies, could have their cases reviewed by a Central Loyalty Review Board in the Civil Service Commission. The standard for removal prescribed by the order was whether,

On all the evidence, reasonable grounds exist for the belief that the person involved is disloyal to the Government of the United States. [The standard of judgment was revised in 1951 to read:] On all the evidence there is a reasonable doubt as to the loyalty of the person involved to the Government of the United States.[5]

Although this standard seemed fair and reasonable on its face, its omissions may seriously endanger civil liberties. The employee is not entitled to know who his accusers are or to confront or cross-examine them. He is, therefore, unable to defend himself against malicious gossip or idle rumor. In the words of Justice Douglas, the critical evidence may be the word of an unknown witness who "is a paragon of veracity, a knave, or the village idiot!" Equally serious is a provision of the order authorizing the Attorney General to draw up a list of organizations which he finds to be

. . . totalitarian fascist, communist or subversive or as having adopted a policy of advocating or approving the commission of acts of force or violence to deny others their rights under the Constitution of the United States, or as seeking to alter the form of government of the United States by unconstitutional means.

In determining a person's loyalty, investigators were directed to consider his membership in, affiliation with, or sympathetic association with organizations thus designated by the Attorney General.

The later Eisenhower loyalty-security program in one respect carried a greater hazard than the Truman program, in that it povided for reopening the cases of all persons in the government whose files contained derogatory information, even though they had received clearance under the earlier program. Considering the diversity of materials and data collected by the F.B.I. from every

[5] Executive Order 10,241, 16 Fed. Reg. 3590.

conceivable source, and of every degree of credibility and incredibility in line with its duty, employees may well have been placed in perpetual jeopardy.

The conflicting views concerning the constitutionality of this program came before the Supreme Court in three cases, but with inconclusive and unsatisfactory results. In *Bailey v. Richardson*,[6] the loyalty order was sustained by an evenly divided Court (Justice Clark not participating), against claims of unconstitutionality on due process and First Amendment grounds. The government had been sustained in the court of appeals by a two to one vote, and the even division of the Supreme Court, of course, affirmed this decision without opinion. In this case a finding of disloyalty was made against Dorothy Bailey, and she was dismissed from her government position on the basis of unsworn reports, based on the unsworn statements of unknown informants. Miss Bailey denied all charges except past membership in one organization listed by the Attorney General. Although she had no power to subpoena witnesses, four appeared on her behalf and others submitted some seventy affidavits. All the evidence of witnesses was in her favor, and no affidavits were introduced against her.

In announcing the decision of the court of appeals,[7] Judge Prettyman stated that Miss Bailey's case is "undoubtedly appealing" because "she was not given a trial in any sense of the word, and she does not know who informed upon her." Nor indeed did the Loyalty Review Board have "the slightest knowledge" about her accusers. However, continued Judge Prettyman, "it so happens that we are presently in an adversary position to a government whose most successful recent method of contest is the infiltration of a government service by its sympathizers." It might be added that we are in that adversary position because we believe in the value of personal freedom and its preservation.

All objections to the dismissal and the methods by which it was effected were brushed aside, including free speech objections, concerning which the Court asserted that the First Amendment does not guarantee government employment. Dismissal of government employees on loyalty-security grounds seems, then, to be no different legally from dismissal on other grounds. This con-

---

[6] 341 U.S. 918 (1951).
[7] 182 F. 2d. 46 (1950).

clusion is rooted in the assumption, well supported by precedent, that no one has a right to public employment and that removal or disqualification is not punishment. The President, in the absence of congressional limitation in certain areas, is free to remove any employee of the government without notice or assigned reason.

Yet, this case could have been decided on the basis of *United States* v. *Lovett*,[8] in which the Supreme Court held invalid as a bill of attainder the provision of a deficiency appropriation act, forbidding the payment of salaries of three designated federal employees from funds carried in the act. A bill of attainder is "a legislative act which inflicts punishment without a judicial trial," and Justice Black declared for the Court in Lovett that "permanent proscription from any opportunity to serve the Government is punishment, and of a most severe type."

The Court did, however, strike down the irregular manner in which the Attorney General made up his list of subversive organizations without a hearing. In 1949 the Joint Anti-Fascist Refugee Committee, along with certain other organizations, sought to restrain the Attorney General from including its name in a list of organizations designated by him to be subversive. The Supreme Court by a five to three vote reversed holdings of the courts below which had denied relief.[9] So great was the diversity of opinion among the majority that it is difficult to determine what the effect of the judgment is. Justice Burton, who announced the judgment of the Court (there was no opinion for the Court as such), took the view, supported by Justice Douglas, that the Attorney General's listing of the complainants was not authorized by the President's Executive Order 9835, which sets forth the procedure for determining the loyalty of federal employees or prospective employees. Justice Black insisted that the Attorney General had violated the First Amendment and that the President's order constituted a bill of attainder. He, along with Justices Frankfurter, Jackson, and Douglas, also held that the Attorney General had deprived the petitioners of due process of law by failing to give them notice and hearing.

There was reason to hope that the uncertain constitutional

[8] 328 U.S. 303 (1946).
[9] *Joint Anti-Fascist Refugee Committee* v. *McGrath*, 341 U.S. 123 (1951).

situation with respect to the loyalty-security program would be resolved when the Supreme Court agreed to review the Peters case.[10] Apparently, however, the Warren Court sought to soften the impact of these programs without challenging the authority of the government in this area. Instead of facing up to the constitutional issues involved, the Court decided the cases on procedural or statutory grounds. Thus, this case was decided in Dr. Peters' favor on a narrow procedural point—that the Loyalty Review Board was limited to cases involving persons recommended for dismissal by the Loyalty Board of the department or agency of the employee, and referred to it by such department or agency. This decision is the more surprising since the Court had granted certioari "because the case appeared to present the same constitutional question left unresolved by the Court's action" in the Bailey case, and also since Dr. Peters had urged the Court to decide the case solely on the constitutional issue.

On the constitutional question, Peters' chief complaints were: (1) that the denial of an opportunity to confront and cross-examine his secret accusers, and his removal and debarment from the government service on their unsworn testimony, deprived him of liberty and property without due processes of law; (2) that rendering him ineligible for government service constituted imposition of a penalty without a fair trial and was, therefore, a bill of attainder; and (3) that his removal and debarment from government service, solely on the basis of his political opinions, denied his right to freedom of speech.

In 1956, the Court, by means of narrow statutory construction, limited the scope of the federal employee fidelity program, again without deciding any of the serious constitutional questions posed in the litigation. In *Cole* v. *Young*,[11] the summary suspension powers of department heads under the Summary Suspension Act of 1950 were held to apply only to those employees who worked "in sensitive positions." The act gives the heads of eleven designated departments and agencies powers of summary suspension and unreviewable dismissal of their civilian employees, when deemed necessary "in the interest of national security." In pur-

[10] *Peters* v. *Hobby*, 349 U.S. 331 (1955).
[11] 351 U.S. 536 (1956).

suance of Section 3 of the act, providing that it would be extended "to such other departments and agencies of the Government as the President may deem necessary in the best interest of national security," the President, by executive order, extended the act to all other departments and agencies of the government. Cole, a preference-eligible veteran under the Veteran's Preference Act, was summarily suspended from his classified civil service position as a food and drug inspector in the Department of Health, Education, and Welfare, on charges of association with alleged Communists and of sympathetic association with an alleged subversive organization. Later he was dismissed, on the ground that his continued employment was not "clearly consistent with the interests of national security." His appeal to the Civil Service Commission under the Veteran's Act was denied, on the ground that the act was not applicable to such discharges.

By a six to three vote, the Court held that Cole's dismissal was not authorized by the Summary Suspension Act and hence violated the Veteran's Preference Act. The Court construed the dismissal procedure of the 1950 act as applicable only if the discharge is in the "interest of national security" and defined this term as relating only to employees' activities "which are directly concerned with the Nation's safety." In arriving at this definition, the Court was influenced by the type of agency to which Congress had specifically granted summary suspension and nonappealable dismissal powers. Since all these agencies were closely connected with the national defense, the inference seems to have been drawn that the President's power to extend the coverage of the act was limited to the so-called sensitive agencies.

It should be noted that the decision in this case in no way limits the substantive power of the government to provide for the dismissal of employees on loyalty grounds. It simply holds that the summary procedures authorized by the act are not applicable in a situation unrelated to the national safety.

At the time of this case it had not yet been judicially conceded that public employees under loyalty investigation have a constitutional right to confrontation, cross examination, and judicial hearing. The loyalty procedure guaranteed them notice, charges, and freedom from summary suspension and nonreviewable dismissal except "in sensitive positions," and they are entitled to no more.

Much more restrictive of the methods of the loyalty-security probers was the 1959 case of *Greene* v. *McElroy* relating to the Industrial Security Program.[12] In 1951 the government had revoked the security clearance of William L. Greene, an officer of Engineering Research Corporation, a firm working on defense contracts for the Navy. This action was followed by Greene's dismissal from the company. After a long fight for reinstatement of his clearance, he finally brought his case to the Supreme Court. He charged that the government had deprived him of his Fifth Amendment right to pursue his private vocation and had violated his Sixth Amendment right to confront and cross-examine adverse witnesses. The government had relied on confidential reports and presented no testimony or witnesses at the open hearings.

Chief Justice Warren emphatically declared that the right to follow a private profession without unreasonable government interference is guaranteed by the Fifth Amendment and that the right of confrontation and cross-examination of hostile witnesses would be available in such a situation. Nevertheless, he announced that there was no occasion here to decide whether the Industrial Security Program was in violation of the Fifth or Sixth Amendments, for the reason that neither the Congress nor the President had authorized the Secretary of Defense to dispense with the right of confrontation and cross-examination. Thus, "We decide only that in the absence of explicit authorization from either the President or Congress the respondents were not empowered to deprive petitioner of his job in a proceeding in which he was not afforded the safeguards of confrontation and cross-examination." [13]

In another case in 1964, Greene petitioned that the government be ordered to make monetary restitution to him for loss of employment under the regulations which were in effect when he began his fight for reinstatement rather than under more restrictive subsequent regulations. The Court in a seven to two decision

[12] 360 U.S. 474 (1959); see also *Vitarelli* v. *Seaton*, 359 U.S. 535 (1959).
[13] See *Cafeteria and Restaurant Workers Union* v. *McElroy*, 367 U.S. 886 (1961), which seemed to weaken the authority of *Greene* v. *McElroy*.

held that he was entitled to restitution under the earlier regulations.[14]

It will be observed that these cases, like most other subversion cases of the Warren Court, were all decided on procedural or statutory grounds without challenging the authority of coordinate branches of the government. The Court sharply criticized the extreme and uncritical procedures that the loyalty security agencies had used, but never questioned the authority of Congress and the President to use their power to cope with the problems of subversion. Still, these cases often accomplished the same specific results as if the legislation had been held invalid.

State Loyalty Oaths

The favorite method of the states for combating Communist subversion among employees during the cold war has been the requirement of a loyalty oath and non-Communist affidavits. Of the state statutory requirements of a loyalty oath that came before the Supreme Court, only one had been held invalid before 1952, and this not because of any lack of power to require a loyalty oath as such. In *Garner v. Board of Public Works* [15] in 1951, the Court upheld a Los Angeles ordinance, barring from city employment any person who would not take an oath swearing that he does not and has not for five years past advised, advocated, or taught the violent overthrow of the government; that he is not, and has not been, a member of any group advocating such activity; and that he will not engage in such forbidden activities while in the employment of the city. The Court also upheld the requirement of non-Communist affidavits required of all city employees.

Seven of the nine justices held that a revelation of party membership was a reasonable requirement, relating to the establishment of qualifications for public office. On the loyalty oath requirement, which in terms made no distinction between knowing and unknowing membership in a subversive organization, the Court divided five to four. The majority, through Justice Clark,

---

[14] *Greene* v. *United States,* 376 U.S. 149 (1964).
[15] 341 U.S. 716 (1951).

upheld the loyalty oath in the belief that *scienter* was implicit in the ordinance and on the assumption that California courts would not so construe the oath as to include innocent membership in subversive organizations. In an earlier case [16] the Court, upholding a part of the Ober Act of Maryland, which required candidates for public office to sign an oath that they are not engaged in any manner in attempting to overthrow the government and that they are not members of any organization engaged in such activity, had stressed that its decision was based on the assumption that what was forbidden was the overthrow of the government by force or violence. Although the Court sustained the loyalty oath in both these cases, it agreed that the doctrine of guilt by association could be carried to the point of denying due process of law.

A year later, however, in *Adler* v. *Board of Education*,[17] Mr. Justice Minton placed the stamp of the Court's approval upon this doctrine. In this case the Court sustained the Civil Service Law of New York, as implemented by the Feinberg Law of 1949. The first denies public employment to persons who willfully advocate or teach the overthrow of government by any unlawful means or who join any group advocating such a policy. The Feinberg Law requires the Board of Regents of the state "after inquiry, and after such notice and hearing as may be appropriate," to prepare a list of subversive organizations to be used, along with similar listing of any federal agency, in removing and barring from the public schools ineligible employees. Membership in any listed organization is *prima facie* evidence of disqualification for employment in the public schools.

After pointing out that listings are made only after full notice and hearing, and that the New York Court of Appeals had ruled that the listed organizations have the right of appeal, the Court held that the Feinberg Law did not violate free speech and free assembly of persons employed or seeking employment in the public schools. It is clear, said Mr. Justice Minton, that such persons have the right to "assemble, speak, think and believe as they will, but it is equally clear that they have no right to employment in the school system on their own terms." If they do not choose to work

[16] *Gerende* v. *Board of Supervisors of Elections*, 341 U.S. 56 (1951).
[17] 342 U.S. 485 (1952).

under "the reasonable terms laid down by the proper authorities," they are "free to retain their beliefs and associations and go elsewhere."

With respect to guilt by association, Mr. Justice Minton said for the majority: "One's associates, past and present, as well as one's conduct, may properly be considered in determining fitness and loyalty. From time immemorial, one's reputation has been determined in part by the company he keeps."

Justice Douglas, with Justice Black agreeing, was unable to "accept the recent doctrine" that public servants may be constitutionally placed "in the category of second class citizens by denying them freedom of thought and expression." The procedure allowed by this law "is certain to raise havoc with academic freedom," said Douglas. Furthermore this law "turns the school system into a spying project." Once membership is established, the view of the teacher must be examined to determine whether his affiliation was or is innocent. Douglas declared:

There can be no academic freedom in such an environment. Where suspicion fills the air and holds scholars in line for fear of their jobs, there can be no exercise of the free intellect. . . . A problem can no longer be pursued with impunity to its edges. Fear stalks the classroom. The teacher is no longer a stimulant to adventurous thinking; she becomes instead a pipeline for safe and sound information. A deadening dogma takes the place of free inquiry. Instruction tends to become sterile; pursuit of knowledge is discouraged; discussion often leaves off where it should begin.

Perhaps Justice Douglas' apprehensions were somewhat relieved by the unanimous decision of the Court the following term in *Weiman* v. *Updegraff*.[18] In this case the Court condemned guilt by association and held unconstitutional, on due process grounds, the Oklahoma Loyalty Oath Act because, as applied to a member of the faculty of Oklahoma A. & M. College, it excluded people from state employment solely on the basis of membership in organizations listed by the Attorney General of the United States as "Communist front" or "subversive." Justice Clark, for the Court, points out that in previous loyalty oath cases the Court had

18 344 U.S. 183 (1952).

made its decision on the understanding that knowing membership in the proscribed organization was an implicit requirement of the statute. Under the Oklahoma law as interpreted by the state court, knowledge was not a factor. Hence mere membership is made a conclusive presumption of disloyalty.

"But membership may be innocent. A state servant may have joined a proscribed organization unaware of its activities and purposes." Such indiscriminate classification of innocent with knowing affiliation is, therefore, condemned "as an assertion of arbitrary power" in violation of due process.

Although this case apparently placed the preceding loyalty oath cases in a less disturbing light from the point of view of the public employee, it in no way challenged the power of the states to impose loyalty tests upon their employees. It merely held this particular loyalty test bad for the reasons indicated. Still, it was encouraging to the public servants to have the Court deny that the unfortunate language of Mr. Justice Minton in the Adler case supports the conclusion "that there is no constitutionally protected right to public employment." Declining to consider whether there is an abstract right to public employment, the Court nevertheless emphasized "that constitutional protection does extend to the public servant whose exclusion pursuant to a statute is patently arbitrary and discriminatory."

In the latest state loyalty case (*Elfbrandt* v. *Russell*, 34 LW 40, 1966), the Court held that even knowing membership in a subversive organization is not sufficient ground for dismissal of an employee unless it can be shown that he joined the organization with the "specific intent to further illegal action."

A variation on the restriction of public employees is illustrated by the case of *Shelton* v. *Tucker* [19] in which an Arkansas statute requiring an annual affidavit detailing all the organizations which teachers and school officials had either joined or contributed to in the preceding five years came before the Court. By a five to four decision the Court held in an opinion by Mr. Justice Stewart that the statute deprived the teachers of their right of "associational freedom" protected by the due process clause of the Fourteenth Amendment, "a right closely allied to freedom of speech and . . .

[19] 364 U.S. 479 (1960).

which, like freedom of speech, lies at the foundation of a free society." The unlimited and indiscriminate sweep of the statute, requiring every teacher to disclose every single organization with which he has been associated over a five-year period, goes far beyond any legitimate inquiry into the fitness and competence of teachers.

A more restrictive attitude toward state loyalty oaths is further illustrated by two cases decided in 1961 and 1964. In *Cramp* v. *Board of Public Instruction*,[20] a Florida statute requiring every employee of the state or its subdivisions to take an oath that he has never lent his "aid, support, advice, counsel or influence to the Communist party," was struck down by a unanimous Court on the ground that the meaning of the required oath is so vague and uncertain that it violates the due process clause of the Fourteenth Amendment. It forces an employee either to take such an oath at the risk of subsequent prosecution for perjury, or face immediate dismissal from the public service.[21]

Boggett v. *Bullitt* [21] involved an action brought by certain members of the faculty, staff, and student body of the University of Washington to enjoin enforcement of a state of Washington statute requiring an oath of teachers and other state employees concerning their activities and membership in subversive organizations and their attitudes toward federal and state laws and institutions. In a seven to two opinion by Justice White, the Court held the oaths void for vagueness. In the "sensitive" area of free speech and association, declared Justice White, restrictive regulations must meet specially high standards of definiteness.

The Privilege Against Self-Incrimination

A less common method of insuring the loyalty of state and local employees is illustrated by the provision of the Charter of the City of New York, which stipulates that whenever any employee of the city invokes the privilege against self-incrimination for the purpose of avoiding disclosure of information relating to his official

---

[20] 368 U.S. 278 (1961).
[21] 377 U.S. 360 (1964).

conduct, he shall be automatically discharged and rendered ineligible for future employment. In *Slochower* v. *Board of Education*,[22] a professor at Brooklyn College was automatically discharged for having pleaded self-incrimination before a U.S. Senate investigating committee with respect to Communist membership and association prior to 1941. Slochower testified that he was not a member of the Communist party and that he was willing to answer all questions relating to such membership subsequent to 1941, but he refused to answer questions about his membership during 1940–41 for fear of self-incrimination.

The Supreme Court, reversing the Court of Appeals of New York, held that Slochower's summary dismissal without charges, notice, hearing, and the right of appeal denied him due process of law.

Although the majority opinion is something less than clear as to which aspects of the discharge procedure failed to satisfy due process requirements, the holding of invalidity seems to rest upon two related considerations: First, under the charter provision a claim of the privilege against self-incrimination creates a conclusive presumption of unsuitability for employment. Second, a provision that bars any weighing of the circumstances in which the privilege was claimed is arbitrary on its face. This point was emphasized by the majority of five.

It should be noted, then, that the Court did not rule that the plea of self-incrimination by an employee could not be made valid ground for dismissal; it held rather that Slochower was entitled to a fair hearing to determine whether in the circumstances of his case such a plea was a proper ground for dismissal.

The principal significance of the Slochower case is its reaffirmation of the proposition of the Wieman case, that "constitutional protection does extend to the public servant whose exclusion pursuant to a statute is patently arbitrary and discriminatory." The decision also refutes the dictum of the Bailey case that public employment is a "privilege" which escapes protection entirely.

The force of this decision was sharply modified by two cases decided by the Court during the congressional assault on the

22 350 U.S. 551 (1956).

Court in 1958. In two five to four decisions the Court upheld dismissal of a public school teacher and a subway employee who refused to answer questions concerning possible subversion affiliations.[23] In the Beilan case the majority reasoned that teaching competence was not limited to classroom performance, but included other factors such as the obligation of frankness and candor to one's superiors. The school board had found Beilan remiss in these duties. In the Lerner case, the New York subway conductor had invoked Fifth Amendment immunity when asked if he were at the time a member of the Communist party. Here Justice Harlan reasoned that the Slochower case was distinguishable on the ground that it involved the loss of state employment rights because of the attempt to exercise a federal constitutional right before an agency of the federal government. On the other hand, Lerner had been dismissed because he refused to give frank answers to questions put to him by state authorities. Somehow this made him a person of doubtful loyalty, and New York law permitted dismissal of such a person. The Fourteenth Amendment did not, at that time, of course, include protection from self-incrimination in a state proceeding.

Another example of withdrawal from the Slochower position is *Nelson and Globe* v. *County of Los Angeles.*[24] Nelson and Globe were Los Angeles County employees who had invoked the Fifth Amendment when asked about subversion and subversive activities by a subcommittee of the HUAC. A California statute required that government employees answer questions about subversion asked by duly authorized state or federal investigating agencies. Both men were discharged by the county on grounds of insubordination, and both sued for reinstatement claiming their dismissals were in violation of the due process clause of the Fourteenth Amendment. On the removal of Nelson, who was a permanent employee, the Court divided four to four, but held five to three that the dismissal of Globe, a temporary employee, did not deny due process. Justice Clark relied on the Beilan and Lerner cases and distinguished the Slochower case on the ground that

[23] *Beilan* v. *Board of Education,* 357 U.S. 399 (1958); *Lerner* v. *Casey,* 357 U.S. 468 (1958).
[24] 362 U.S. 1 (1960).

Globe had been dismissed for insubordination, that is, for failure to give information which the state had a proper interest in securing, whereas New York had removed Slochower solely because he had invoked the Fifth Amendment. Globe had been warned before he invoked immunity that he would be dismissed if he failed to answer the subcommittee's questions. This distinction was too thin in the eyes of the dissenters.

Bar Admission Cases

A further switch in the position of the Court is illustrated by the Bar Admission Cases. In 1957 and 1958, the Court struck down on due process grounds the state decisions denying admission respectively to the New Mexico and California bars, of applicants who had failed to demonstrate good moral character. Their character deficiency grew out of certain allegedly subversive activities and associations casting doubt on their loyalty.[25] These cases, among others, were the subject of a vigorous attack by the 1958 Conference of State Chief Justices, and soon thereafter the Court took a much milder position on these same issues.

In the second Konigsberg case in 1961, the Court sustained rejection of Konigsberg's application because he refused to answer questions about membership in the Communist party on First Amendment grounds. The Court took the position that in the circumstances of this case the state's interest in securing a competent bar of good character outweighed the applicant's free speech interest.[26]

State Legislative Investigation

The case of *Sweezy v. New Hampshire*,[27] which will be considered later in connection with congressional powers of investigation, fur-

---

[25] *Schware v. Board of Bar Examiners*, 353 U.S. 232 (1957), and *Konigsberg v. California*, 353 U.S. 252 (1957).
[26] *Konigsberg v. State Bar*, 366 U.S. 36 (1961); see also In re *Anastoplo*, 366 U.S. 82 (1961).
[27] 354 U.S. 234 (1957).

ther limited the power of the states to encroach upon the rights of public employees in their search for subversives. The legislature of New Hampshire had in 1951 enacted a comprehensive Subversive Activities Act and in 1953 authorized and directed the attorney general of the state to make full and complete investigation of subversive activities and persons. He was authorized to act on his own motion upon such information as in his judgment was reasonable and reliable, and he was given the further authority to subpoena witnesses and documents. Although he did not have power to hold witnesses in contempt, he could invoke the aid of a state superior court for this purpose.

Sweezy, a university professor, was summoned to testify before the attorney general. Although he had previously testified that he had never been a member of the Communist party, that he had no knowledge of any violations of the Subversive Activities Act or of the presence of subversive persons within the state, he refused to answer, both before the attorney general and before the superior court, questions relating to the content of a lecture he had delivered at the University of New Hampshire and questions concerning his and others' association with the Progressive party. His refusal to answer those questions was based on his contention that they were not pertinent to the subject of the inquiry and that they infringed upon an area protected by the First and Fourteenth Amendments. For this refusal to answer, Sweezy was held guilty of contempt. The Supreme Court reversed the conviction on the ground that it had denied the defendant due process of law.

The meaning of this decision is not unmistakably clear because of the division in the opinion of the six majority justices. Four justices (Warren, Black, Douglas, and Brennan), although placing great emphasis on the infringement of Sweezy's academic freedom and his right of political association, seemed to hold that the conviction was bad because the legislature, in its sweeping grant of discretionary authority to the attorney general, had divested itself of all responsibility for the direction of the investigation. So broad and uncertain is the mandate of the attorney general that the matters to be investigated, the witnesses to be summoned, and the questions to be asked are all left to his discretion. "In this circumstance," said the Chief Justice, "it cannot be determined authoritatively that the legislature asked the attorney general to gather the kind of facts comprised in the subjects upon which petitioner was interrogated." Justices Frankfurter and Harlan agreed that the conviction should be set aside, but on the ground that the questions asked of Sweezy deprived him of his constitutionally protected rights of academic freedom and political association.

Although the precise manner in which the Fourteenth Amendment was violated does not emerge clearly from the divided opinions of the justices, all six members of the majority seem to agree that the academic freedom of a university teacher and the political freedom of a citizen are constitutionally protected against the state investigatory power through the due process clause of the Fourteenth Amendment, unless the state can show a very strong countervailing interest.

In *Uphaus* v. *Wyman* [28] the Court apparently pulled some of the teeth of the Sweezy case. This case, too, involved the power of the attorney general of New Hampshire, sitting as a one-man legislative investigating committee, to require Uphaus to supply the names of all persons who had been guests at a summer camp maintained by World Fellowship, Inc., of which Uphaus was executive director. Dividing five to four, the Court held that due process was not denied in this case. Since World Fellowship was neither a university nor a political party, the academic and political freedoms considered in Sweezy were not involved here in the same measure. The main federal question was whether the public interest of the state in security overbalanced the private interest in associational privacy. On this point Justice Clark, for the majority, noted that the state attorney general had reason to believe that some of the guests might have been subversive persons, since at least nineteen speakers at the camp had Communist connections.

The investigative power of the state, he argued, need not be restrained until sufficient evidence is secured to justify the institution of criminal proceedings for subversion. The governmental interest in self-preservation, the ultimate value in any society, "out-

[28] 360 U.S. 72 (1959).

weighs individual rights in an associational privacy, which, however real in other circumstances, . . . were here tenuous at best."
The camp was open to the public and operated under a state law
requiring the maintenance of a register open to police inspection.

A 1963 case seems to represent a wide swing from the Court's
attitude of restraint reflected in Uphaus and other cases. A committee of the Florida legislature was investigating the NAACP
as a part of an investigation of subversive activities. In this connection the committee sought by subpoena to obtain the entire
membership list of the Miami branch of the NAACP. The branch
president refused the list and was cited for contempt. The contempt action was challenged as violating First Amendment rights.
The Court in a five to four opinion by Justice Goldberg agreed
and held that groups which themselves are neither engaged in
subversive or other illegal or improper activities, nor are demonstrated to have any substantial connections with such activities
are to be protected in their right of free and private association.[29]

Deportation of Aliens and Denaturalization of Citizens

Where subversive control programs have related to aliens or to
naturalized citizens, the Court has been especially reluctant to
intervene in behalf of individual freedoms. The complete power
of Congress over the admission of aliens to this country and the
responsibility of the Executive for the conduct of foreign affairs
make it easy for the Court to maintain a role of passivity with
respect to subversive control relating to aliens. The virtually absolute power of Congress to prescribe the standards for admission
of aliens into the United States has been well established for more
than a half-century,[30] and with this power goes also a broad control of aliens after their admission to the country. By the Alien
Registration Act of 1940, for example, it was provided that all
aliens fourteen years of age and over, residing in the United
States, submit to registration and fingerprinting. Failure to comply

---

[29] *Gibson* v. *Florida Legislative Investigation Committee*, 372 U.S. 539
(1963).

[30] See *Turner* v. *Williams*, 194 U.S. 279 (1904).

was made a criminal offense against the United States.[31] Should he, while residing in the United States, violate the rules and regulations laid down by Congress for the control of his conduct, the alien may be deported.

The attitude of judicial restraint on the part of the Court in alien cases became much more pronounced in the postwar period than during World War II. In the earlier period it had been held, for example, that Communist belief and affiliation which had ceased at the time of the defendant's arrest was not a proper ground for deportation under the Immigration Act of 1918.[32] Furthermore, cooperation with the Communist party in lawful activities did not constitute affiliation within the meaning of the Alien Registration Act of 1940, which authorized the deportation of any alien affiliated with an organization believing in or advocating the overthrow of the government by force or violence.[33]

On the other hand, in 1952, a provision of the Internal Security Act of 1950, authorizing the Attorney General, in his discretion, to hold in custody without bail alien Communists pending determination of their deportability was sustained by the Court in a five to four vote.[34] The Court had no doubt of the validity of the provision of the law making membership in the Communist party alone a cause for deportation, for "so long as aliens fail to become and remain naturalized citizens, they remain subject to the plenary power of Congress to expel them under the soverign right to determine what non-citizens shall be permitted to remain within our borders." Detention, even for life, was held to be a necessary part of deportation procedure.

Justice Black, in dissent, thought that condemning people to jail was a job for the judiciary, not the Attorney General, and that to keep people in jail because of what they said was a clear violation of the First Amendment.

On the same day, the Court, with only Douglas and Black dissenting, sustained a provision of the Alien Registration Act of 1940, authorizing the deportation of legally resident aliens on

---

[31] 54 Stat. 670, 673.
[32] *Kessler v. Strecher*, 357 U.S. 22 (1939).
[33] *Bridges v. Wixon*, 326 U.S. 135 (1945).
[34] *Carlson v. Landon*, 342 U.S. 524 (1952).

account of membership in the Communist party, which terminated before the enactment of the act. The Court in *Harisiades* v. *Shaughnessy* [35] held that such deportation did not deprive the alien petitioners of liberty without due process of law, even though it might be unreasonably and harshly exercised under this statute, (1) because the power to expel aliens is a weapon of defense and reprisal, confirmed by international law as a power inherent in every sovereign state; (2) because the policy toward aliens is so exclusively entrusted to the political branches of the government as to be largely immune from judicial inquiry or interference. As Justice Frankfurter observed in a concurring opinion, "the place to resist unwise or cruel legislation touching aliens is the Congress, not this Court."

The Court also held that the act did not abridge the aliens' rights of free speech and free assembly in contravention of the First Amendment. Under the First Amendment, said Justice Jackson for the majority, Congress may make a distinction between advocacy of change by lawful elective processes and change by force and violence.

In 1954, in *Galvan* v. *Press*,[36] the Court held that an alien was deportable even if he had no knowledge of the illegal purposes of the Communist party.

But this case was seriously eroded as a precedent in 1957 by *Rowaldt* v. *Perfetto*.[37] Justice Frankfurter, writing for the Court, held that although the petitioner had admitted a brief membership in the Communist party in 1935, the record was still "too insubstantial" to support the order of deportation under the law. "There must," said Justice Frankfurter, "be a substantial basis for finding that an alien had committed himself to the Communist party" in the knowledge of its nature and purpose.

In a case decided in 1957, a point is scored in favor of the alien, in a holding that the Attorney General is forbidden to ask an alien, under order of deportation, questions that do not relate to his availability for expulsion.[38]

---

[35] 342 U.S. 580 (1952).
[36] 347 U.S. 522 (1954).
[37] 355 U.S. 115 (1957).
[38] *United States* v. *Witkovick*, 353 U.S. 194 1957).

Denaturalization and Deportation

Even naturalized citizens are subject to serious disabilities when the question of defense against charges of subversion arises. Chief Justice Marshall asserted, in 1824, that a naturalized citizen becomes a full-fledged member of the society into which he is admitted, "possessing all the rights of a native citizen, and standing, in the view of the Constitution, on the footing of a native. The Constitution does not authorize Congress to enlarge or abridge those rights" [39] other than to prescribe a uniform rule of naturalization. Justice Douglas expressed a similar view for the Court in 1946:

Citizenship obtained through naturalization is not second class citizenship. . . . [It] carried with it the privilege of full participation in the affairs of our society, including the right to speak freely, to criticize officials and administrators, and to promote changes in our laws including the very charter of our government.[40]

Nevertheless, the device of denaturalization can and has been used against naturalized citizens who express unorthodox political views.[41] The power to denaturalize is, of course, implied from the power of Congress to provide a uniform rule of naturalization and is based on the charge that naturalization was obtained through fraud or illegality. There has never been any question of the legality of canceling certificates of naturalization thus obtained. If it can be shown that the applicant has sworn falsely that he was "attached to the principles of the United States, and well disposed to the good order and happiness of the same," his certificate may be canceled. In determining the standards of proof that must be observed to support the government's charges in such cases, the courts enlarge or contract the civil liberties of naturalized citizens. Enlargement was achieved in some denaturalization cases of World War II, the leading one being *Schneiderman* v. *United States.*[42]

---

[39] *Osborn* v. *Bank of United States,* 9 Wheat 738, 827 (1824).

[40] *Knauer* v. *United States,* 328 U.S. 654, 658 (1946).

[41] See C. H. Pritchett, *Civil Liberties and the Vinson Court* (Chicago, University of Chicago Press, 1954), p. 103.

[42] 320 U.S. 118 (1943).

Here, the Court held that before the citizenship of a naturalized citizen could be canceled, the government must present evidence of his failure to meet the statutory requirements of attachment to the principles of the Constitution that is "clear, unequivocal, and convincing." A mere preponderance of evidence is not enough. The government had failed to meet this standard of proof in its case against Schneiderman, and the denaturalization decree of the lower court was set aside. Because of our firmly rooted tradition of freedom of belief, the Court in construing the denaturalization acts refused to presume "that Congress meant to circumscribe liberty of political thought by general phrases in those statutes." [43]

Here, the Court had required a burden of proof of the government in denaturalization cases which in effect approximates the burden demanded for conviction in criminal cases, namely, proof beyond a reasonable doubt of the charges alleged. Yet, five years after Baumgartner, in 1949, the Court ruled in *Klaprott* v. *United States* [44] that the strict procedural standards of a criminal trial need not be observed in denaturalization cases. But the cases decided in 1956 and 1957 mark reversion of the Court to a more favorable attitude to the citizen. For example, in *United States* v. *Miniker* [45] it was held that the provision of the Immigration and Nationality Act of 1952, relating to the compulsion of testimony in deportation and denaturalization proceedings, does not empower an immigration officer to subpoena a naturalized citizen to testify in an administrative proceeding in which determination of his denaturalization is the subject of the investigation. Again, in 1958, the Court insisted on strict standards of proof in denaturalization cases. In *Maisenberg* v. *United States* [46] the government sued under a provision of the Nationality and Immigration Act of 1952 to set aside the naturalization decree of Maisenberg on the ground that it had been obtained by the "concealment of a material fact" and "willful misrepresentation." The Supreme Court reversed lower court decisions in favor of the government

[43] See also *Baumgartner* v. *United States,* 322 U.S. 665 (1944).
[44] 335 U.S. 601 (1949).
[45] 350 U.S. 179 (1956); see also *United States* v. *Zucca,* 351 U.S. 90 (1957).
[46] 356 U.S. 670 (1958); see also Novak, 356 U.S. 660 (1958).

because, under the Schneiderman rule, it had failed to prove its charge by "clear unequivocal and convincing evidence." Although the government proved that the petitioner for five years preceding her naturalization had been a member of the Communist party, it did not prove by proper evidence that she knew that the party advocated the violent overthrow of the government. A further liberalization of judicial attitude in favor of the citizen was reflected in two later cases decided in 1964. In *Schneider* v. *Rusk*,[47] a German national by birth who had acquired derivative American citizenship through her mother at age sixteen and who had returned to Germany after graduation from college and lived there for eight years, except for two visits to the United States, was denied a passport by the State Department on the ground that she had lost her citizenship by continuous residence for three years in the country of her nativity as required by act of Congress. The Court held the statute void as violative of the due process clause of the Ffth Amendment. The Court rejected the discriminatory "assumption of the statute that naturalized citizens as a class are less reliable and bear less allegiance to this country than do the natural born."

In the other case the Court intercepted the deportation of Frank Costello. It held that the provision of the Immigration and Nationality Act of 1952 authorizing deportation of an alien who had been twice convicted of crimes involving moral turpitude did not apply to a denaturalized alien whose criminal acts had been committed while he was a citizen.

The troublesome question of loss of citizenship by an American national confronted the Court again in a 1963 case. The Court struck down provisions of the Immigration and Naturalization Act of 1952 and the Nationality Act of 1940, which automatically deprive native-born Americans of their citizenship for "departing from or remaining outside of the jurisdiction of the United States in time of war or . . . national emergency for the purpose of evading or avoiding military service." Such powers of the Congress are subject to the constitutional requirements of due process, and "Congress may not employ the deprivation of nationality as a punishment for the above mentioned offense without affording

[47] 377 U.S. 163 (1964).

the procedural safeguards guaranteed by the Fifth and Sixth Amendments." [48]

Congressional Investigatory Power

The legislative response to the Communist menace that has provoked perhaps the sharpest controversy in the postwar years took the form of the legislative investigatory power. There can be no question, of course, that few things should be of greater concern to Congress than the security of the nation and its protection against subversion and conspiracy. But of equal importance is protection of the rights of the individual against possible abuses of the investigatory power. Since 1937, there have been many complaints that some legislative committees were guilty of such abuses.

On the basis of well-established precedents, it is clear that the courts can exercise no substantial restraint upon the exercise of this legislative function. Investigative powers are, of course, not specifically stated in the Constitution but are derived by implication from the delegated powers of Congress as incidental to the effective exercise of those powers. Until the Watkins case, there had actually been only one case [49] in which the Supreme Court failed to find relevance to the delegated powers of Congress.

It was nearly a century after the framing of the Constitution before the first case to challenge the securing of information by compulsory legislative process reached the Supreme Court. In the case of *Kilbourne v. Thompson*,[50] in 1881, the Court held an investigation invalid because Congress was without power to legislate with respect to the subject of the investigation. The investigation involved an effort to pry into purely private affairs, with which the judiciary alone was empowered to deal, and hence violated the principle of the separation of powers. The Court also indicated that the investigating committee's authorizing resolution must recite a proper legislative purpose, but in *McGrain v.*

[48] *Kennedy v. Mendoza-Martinez*, 372 U.S. 144 (1963); see also *Marks v. Esferdy*, 377 U.S. 214 (1964).
[49] See note 50.
[50] 103 U.S. 168 (1881).

Daugherty,[51] in 1927, the rule was enunciated that when the subject matter of the investigation is one from which valid legislation might ensue, a proper legislative purpose will be presumed, whether or not this were the actual situation. Here the Court declared "that the power of inquiry—with process to enforce it—is an essential and appropriate auxiliary to the legislative function."

Aided by the aforementioned presumption of regularity, and the consequent reluctance of courts to find in contempt proceedings that investigations were conducted for improper purposes, the committees have been able to carry on investigations aimed at exposure rather than at corrective legislation. For many years both the legislatures and the courts seem to have overlooked the qualifications of the McGrain case, namely, that the investigation must be in aid of a valid legislative function, and that the questions asked must be pertinent to the subject of the inquiry.

This broadening of the investigatory power assumed a form, in the post-World War II years, hitherto unknown. The investigations of this period were concerned almost exclusively with the problems of subversion, and they brought before the courts new questions of the appropriate limits of congressional investigation. The central issue here was the application of the Bill of Rights as a restraint upon the assertion of the investigatory powers of Congress.

The activities of the House Committee on Un-American Activities were challenged in several cases, in 1947, on substantive constitutional issues. The Supreme Court refused to review all but one of these cases, and in that one, the flight of the defendant from the country prevented the Court's rendering a decision on the merits of the controversy. In this and the four other cases, the constitutional issues were decided by the court of appeals in favor of the committee.[52] With respect to the four cases finally deter-

---

51 273 U.S. 135 (1927).

52 *United States* v. *Josephson,* 165 F. 2d. 82 (1947), cert. denied 333 U.S. 838 (1948); *Barsky* v. *United States,* 167 F. 2d. 241 (1948), cert. denied 334 U.S. 843 (1948); *Eisler* v. *United States,* 170 F. 2d. 273 (1948), cert. granted 335 U.S. 857 (1948); *Lawson* v. *United States,* 176 F. 2d. 49 (1949), cert. denied 339 U.S. 934 (1950); *Marshall* v. *United States,* 176 F. 2d. 473 (1949), cert. denied 339 U.S. 933.

mined by the court of appeals, the Supreme Court apparently saw no reason to question the holdings and reasoning of the lower courts. The fact that the committee showed little, or no, interest in legislation made no difference to the court of appeals. It followed McGrain v. Daugherty in regarding the declaration by Congress that the information sought by it in creating the committee was for a legislative purpose as binding on the courts.

In these cases a new attack was made on the work of investigative committees by attempts to show that the results achieved by this committee violated the First Amendment. For example, the argument of the appellant in the case of United States v. Josephson [53] ran substantially in this fashion: The committee's power to investigate is limited by Congress' power to legislate; Congress is without power to legislate upon matters of thought and speech; therefore, a statute empowering a congressional committee to investigate such matters is unconstitutional. One of the three judges of the court of appeals accepted this argument, but the response of the majority was that Congress clearly can and should legislate to curtail this freedom, where there is a clear and present danger that its exercise would imperil the safety of the country and its constitutional system, and that courts cannot anticipate that Congress will enact legislation in violation of the First Amendment.

The contention that the committee's questioning of witnesses as to their political affiliation violated their First Amendment rights to privacy and to freedom from inquiry into political beliefs was likewise rejected by the court of appeals. Such questioning is incidental to the committee's principal function of securing information with a view to determining whether party affiliations or activities do in fact constitute a clear and present danger. In such circumstances the right to privacy must give way to the congressional interest in safeguarding the public welfare. Rejected also was the argument that the authorization to the committee to examine into "the extent, character, and objects of un-American propaganda activities in the United States" was so vague as to deny due process.

Apparently the Supreme Court at this time had no desire to

[53] 165 F. 2d. 82 (1947).

become involved in the problem of determining the boundaries of legislative inquiry. At any rate, it had placed no restraint upon any committee investigating Communist activity. The Court did, however, rule against the House Select Committee on Lobbying in its attempt to secure information from the secretary of the self-styled Committee on Constitutional Government with respect to the names of the purchasers of its propaganda materials in bulk. The Regulation of Lobbying Act of 1946 requires the reporting of all contributions of $500 or more received or expended for the purpose of influencing legislation. The Committee on Constitutional Government, commonly regarded as a right-wing propaganda organization, adopted the policy of accepting payments of over $490 only if the contributor specified that the money was to be used for the distribution of books and pamphlets. The organization described these practices as sales and hence refused to report them. The Committee on Lobbying responded to what it regarded as a transparent attempt at evasion of the law by citing the secretary Rumely, for contempt. In *United States* v. *Rumely*,[54] the Supreme Court unanimously reversed the conviction of Rumely for contempt, but the decision seemed to be of little value as a precedent, for only Douglas and Black were willing to face the constitutional issue of First Amendment violation. The Court evaded this issue, as indicated in Chapter 4 by holding that the committee was authorized by Congress to investigate lobbying, that lobbying as defined in the statute means only the direct attempt to influence legislation and does not extend to general efforts to influence the opinion of the community by the circulation of books and pamphlets.

Before the cases beginning in 1955, it appears then that the position of the Court on judicial review of the scope of the legislative investigatory function could be summed up in the statement of Justice Frankfurter, in *Tenney* v. *Brandhove*,[55] that to justify a judicial finding that a committee's investigation has exceeded the bounds of legislative power, "it must be obvious that there was a usurpation of functions exclusively vested in the executive or the courts."

[54] 345 U.S. 41 (1953).
[55] 341 U.S. 367, 378 (1951).

However, a redefinition of the scope of legislative investigation was in the making, and even the charge of First Amendment violation made in the Josephson case [56] was destined to bear fruit. In a series of cases decided in the 1955 term, the Court recognized the privilege against self-incrimination as a legal limitation on the powers of congressional investigating committees.

In three companion cases,[57] the Court faced the problem of recalcitrant witnesses before congressional investigating committees. Each defendant had been convicted of contempt of Congress for refusing to answer questions put to him by a subcommittee of the House Committee on Un-American Activities. The Court in three opinions by Chief Justice Warren reversed the convictions.

The controlling issues, as framed by the Court were: (1) whether the defendants had invoked their constitutional privilege against self-incrimination with a sufficient degree of specificity (this issue was not involved in the Bart case); and (2) whether, assuming that they had not, the committee had made its refusal to accept the defendant's objections sufficiently clear to support a finding that they had intended to defy the committee's authority. Despite the fact that Quinn and Emspak had stated their reasons for refusal to answer in something less than unequivocal terms, the Chief Justice nevertheless declared that the responsibility for clarification of ambiguities in the witness' position rests on the interrogator. A valid claim of the privilege does not depend upon any special combination of words. Thus Emspak's refusal based on "primarily the first Amendment, supplemented by the fifth," was sufficient. The Court pointed out that, in common parlance today, the Fifth Amendment is taken to mean privilege against self-incrimination. On the issue of criminal intent to defy the committee, the Court ruled that the committee had failed to make it sufficiently clear that it was not willingly abandoning those questions to which objection had been made. Thus the witness may have thought that his objections had been sustained. In short, there must be a clear disposition of the witness' objection before

---

[56] See note 52, p. 230.
[57] Quinn v. United States, 349 U.S. 155 (1955); Emspak v. United States, 349 U.S. 190 (1955); Bart v. United States, 349 U.S. 219 (1955).

there can be a prosecution for contempt. The committee's failure to rule on the objections was fatal to a citation for contempt.

Although it had previously been assumed that the privilege against self-incrimination could be invoked by witnesses called before congressional investigating committees, the Supreme Court had not ruled on this question up to this point. These decisions, however, imposed no important substantive limitations on congressional investigative procedures. Their significance lay in the fact that they made it less likely that the constitutional rights of a witness would be lost through entrapment or confusion.

It has been long and firmly established that the sole purpose of the immunity from self-incrimination clause of the Fifth Amendment is to protect persons from compulsion to give evidence which will expose them to the danger of criminal prosecution. Significantly affecting both the power of the government to investigate subversion and the right of witnesses under the Fifth Amendment is the case of *Ullmann* v. *United States*,[58] which sustained the Immunity Act of 1954, even as applied to state prosecutions.

The act [59] provides that when a U.S. attorney believes it necessary in the public interest to secure testimony or papers of a witness in any judicial proceeding in connection with threats to the national security or defense, he may, upon approval of the Attorney General, apply to the Court for an order, directing the witness to testify or produce the evidence, provided that:

. . . no such witness shall be prosecuted or subjected to any penalty or forfeiture for or on account of any transaction, matter or thing concerning which he is compelled, after having claimed his privilege against self-incrimination, to testify or produce evidence, nor shall testimony so compelled be used as evidence in any criminal proceeding against him in any Court.

Ullmann, who had refused on Fifth Amendment grounds to testify before a grand jury concerning his alleged Communist party membership and activities, persisted in his refusal, in response to a Court order issued under the Immunity Act, on the

58 350 U.S. 422 (1956).
59 18 U.S.C., 68 Stat. 746; (Supp. II), Sec. 3486.

ground that the act was unconstitutional. On appeal to the Supreme Court, the act was upheld and his conviction for contempt was sustained. The Court, speaking through Justice Frankfurter, held that the government may trade the right to prosecute for the privilege against self-incrimination, since the immunity need only remove the fear of criminal prosecution. Thus, if the defendant is rendered safe from prosecution, he cannot claim immunity on the ground that his testimony will disgrace, embarrass, or expose him to public disapprobation. Quoting from the sixty-year-old precedent of *Brown* v. *Walker*,[60] upholding a similar statute of 1893, Justice Frankfurter asserted that "the object of the constitutional immunity from self-incrimination is fully accomplished by the statutory immunity." Since this displaces the danger of criminal prosecution, the reason for the privilege, it displaces the privilege itself. "Once the reason for the privilege ceases, the privilege ceases."

Nor is the principle of *Brown* v. *Walker* altered by new disabilities, not then existent, such as expulsion from a union, loss of employment, or adverse public sentiment. Immunity need only remove the sanction that causes the fear of criminal punishment.

More significantly, the Court further held that the provision of the act rendering the petitioner immune from prosecution "in any Court" frees him from the danger of state prosecution, and that Congress has the power to grant such immunity under its power to provide for the national security as aided by the necessary and proper clause. Congress is clearly under no constitutional obligation to afford witnesses such immunity from state prosecution in order to exercise over them its power of compulsory process, but it may do so if it wishes.

In the spring of 1957, the Court, in a highly significant and controversial case, reaffirmed some long-established but more recently ignored limitations on the investigative process, and apparently took the first step toward another and more far-reaching limitation, based on the First and Fourteenth Amendments. In the case of *Watkins* v. *United States*,[61] a labor union officer appeared before the House Committee on Un-American Activities

[60] 161 U.S. 591 (1896).
[61] 354 U.S. 178 (1957).

and testified at length and with complete candor about his earlier associations and activities with respect to the Communist party. He refused, however, to answer questions about similar associations and activities of others with whom he had associated but who had "long since removed themselves from the Communist movement." Watkins rested his refusal to answer questions on the ground that they were not relevant to the work of the committee and that the committee was without authority to undertake public exposure of persons for their past activities.

The Court sustained Watkins in his refusal to answer the questions put to him by the committee on the ground of lack of pertinency to the subject under inquiry. Both the resolution of the House establishing the committee and the statements of the sub-committee chairman on the day of questioning were too vague and uncertain to give Watkins sufficient indication of the matter under inquiry. The resolution setting up the committee in 1938 authorized it, among other things, to examine into "the extent, character, and objects of un-American propaganda activities in the United States," and propaganda that attacks "the principle of the form of government as guaranteed by our Constitution." How is the witness to know what the vague term "un-American" embraces? How is he to know what is "the single principle of the form of government as guaranteed by our Constitution"?

Since the contempt statute under which witnesses may be cited to the courts provides that a witness may be punished "if he willfully makes default" by failing to respond to the subpoena or if he "refuses to answer any questions pertinent to the question under inquiry," [62] and since he must decide at the time the questions are propounded whether or not to answer, "fundamental fairness demands that no witness be compelled to make such a determination, with so little guidance as is available in this case." It is the duty of the interrogator, when the witness protests on the ground of pertinency, to state clearly for the record the subject under inquiry at the time and how the propounded questions are pertinent.

The statement of the subcommittee chairman in this case failed to convey to the petitioner sufficient information on the

[62] U.S.C. Sec. 192.

pertinency of the questions to enable him to determine whether he was within his rights in refusing to answer. The fundamental defect in such vague grants of authority to investigating agents is that it insulates the House authorizing the investigation from the witnesses subjected to the sanction of compulsory process. Thus responsibility for the use of investigative power is divorced from the actual exercise of such power. The Court argued that this situation places constitutionally protected freedoms in a danger that cannot be justified under the Bill of Rights.

Although, precisely speaking, the Court confined its holding to the narrow point of lack of pertinency and consequent denial of due process, the Chief Justice went far beyond this narrow holding and, in broad and unequivocal declarations, announced principles defining limitations on the power to investigate, including those springing from the First Amendment. He reiterated the long-established principle that the power of Congress to conduct investigations is implicit in the legislative process and is so broad as to encompass "inquiries concerning the administration of existing laws as well as proposed or possible needed statutes," surveys of defects in our social or political system with a view to finding remedies therefor, and "probes into the departments of the Federal Government to expose corruption, inefficiency, or waste."

Still, Congress is not a law enforcement or trial agency. Every inquiry must be related to its legitimate function. Consequently, there is no general authority to expose the private affairs of individuals without clear justification in terms of the functions of Congress. Moreover, the Bill of Rights limits the power of investigation, as it limits the exercise of all other powers of government. For example, witnesses may not be compelled to give evidence against themselves, nor may they be subjected to unreasonable search or seizure. Most significantly, an investigation is subject to the requirements of the First Amendment. The Court emphasized that the power to investigate in the constitutionally protected areas of "speech, press, religion, or political belief and association" may not be delegated to committees by resolutions so broad that they provide no standards for the interrogators and no measure of the need for the data, which can be balanced against the competing demands of individual freedom. Thus, congressional committees are forbidden to ask questions which violate the rights of witnesses under the First Amendment.

Although the last point may be regarded as dictum with respect to the precise holding in the Watkins case, the Court seems to have made it the basis of decision in *Sweezy* v. *New Hampshire*,[63] decided on the same day. As has been pointed out previously in connection with state loyalty programs, all six members of the majority in this case agreed that academic and political freedoms are constitutionally protected against state investigatory power through the medium of the Fourteenth Amendment. In the words of the Court, "There is no doubt that legislative investigations, whether on a federal or state level, are capable of encroaching upon the constitutional liberties of individuals."

Indeed, it was regarded by the Court as particularly important that the power of compulsory process be carefully confined when an investigation tends to encroach upon the freedoms of teaching and of political expression and association. The interest of the state in compelling Sweezy to testify concerning the content of his lecture was insufficient when weighed against "the grave harm resulting from governmental intrusion into the intellectual life of a university." On this point, the Court made the following general observation:

The essentiality of freedom in the community of American universities is almost self-evident . . . . To impose any strait jacket upon the intellectual leaders in our colleges and universities would imperil the future of our nation. . . . Scholarship cannot flourish in an atmosphere of suspicion and distrust. Teachers and students must always remain free to inquire, to study, and to evaluate, to gain new maturity and understanding; otherwise our civilization will stagnate and die.

On Sweezy's right to refuse to answer questions concerning his association with the Progressive party, the Court observed:

Equally manifest as a fundamental principle of a democratic society is political freedom of the individual. Our form of government is built on the premise that every citizen shall have the right to engage in political expression and association. This right was enshrined in the First Amendment of the Bill of Rights . . . . [and, of course, is made operative on the states through the Fourteenth Amendment].

[63] 354 U.S. 234 (1957).

Notwithstanding the divisions of the Court in the Sweezy case and the narrow grounds of decision in the Watkins case, the Court seems, in the combination of these two cases, to have expressly recognized the proposition that the First Amendment limits the power of congressional investigative committees, and that this limitation is made operative upon the states through the due process clause of the Fourteenth Amendment.

A Tactical Retreat?

Although in most of the preceding subversion cases the Court had made no effort to limit the authority of Congress to cope with problems of subversion, the specific results flowing from them had greatly antagonized many members of Congress and certain highly vocal elements of their constituents. This in turn led, in 1957–58, to a determined and prolonged effort in the Congress to curb and discipline the Court.[64] This threatened retaliation from Congress followed Watkins, Sweezy, and other cases to be considered later, and apparently caused something of a tactical retreat by the Court. At any rate, by 1959 the Court was taking a more restrained position with respect to the power of investigation of alleged subversive activities, apparently without retreating from the doctrinal stand taken in Watkins and Sweezy, but not without substantially weakening the effective application of the doctrine. In *Barenblatt* v. *United States* [65] and *Uphaus* v. *Wyman* [66] the Court majority upheld broad federal and state legislative investigations; and in two cases [67] decided in 1961, it sustained even more drastic investigatory authority of the House Committee on Un-American activities.

Barenblatt was convicted for contempt of Congress arising from his refusal to answer certain questions put to him by a subcommittee of the HUAC, during the course of an investigation

[64] For an able and thorough study of this congressional-judicial conflict, see Walter F. Murphy, *Congress and the Court* (University of Chicago Press, Chicago, 1962).

[65] 360 U.S. 109 (1959).

[66] 360 U.S. 72 (1959).

[67] *Wilkinson* v. *United States*, 365 U.S. 399 (1961), and *Braden* v. *United States*, 365 U.S. 431 (1961).

of alleged Communist infiltration into the field of education. The inquiry related solely to the period 1947 to 1950, when Barenblatt had been a graduate student and teaching fellow at the University of Michigan. The Court considered only those aspects of the charge against Barenblatt relating to his refusal to answer whether he was then or had ever been a member of the Communist party.

In reply to questions concerning his Communist membership and associations, Barenblatt expressly disclaimed any reliance on the Fifth Amendment, and he based his refusal to answer solely on the First Amendment. He contended that the committee's statutory grant of authority was too broad and vague, that the pertinency of the questions to the subject under inquiry had not been made clear to him, and that the asking of the questions violated his First Amendment rights.

Justice Harlan, for the five to four majority, reiterated the broad declarations of the Watkins opinion that the power of congressional inquiry is not unlimited. It may not invade the province of the executive or the judiciary nor violate the Bill of Rights. Especially may it not encroach upon academic freedom—"teaching freedom" and "learning freedom"—which is regarded as so essential to the well-being of the nation that the Court "will always be on the alert against intrusion by Congress into this constitutionally protected domain." However, this does not mean that a congressional committee is forbidden to interrogate a witness merely because he is a teacher.

As the Court viewed Barenblatt's claim, his reliance upon the Watkins case was misplaced. Justice Harlan pointed out that the Watkins decision had not held that the statutory authority of the committee alone was the basis of the invalid vagueness. The vagueness derived from this plus the remarks of the chairman or members of the committee, or perhaps even the nature of the proceedings. And furthermore, there is no evidence that Congress ever intended to exclude the field of education from the committee's authority. The Court held that the pertinency of the questions had been made incontestably clear, since it was carefully announced at the outset of the investigation that the subject of the inquiry was Communist infiltration into the field of education.

On the important First Amendment constitutional issue, the

Court applied the "balancing theory" which, indeed, Chief Justice Warren had recognized in the Watkins case. Justice Harlan declared that the protections of the First Amendment do not afford a witness the right to refuse information in all circumstances. Where this amendment is advanced to bar governmental interrogation, the resolution of the issue always "involves a balancing by the courts of the competing private and public interests" in the particular circumstances shown. The Court held that in the context of the circumstances of this case the balance lay on the side of the public interest in the investigation.

Furthermore, the investigation must be deemed to have been in furtherance of a valid legislative purpose, because there is no question that Congress has wide power to legislate in the field of Communist activity and has done so. Such a power rests in the last analysis upon the right of self-preservation, "the ultimate value of any society," and the justification for it in the circumstances of this case "rests on the long and widely accepted view that the tenets of the Communist Party include the ultimate overthrow of the Government of the United States by force and violence . . ."

The Court also rejected Barenblatt's argument that this investigation was directed not at the revolutionary aspect of Communism but at the theoretical and philosophical classroom discussion of it. The Court somewhat vaguely replied that this was too restricted a view of the nature of the investigatory process. "An investigation of advocacy of or preparation for overthrow certainly embraces the right to identify a witness as a member of the Communist Party . . . and to inquire into the various manifestations of the Party's tenets. The strict requirements of a prosecution under the Smith Act . . . are not the measure of the permissible scope of a congressional investigation into the overthrow, for of necessity the investigatory process must proceed step by step."

The Court finally rejected the argument that this investigation was not in furtherance of a valid legislative purpose because the real purpose of the committee was exposure. On this point Justice Harlan replied: "So long as Congress acts in pursuance of its constitutional power, the judiciary lacks authority to intervene on the basis of the motives which spurred the exercise of that power."

Whether or not one regards the Barenblatt case as a substantial retreat from Watkins depends in large measure on whether one looks to the precise holding in the latter case or to the broad libertarian dicta of the opinion. There is, of course, little doubt that Barenblatt loosened the shackles which the Watkins case was thought to have placed upon the investigatory power of Congress. Yet on the narrow, but controlling, point of pertinency the two cases can be distinguished. Although Watkins declined to testify about his earlier associates who, he insisted, were no longer connected with the Communist movement, he showed no lack of candor in testifying about his own current relationships and activities. Barenblatt, however, flatly refused to answer the question whether he was at the time of the interrogation a member of the Communist party.

On the broader First Amendment constitutional issue, however, the Court seemed to balance an assumption against a reality—the assumption that the public interest involved was nothing short of the safety of the nation against the reality of encroachment upon the individual freedom of speech and association.

The Wilkinson and Braden cases [68] decided in 1961 presented the same issues involved in Barenblatt, but introduced a new factor into the problem of legislative investigations. Here it was contended, in addition, that the legislative purpose of the investigation had been corrupted by a punitive motive on the part of the investigating committee. The House Committee on Un-American Activities had been adversely criticized by the petitioners for undertaking an investigation of the infiltration of Communism into southern industry. Later when the subcommittee met in Atlanta they were called before it and asked about their party membership. They refused to answer partly on the ground that they were being questioned, not for the sake of gaining public information, but for the purpose of punishing them for their criticism of the committee.

Mr. Justice Harlan, in upholding the convictions for the

[68] *Ibid.*

Court, argued that even if the charge of punitive motive were true, the inquiry would still be valid. For as the Watkins opinion asserted, "motives alone would not vitiate an investigation . . . by a House of Congress if that assembly's legislative purpose is being served." And in these cases the subcommittee had "probable cause" to believe that the witnesses had information that would serve that purpose. The dissenting justices asserted that the committee in each of these cases was simply seeking to harass its critics and to expose them for the sake of exposure, and not for the purpose of eliciting information for legislative purposes.

Soon the Court swung in the other direction, and in two cases [69] reinforced and extended the procedural aspect of the Watkins holding. It will be recalled that the Watkins case held that an investigating committee, when challenged by a witness, must state clearly the subject of the investigation. In the Russell case the Court held that the failure of a grand jury indictment to identify the subject matter of an inquiry is fatal to a citation for contempt.

In the Deutch case [70] the pertinency of the questions which Deutch had refused to answer was at issue. The questions had to do with the Communist activities of other persons with whom he had been associated in Cornell University. In a five to four opinion Mr. Justice Stewart held for the Court that under the due process clause of the Fifth Amendment, "the pertinency of the interrogation to the topic under the Congressional Committee's inquiry must be brought home to the witness at the time the questions are put to him." The government here had failed to prove the questions pertinent.

As already indicated, the Court had in the early cold war years declined to consider the First Amendment as a safeguard of the right of witnesses before legislative committees. Even in the later Rumely case, only by implication did it acknowledge such an application of the amendment. Although the limits imposed upon investigative process by the First Amendment are not clearly defined in the Watkins and Sweezy cases, they are expressly recognized and applied for the first time.

[69] *Russell* v. *United States*, 369 U.S. 749 (1964).
[70] *Deutch* v. *United States*, 367 U.S. 456.

In attempting to appraise the consequences of these cases, however, it must not be assumed that they place any serious handicaps in the way of proper legislative investigation. There is no reason to believe that a Congress, bent upon the investigation of any phase of Communist activity which affects the safety of the nation, will find the Watkins case any more of an obstacle than important cases of the past have been, unless the probable necessity for a more scrupulous regard for First Amendment freedoms is regarded as a handicap. Nor is New Hampshire in danger of being overrun by subversives because of Sweezy.

The Supreme Court did not maintain in the Watkins case that Congress could not compel witnesses to appear before its committees and to testify on matters relevant to the constitutional functions of that body. It did hold that the purpose of an inquiry must be clearly stated in the authorizing resolutions, that the questions asked of witnesses must be pertinent, and that Congress must not "unjustifiably encroach upon an individual's right of privacy nor abridge his liberty of speech, press, religion or assembly." The purpose of the inquiry in this case was to expose Watkins to "the violence of public reaction" because of his past beliefs without serving any public purpose. Congress may not grant to any committee the power to expose for the sake of exposure.

It seems probable then that, in the future, resolutions authorizing investigations will have to be drawn with more particularity or that committee chairmen will have to state for the record the subject under inquiry at the time of the questioning and the manner in which the questions are pertinent thereto.

8

THE COLD WAR
AND INTERNAL SECURITY: II

FEDERAL LEGISLATIVE CONTROL
OF SUBVERSION

The preceding chapter was concerned with the Court's response to such cold war measures as the loyalty-security programs of the federal and state governments, the application of subversive control programs to aliens and naturalized citizens, and federal and state legislative investigatory powers. There remains to be considered in this chapter the Court's response to federal antisubversive legislation.

The Taft-Hartley Act: Political Strikes

Section 9(*h*) of the Taft-Hartley Act provides that no labor union shall have access to the privilege of the National Labor Relations Act or to the facilities of the National Labor Relations Board unless each of its officers files an affidavit swearing: (1) "that he is not a member of the Communist Party or affiliated with such party," and (2) "that he does not believe in, and is not a member of or supports any organization that believes in or teaches the overthrow of the United States government by force or by any illegal or unconstitutional methods."

These regulations as they affect free speech were upheld by the Court in *American Communications Association* v. *Douds*.[1] Chief Justice Vinson, at the outset of his opinion, said that the purpose of Congress in setting up the oath requirement was to eliminate the political strike as an obstruction to interstate commerce. On this ground the provisions of the statute were sustained against the contention that they violated freedom of speech and political opinion.

In his opinion the Chief Justice proceeded to reduce the clear and present danger doctrine to a device for the judicial balancing of interests between First Amendment freedoms, on the one hand, and the public order, on the other. Of course, the evil threatened by free speech must be serious and substantial, but this does not mean an absolutist test in terms of danger to the nation. Indeed, Vinson continued, "When the effect of a statute or ordinance upon the exercise of First Amendment freedoms is relatively small and the public interest to be protected is substantial, it is obvious that a rigid test requiring a showing of imminent danger to the security of the Nation is an absurdity."

In effecting this balancing process in the instant case, the preferred status formula of earlier cases necessarily gave way to deference to legislative judgment. The problem here was simply that of balancing what was considered to be the relatively small effects of the statute upon those freedoms, against the judgment of Congress that political strikes were evils of conduct causing substantial harm to interstate commerce. This, argued the Court, was a matter with which Congress, not the courts, was primarily concerned, and there was ample justification for the decision of Congress in this case.

The provision of the statute concerning belief in the overthrow of the government by force was construed to relate not to the ultimate overthrow of the government as a vision of the future, but to belief in the "objective overthrow" of the government as it now exists under the Constitution, by force or other illegal means. Interpreted thus, the belief provision of the oath was held

[1] 339 U.S. 382 (1950).

to present a problem no different from that involved in the provision relating to membership in the Communist party. It was vigorously denied that thought control was involved or that beliefs were in any way to be punished, since the only result of the statute was the possible loss of one's position as a labor leader. This, interestingly enough, was not regarded as punishment.

In the principal opinion, Chief Justice Vinson spoke only for Justices Reed and Burton. Justices Douglas, Minton, and Clark did not participate in the decision. Justices Frankfurter and Jackson concurred with the majority on the first part of the oath law, relating to membership in the Communist party, but dissented from the portion of the opinion that upheld provisions concerning belief in the overthrow of the government by force. Justice Black dissented from the entire opinion on the ground that Section 9 (h) was completely invalid. Thus, the six participating justices divided five to one in sustaining the first part of the section and three to three in sustaining the second part. In his dissent, Justice Frankfurter declared that Congress had here "cast its net too indiscriminately" and had opened "the door too wide to mere speculation of uncertainty." Every rational indulgence should be made in favor of the constitutionality of a congressional enactment, but it is not within the authority of Congress to probe into opinions which indicate no certain relationship to the Communist party and the dangers which the statute as a whole sought to avert. Justice Jackson vigorously denounced the thought control provision, because Congress in his view has no power

. . . to proscribe any opinion or belief which has not manifested itself in any overt act. . . . Only in the darkest periods of human history has any Western government concerned itself with mere belief . . . when it has not matured into overt action; and if that practice survives anywhere, it is in the Communist countries whose philosophies we loathe.

Rejecting the assumption that the power to forbid acts includes the power to forbid their contemplation, he asked rhetorically, "Can we say that men of our time must not even think about the propositions on which our own Revolution was justified? Or, may they think, provided they reach only one conclusion—and that the opposite of Mr. Jefferson's?" Thus Jackson asserted the unrestricted constitutional right of each member of our society to think as he will. "Thought control is a copyright of totalitarianism, and we have no claim to it."

The Smith Act: Dennis and Illegal Advocacy

The new interpretation of the clear and present danger rule in the Douds case and the Court's disposition of the preferred status principle easily paved the way for the decision a year later in the famous Dennis case.[2] It was this case which offered the Supreme Court its first opportunity to pass upon the validity of the Smith Act, Sections 2 and 3 of which forbid the willful advising, teaching, or advocacy of the overthrow of any government in the United States by force or violence, and conspiring to do so. In 1948, eleven top leaders of the Communist party of the United States were indicted under the act for willfully and knowingly conspiring to teach and advocate the overthrow of the government by force and violence, and for conspiring to organize the Communist party for such purpose. The trial, which ran for more than eight months before District Judge Medina in New York, resulted in conviction. In his charge to the jury, Judge Medina stated that:

. . . it is not the abstract doctrine of overwhelming or destroying organized government by lawful means which is denounced by this law, but the teaching and advocacy of action for the accomplishment of that purpose, by language reasonably and ordinarily calculated to incite persons to such action . . . as speedily as circumstances would permit.

He stated further that the duty of the jury was confined to determining whether the evidence showed a violation of the statute, as he had interpreted it, and that the question of whether there was a clear and present danger of an evil, which Congress might prevent without violating the First Amendment, was a matter of law with which the jury had no concern. Both the charge to the jury and the conviction were upheld by the court of appeals in an opinion by Judge Learned Hand.

[2] *Dennis* v. *United States*, 341 U.S. 494 (1951).

In granting *certiorari*, the Supreme Court limited the scope of its review to the constitutional questions of free speech under the First Amendment and due process under the Fifth Amendment. It did not review the sufficiency of evidence for supporting the jury's verdict or certain allegations relating to the conduct of the trial.

The judgment of the Court sustaining the convictions, against free speech and free assembly objections, was supported by three different opinions representing three interpretations of the clear and present danger test, not to mention a fourth by dissenters Black and Douglas.

Chief Justice Vinson, announcing the judgment of the Court and speaking also for Justices Reed, Burton, and Minton, stressed the substantial character of the government's interest in preventing its own destruction by force. This, he said, "is certainly a substantial enough interest for the Government to limit speech." Indeed, this is the ultimate value of any society, for if it is unable to protect itself from armed internal attack, it is certain that no subordinate value can be protected. The Chief Justice spoke here as though the defendants had been indicted for an overt act of attempting to overthrow the government by force, which was not the charge. They had been accused of conspiring to teach and advocate and to form a party to teach and advocate overthrow of the government by force and violence.

Considering the meaning of the phrase "clear and present danger" in such circumstances, the Chief Justice declared that it "obviously cannot mean that before the Government may act it must wait until the *putsch* is about to be executed, the plans have been laid and the signal is awaited." Vinson paid warm tribute to the Holmes-Brandeis version of clear and present danger and purported to apply it, but in reality he had adopted in its place a very different test, suggested by Judge Learned Hand in his court of appeals opinion. "In each case," said Judge Hand, "Courts must ask whether the gravity of the 'evil,' discounted by its improbability, justifies such invasion of free speech as is necessary to avoid the danger." Accepting this test, the Chief Justice argued that Holmes and Brandeis were not confronted with a situation comparable to that of this case, namely, a highly organized conspiracy of rigidly disciplined members "dedicated to the overthrow of the government" in the context of recurring world crises. Under the Hand formula, the danger need not be imminent. It was not important, then, that no attempt had been made here to overthrow the government. It was enough that the defendants were ready and willing to make the attempt "as soon as circumstances will permit." If, then, the evil legislated against is serious enough, advocacy may be punished, even though there is no clear and present danger of success. Put another way, the gravity of the evil decreases the necessity for its clarity and imminence. In this opinion, then, Chief Justice Vinson substituted the Hand test of "grave" and "probable" for the Holmes-Brandeis test of "clear and present danger." He thus divested the traditional test of the vital element of "imminence" and seriously blurred the element of "clarity." Vinson's attempt to square the Hand formula with the Holmes-Brandeis version of clear and present danger is something less than impressive. It is essentially the bad tendency test in a different garb.

Yet, as if to save something of the clear and present danger test, Vinson brings up the question of conspiracy, which he had not hitherto stressed. Rejecting the argument that a conspiracy to advocate, as distinguished from advocacy itself, cannot be constitutionally restrained since it comprises only preparation, the Chief Justice asserts: "It is the existence of the conspiracy which creates the danger," and, after all, clear and present danger "is a judicial rule to be applied as a matter of law by the courts."

In his concurring opinion, Justice Frankfurter reiterated his well-known antagonism to the clear and present danger doctrine which, through recent decisions, he thought, had become nothing more than "a sonorous formula which is in fact only a euphemistic disguise for an unresolved conflict," an inflexible dogma supporting "uncritical libertarian generalities."

Justice Jackson, who had earlier been a vigorous and eloquent defender of the clear and present danger doctrine, set forth an entirely new notion of the formula in his concurring opinion. Cases like this one, he said, require the Court "to reappraise, in the light of our own times and conditions, constitutional doctrines devised under other circumstances to stake a balance between authority and liberty." The clear and present danger test, as originally enunciated by Mr. Justice Holmes and later refined by him and Mr. Justice Brandeis, was used as a rule of evidence in particular cases involving relatively simple issues, such as the "criminality of a hot headed speech on a street corner, or circulation of a few incendiary pamphlets, or parading by some zealots behind a red flag. . . ." This was before the era of World War II had revealed "the subtlety and efficacy of modernized revolutionary techniques used by totalitarian parties." In these earlier and simpler situations it was not beyond the capacity of courts to comprehend and weigh the evidence "for decision whether there is a clear and present danger of substantive evil or a harmless letting off of steam." In such cases the danger, if there ever was a danger, has already matured by the time of the trial and does not involve prophecy. Thus Jackson would save the clear and present danger test for the relatively trivial situations involving speech and publication by individuals. But he bluntly rejected the applicability of the test to a nationwide, organized conspiracy, such as that of the Communist party.

In this connection he emphasized, as did none of his colleagues, that this was a conspiracy case. He accurately pointed out that what the Court was really reviewing here "is a conviction of conspiracy, after a trial for conspiracy on an indictment charging conspiracy, brought under a statute outlawing conspiracy." He noted further that the Constitution does not make conspiracy a civil right, and the Court ought not to make it one now. The essence of the concept of conspiracy is that it may be an evil in itself, independent of any evil it hopes to accomplish. Conspiracy is the plotting of an unlawful act, and the execution of the act is not a part of the conspiracy unless required by statute. Thus, if Congress makes conspiracy a crime without the requirement of an overt act to establish it, as it did in the Smith Act, it is ridiculous, Jackson argued, to hold that it can punish the former only if there is a clear and present danger of the latter. Furthermore, it makes no difference that speech was used in the course of this conspiracy, for "communication is the essence of every conspiracy."

Jackson's theory seems to hold serious hazards for persons speaking or writing in concert with others, or for speech in combination with assembly, and much speaking and writing fall within these classes. Justice Jackson recognized this danger in the frank admission that he considered criminal conspiracy "a dragnet device capable of perversion into an instrument of injustice in the hands of a partisan or complacent judiciary," but it has an established place in our law and ought to be available for application against plots to undermine the whole government.

It is significant that Frankfurter and Jackson, whose votes were necessary to the majority position in this case, both expressed doubt as to the wisdom and effectiveness of the Smith Act as a method of combating Communism. Although Jackson thought the Court could not hold the act unconstitutional, he took the pains to add: "I have little faith in the long-range effectiveness of this conviction to stop the rise of the Communist movement. Communism will not go to jail with those Communists."

Justice Frankfurter likewise warned that his holding of constitutionality in no way implied that he favored "the implications that lie beneath the legal issues." He rather thought that legislation of this kind tends to become "a formidable enemy of the free spirit."

There seemed to be little doubt, however, that the Court, in affirming these convictions, had narrowed the scope of protection of freedom of speech and assembly under the First Amendment. It so interpreted the clear and present danger test as to leave Congress largely free from the restrictions of the First Amendment in meeting the Communist problem. If the effect of this were confined to Communist party cases, there would be nothing to deplore but it would be naïve to anticipate such a happy result. The contrary was forcefully put by Mr. Justice Frankfurter in his concurring opinion, just considered. Said he:

Suppressing advocates of overthrow inevitably will also silence critics who do not advocate overthrow but fear that their criticism may be so construed. No matter how clear we may be that the defendants now before us are preparing to overthrow our Government at the propitious moment, it is self delusion to think that we can punish them for their advocacy without adding to the risks run by loyal citizens who honestly believe in some of the reforms these defendants advance. It is a sobering fact that in sustaining the conviction before us we can hardly escape restrictions on the interchange of ideas.

Yates Case Limits Effect of Dennis

The Department of Justice, not without reason, seems to have interpreted the Dennis decision as holding that the Communist party is a criminal conspiracy, dedicated to the overthrow of the government of the United States by force and violence, and that its leaders and members may therefore be constitutionally punished. Since the Dennis decision, nearly one hundred convictions and many more indictments had been obtained for violation of the Smith Act.[3]

But in the Yates case [4] of June, 1957, the Supreme Court demonstrated that the government had taken too expansive a view of its powers under the Smith Act to prosecute Communists. The fourteen Communist leaders in the case were convicted after a jury trial in the District Court for the Southern District of California, on a single-count indictment charging them with conspiracy (1) to advocate and teach the duty and necessity of overthrowing the government by force and violence, and (2) to organize the Communist party for such advocating and teaching, both with the intention of causing the overthrow of the government by force and violence as speedily as circumstances would permit doing so.

In Yates, the Court was faced, among other things, with the question whether the Smith Act forbids advocacy and teaching of forcible overthrow as an abstract principle, divorced from any effort to incite action to that end, provided that such advocacy and teaching are done with evil intent. The Court held that it does not. Since the government had relied upon the Dennis case in presenting its case against the petitioners in Yates, the Court declared that its reliance on Dennis showed a misinterpretation of that case. Indeed, it would appear that the Court in the later case was interpreting the Dennis opinion as much as it was the Smith Act.

The Court found the district judge's charge to the jury defective, because it did not state clearly that advocacy of violent over-

[3] Robert E. Cushman, *Leading Constitutional Decisions*, 11th ed. (New York, Appleton-Century-Crofts, 1958), p. 459.

[4] *Yates v. United States*, 354 U.S. 298.

throw, to escape the restrictions of the First Amendment, must involve an urging to action presently or in the future. The charge to the jury in the Dennis case had met this test, argued the Court. The important and essential distinction here is that those to whom advocacy is directed must be urged to action now or in the future, and not merely to belief in something.

Dennis was concerned with a conspiracy to advocate presently the forcible overthrow of the government in the future. Action, not advocacy, was to be postponed "until circumstances would permit."

The Court emphasized that Dennis still stands, and that its reasoning, properly viewed against the facts of the case, is not in conflict with the opinion in Yates.

Yet the Yates opinion seems to represent a departure from the belief, expressed by a majority of the justices in Dennis, that the secret nature of the Communist party and its indoctrination activities make any distinction between advocacy of action and advocacy of belief somewhat thin, when the defendants are members of such a tightly disciplined organization as the Communist party. Moreover, the Dennis case seems clearly to indicate that when a conspiracy itself is a clear and present danger, little evidence is required to show that the nature of the advocacy by the conspirators presents a clear and present danger.

On its face, the Smith Act does not indicate the distinction here made by the Court, but it is argued that the history of the act shows it was aimed at the advocacy and teaching of concrete action for the forcible overthrow of the government, and not of principles divorced from action. Moreover, since the word *advocate* in the free speech area has traditionally meant advocacy of action,[5] Congress must have intended such a meaning in the act. "In construing the Act," the Court declared, "we should not assume that Congress chose to disregard a constitutional danger zone so clearly marked" as the free speech guarantees of the First Amendment. Thus the Court construes the Smith Act as forbidding the only kind of advocacy it could constitutionally forbid,

[5] Citing *Fox* v. *Washington*, 236 U.S. 273, *Schenck* v. *United States*, 249 U.S. 47, and *Gitlow* v. *New York*, 268 U.S. 652.

namely, that which amounts to actual incitement to action directed to the forcible overthrow of the government.

Were Congress to amend the Smith Act to forbid, in precise terms, advocacy of forcible overthrow of the government with the intent to bring about such an end, would the Court hold the act unconstitutional? On the basis of its opinion in Yates, and the interpretation there given of the Dennis opinion, it would logically so hold. Still, it would be hazardous to predict that logic would prevail in these circumstances, for the pull of judicial self-restraint has in the past been at its maximum when the Court was dealing with the validity of acts of Congress relating to national security. Under the Yates rule of interpretation, the government will no longer be able to convict and punish members of the Communist party for expressing a mere belief in the violent overthrow of the government. It will have to prove that the defendants actually intended to overthrow the government, or to persuade others to do so by language calculated to incite action to that end either immediately or in the future.

In the light of Yates one might have guessed that the punishment of simple membership in the Communist party would involve an unconstitutional application of the Smith Act, but the guess would have been wrong. In the Scales case,[6] the Court by a five to four vote, upheld the membership section of the Smith Act, but punishable membership was construed by Justice Harlan to include only "active" members, having also guilty knowledge and "a specific intent to bring about violent overthrow of the government as speedily as circumstances would permit." This ingenious construction was necessary to escape the application of the principle of guilt by association and to avoid conflict with a section of the McCarran (Internal Security) Act of 1950, which provides that "neither the holding of office nor membership in any Communist organization . . . shall constitute *per se* a violation of . . . this section or of any other criminal statute."

On the same day that Scales was decided, the Court, applying the Yates doctrine, set aside a conviction under the Smith Act for membership in the Communist party, because the evidence against the petitioner showed that the Communist organization

[6] *Scales* v. *United States*, 367 U.S. 203 (1961).

to which he belonged had done nothing more than engage in the "abstract teaching of Communist theory." [7]

Internal Security Act of 1950: Registration of Communists

A more difficult problem confronted the Court in determining the validity of the registration requirement of the Internal Security Act of 1950. The registration section of the act requires "Communist action" organizations to register with the Attorney General, and to file a substantial body of information including the names of officers and members. Once registered, or properly ordered to do so, the organization and its members become subject to certain handicaps and obligations.

In *Communist Party* v. *Subversive Activities Control Board*,[8] in 1961, the Communist party faced an order to register, and the Supreme Court upheld the validity of the order. The more serious challenges against the order were based on the First Amendment and the immunity clause of the Fifth Amendment. Applying the balancing theory the Court held that the registration requirement of the act neither on its face nor as applied in this case violates the First Amendment. This amendment, said the Court, does not prohibit "Congress from requiring the registration and filing of information, including membership lists, by organizations substantially dominated or controlled by the foreign powers controlling the world Communist movement and which operate primarily to advance the objectives of that movement: the overthrow of existing government by any means necessary and the establishment in its place of a Communist totalitarian dictatorship." The Court saw the public interest in thwarting this threat as greatly outweighing the private interest of the party members in freedom of speech and association. It was these considerations which distinguished this case from *NAACP* v. *Alabama* [9] in which the privacy of the membership list was protected by the Court.

On the more touchy issue of Fifth Amendment immunity

[7] *Noto* v. *United States,* 367 U.S. 290 (1961).
[8] 367 U.S. 1 (1961).
[9] 357 U.S. 449 (1958).

from self-incrimination the Court was able to postpone the determination on the ground that the issue was prematurely raised. The privilege could not be invoked by the Communist party on behalf of its officers, and they had not invoked it as individuals.

But the Communist party persisted in its refusal to register, and the Department of Justice secured an indictment and won a conviction and fine against the party. The Court of Appeals of the District of Columbia reversed the conviction, holding that Communist party officers could not be required to register under the McCarran Act because anyone who filed a registration statement would be opening the way for his own prosecution under the Smith Act, which makes it a crime to belong to organizations which advocate violent overthrow of the government.[10] The government had failed to prove the existence of a volunteer who would be willing to risk self-incrimination by filing the required registration statement on behalf of the party. The Supreme Court declined to review this case.

Again, in April, 1965, the Court avoided the constitutional issues presented by an order for registration because the SACB's findings that the petitioner was a "Communist front" were based primarily upon evidence taken at a hearing in 1955. These findings rested substantially on evidence of a Communist party member who was executive secretary of the organization, and there was no evidence concerning the organization's activities after his death in 1959. Since an order of the SACB operates prospectively, the Court held that reasonably current aid to and control by the Communist party must be established to justify an order to register as a Communist front. For these reasons "the decision of serious constitutional questions raised by the order was neither necessary nor appropriate." [11]

Finally, the Supreme Court itself met the issue head on in *Albertson* v. *United States* (86 S. Ct. 194, 1966) and held the registration requirement to be violative of the immunity clause of the Fifth Amendment, because such admission of membership

[10] *Communist Party* v. *United States*, 33 F. 2d. 807 (1964); cert. denied, 377 U.S. 968 (1964).
[11] *American Committee for Protection of Foreign Born* v. *Subversive Activities Control Board*, 380 U.S. 505 (1965).

in the Communist Party would render the registrant liable to criminal prosecution under the membership clause of the Smith Act.

Federal Sedition Statutes Supersede State Sedition Laws

In 1956, the Court adopted the device of statutory construction to limit the applicability of state sedition laws. In *Pennsylvania* v. *Nelson*,[12] Chief Justice Warren, speaking for the Court, found Pennsylvania's antisubversive legislation, to the extent that it punished subversion against the United States, to be unconstitutional for the following reasons: (1) the scheme of federal regulation is so pervasive as to make reasonable the inference that Congress left no room for the states to supplement it; (2) the federal statutes touch a field in which the national interest is so dominant that the federal system must be assumed to preclude enforcement of state laws on the same subject; and (3) "Enforcement of state sedition acts presents a serious danger of conflict with the administration of the federal program." The Chief Justice was careful to point out that this decision did not affect the right of the state to enforce its sedition laws when the federal government has not occupied the field, that it did not limit the right of the state to protect itself against violence and sabotage at any time, and that it did not preclude the state from prosecution where the same act is both a state and a federal offense. Here, however, there was no evidence, in a long record, of sedition against the government of Pennsylvania.

Although the Court had in this case stated that the pre-emption issue turned upon the Smith Act alone, it supported its decision by relying not on the Smith Act alone, but also on the Internal Security Act of 1950 and the Communist Control Act of 1954, which together constituted a comprehensive system of Communist control. In determining the pre-emptive effect to be given this scheme of legislation, the Court relied on criteria developed in commerce clause cases.[13] Under the doctrine of na-

[12] 350 U.S. 497 (1956).
[13] See, for example, *Rice* v. *Sante Fe Elevator Corp.*, 331 U.S. 218, 219–230 (1947).

tional supremacy, it would seem clear that Congress has the power to bar state prosecution in the interest of national security. In the Ullmann case, previously discussed, the Court had found that a federal immunity statute precluded state criminal prosecution on this ground.

SUMMARY ANALYSIS OF CHAPTERS 7 AND 8

The generally strong libertarian spirit which characterized the opinions of the Court during the decade after 1937 rapidly subsided with the onset of the cold war, except with respect to Negro rights and certain procedural guarantees. This change in judicial attitude then coincided with what was apparently a marked change in public opinion with respect to the seriousness and scope of the Communist threat.

The reluctance of the Vinson Court to interpose judicial power against legislative investigation or criminal prosecutions of Communists was not shared by the Warren Court in 1956–1957, but this libertarian boldness was not consistently maintained on the part of the latter. Indeed, the preceding pages have recounted a state of flux in the Warren Court from the early 1950's to 1965. These shifts in the position of the Court have roughly coincided with public and congressional reactions to the decisions of the Court on cold war issues, and have been aided by occasional changes in the personnel of the Court.

One or two examples will suffice at this point. The Bar Admissions Cases, in which the Court reversed the action of two states in barring from the practice of law a former Communist who refused to reveal his political beliefs to bar examiners, met with bitter criticism from bar associations and lawyers in general. Four years later (1961) in the second Konigsberg case and *In re* Anastoplo the Court sustained rejections of applicants to the bar because of their refusal to answer questions concerning their character and other qualifications to practice law.

In the field of legislative investigation the significant libertarian advances made by the Court in Watkins and Sweezy were limited by Barenblatt, Uphaus, Wilkinson, and Braden. These and other earlier subversive cases, along with the racial segregation cases, set off a violent protest in Congress which found expression in persistent and determined efforts to reverse the Court's rulings and to limit its appellate powers. Although this ill-fated threat failed in the closing days of the 1958 session of the Congress, it was apparently the principal cause of the shift of the Court from its earlier position.

Such clashes between the Court and the Congress, or between the Court and the Executive, are not new. Walter F. Murphy, in his excellent study, *Congress and the Court*, points out that this latest Congress-Court clash followed a historic pattern. Roughly, according to Murphy, first, there were decisions on important aspects of public policy; next, severe criticisms of the Court were coupled with threats of retaliatory or remedial legislation; and the final "step has usually been a judicial retreat." [14] With some differences and with some allowance for oversimplification, this was also the pattern of the dramatic battle between the New Deal and the Hughes Court in 1937.

In the 1961 term of the Court, the pendulum began to swing back. By that time the heat of congressional antagonism toward the Court had simmered down; and with the appointment in 1962 of Byron M. White and Arthur J. Goldberg to take the vacated seats of Justices Whittaker and Frankfurter respectively, there seemed to be a clear majority for the more liberal position on the Court. (The more recent appointment of Justice Fortas to succeed Justice Goldberg does not seem to have altered this situation.)

However, the principal technique of the Warren Court is still to achieve its libertarian results through nonconstitutional processes without challenging the power of the political branches of the government, although it has done this in some cases. For example, with respect to legislative investigation, the Court in 1962 invalidated contempt convictions of nine men who had refused to answer congressional committee questions concerning Communist infiltration of the newspaper business. The reason as

[14] Murphy, *op. cit.*, p. 247.

set forth in the Russell case was that in the prosecution for contempt, the grand jury indictment had not clearly identified the subject of the inquiry. Thus, as pointed out above, the procedural features of the Watkins case were reinforced and expounded.

SUMMARY OF COLD WAR HOLDINGS

It is not easy to take stock of the current state of cold war holdings of the Court, but perhaps the effort should be made. The situation, then, seems to be approximately as follows.

Loyalty-Security Cases

On the national level, the Court has condemned the listing of organizations by the Attorney General as subversive without a hearing; it has limited the authority of the Loyalty Review Board to review cases on its own motion; and has denied the applicability of summary suspension and dismissal procedures to employees in nonsensitive positions. More significantly it has held with respect to the Industrial Security Program that one may not be deprived of the right to pursue one's private vocation without the opportunity to confront and cross-examine adverse witnesses in the absence of explicit authorization by Congress or the President. One thus denied is entitled to monetary restitution for loss of employment. At the state level the Court has condemned state loyalty statutes, embodying the doctrine of guilt by association by making mere membership in a subversive organization a conclusive presumption of disloyalty. It has also held that no state employee may be automatically dismissed without charges, notice, hearing, or the right of appeal, merely because he invokes the privilege against self-incrimination in a federal investigation. Furthermore, loyalty oath requirements may not be so vague in meaning as to compel an employee either to take the oath at the risk of a perjury prosecution, or to refuse and face dismissal from the public service.

Finally, freedom of expression and association of state employees seems to be protected against the state investigatory power unless the state can show that an overriding public interest is threatened.

Aliens, Naturalized Citizens, and Subversion

The complete power of Congress over the admission of aliens to the country and the equally complete responsibility of the Executive for the conduct of foreign affairs have caused the Court to hesitate to intervene in behalf of the basic freedoms of aliens and denaturalized citizens. Nevertheless, these points seem to have been established in favor of the alien. The Attorney General is forbidden to ask an alien, under an order of deportation, questions unrelated to his availability for expulsion.

The extreme holding of the Galvan case that past membership in the Communist party without knowledge of the party's advocacy of violent overthrow of the government could be made the basis for deportation, was sharply curtailed by the Rowaldt case. Under the rule of this case, before an alien can be deported for membership in the Communist party, the record must show substantial evidence that he has committed himself to the party with knowledge of its nature and purpose.

With respect to denaturalization and deportation, it has been held that the pertinent provision of the Immigration and Nationality Act of 1952 does not authorize an immigration officer to subpoena a naturalized citizen to testify in an administrative proceeding in which his denaturalization is the subject of the investigation.

Cancellation of a naturalization decree on the ground that it was obtained by the "concealment of a material fact" and "willful misrepresentation" is not permissible unless the charge is supported by "clear, unequivocal, and convincing evidence." A mere preponderance of evidence is not enough.

It was a deprivation of liberty under the Fifth Amendment for Congress to decree loss of citizenship to an American citizen who returned to her native land for more than three years.

Congress may not constitutionally authorize the deportation of a denaturalized alien for the commission of crimes involving moral turpitude committed while he was a citizen.

Nor, finally, may Congress validly enact legislation which automatically deprives native-born American citizens of their citizenship for "departing from or remaining outside of the jurisdiction of the United States in time of war or . . . national emergency for the purpose of evading or avoiding military service." Such punishment may not be inflicted without the procedural safeguards guaranteed by the Fifth and Sixth Amendments.

Legislative Investigation

Despite the setbacks of a series of cases beginning with Barenblatt in 1959, the following limitations on the power of investigating committees seem to have been established—in some cases firmly, in others, perhaps tentatively.

The investigation must be clearly in aid of a valid legislative function. The questions asked of witnesses must be pertinent to the subject of the inquiry. The valid purpose of the inquiry must be clearly stated in the authorizing resolution. Witnesses may not be compelled to give evidence against themselves, unless they are protected from the danger of criminal prosecution by an immunity statute; nor may a witness be subjected to unreasonable search and seizure. True, the privilege against self-incrimination must be claimed by the witness, but no special formula of words is required so long as his intention is made reasonably clear. Moreover, criminal intent on the part of the witness must be shown by a clear disposition of his objection to questions, before he can be cited for contempt. There can be no investigation into the private affairs of a person for the sole purpose of exposure. Most significantly, it appears that both congressional and state legislative investigating committees are forbidden to ask questions that violate the rights of witnesses to freedom of expression and association under the First and Fourteenth Amendments, unless the danger to the public safety and welfare overbalances the private interest in freedom of expression.

Furthermore, the Watkins principle that an investigating committee, when challenged by a witness, must make clear the subject of the investigation has been extended to grand jury indictments in the prosecution of legislative contempt cases. The indictment must make clear the subject of the inquiry.

Antisedition Legislation and the Modification of "Clear and Present Danger"

The tendency toward judicial self-restraint during the early cold war years was equally marked with respect to substantive legislation aimed at the control of subversion. In the Douds case the Court abandoned the preferred position principle in favor of deference to legislative judgment, in the question of the anti-Communist oath provisions of the Taft-Hartley Act. Only Douglas and Black still pleaded for the preferred status of First Amendment freedoms.

Then, in the famous Dennis case, the substantial majority of the Court seemed to go all the way in rejecting the Holmes-Brandeis version of the clear and present danger test, in favor of the old reasonable tendency test, although it was clothed in the garb of a new clear and present danger test. Whereas under the Holmes-Brandeis theory, immediate danger to a substantial interest was necessary to justify invasion of free speech, Vinson argued in Dennis that if the interest be substantial, the danger need not be imminent. It was not important in this case that the defendants had made no effort to overthrow the government; it was sufficient that they were willing to make the attempt when circumstances permitted. The intention to bring about the overthrow of the government by violence at an indefinite time in the future, when combined with conspiracy to advocate such overthrow, presented a sufficient danger to justify punishment without the necessity of proving any immediate danger from advocacy. In a word, the Court substituted for the clear and present danger doctrine the grave and probable test of Judge Learned Hand.

There seemed little doubt at the time that this reinterpretation of constitutional doctrine had narrowed the scope of protection of freedom of speech and assembly; that the clear and present danger test had been divested of its substance so far as congressional legislation was concerned, and that Congress had been given a free hand on legislation against subversion.

The force and effect of Dennis was substantially modified by the Yates case in which the Court found serious flaws in the Smith Act conviction of fourteen leaders of the Communist party. Here the Court declared that advocacy and teaching of violent overthrow of the government even with intent to bring about that result is not forbidden by the Smith Act unless some effort is made to incite to action. Thus the act was interpreted as being intended to preserve "the distinction between advocacy of abstract doctrine and advocacy directed at promoting unlawful action."

Not many cases involving antisubversion legislation have reached the Court since the Congress-Court battle, but these indicate a tendency on the part of the Court to allow a free flow of ideas in spite of "un-American" content. In 1961 the Court finally upheld the registration provision of the Subversive Activities Control Act but without reaching the problem of self-incrimination under a provision of the Smith Act making membership in the Communist party a crime. In 1964, however, the Court refused to review the court of appeals decision holding that Communists could not be required to register under the 1950 act.

Also in 1964, the Court struck down the passport section of the Subversive Activities Control Act. Justice Goldberg, writing for the majority, held that in preventing Communist-dominated organizations from securing passports and in making it criminally punishable for them even to apply for passports, the statute "too broadly and indiscriminately restricts the right to travel and thereby abridges the liberty guaranteed by the Fifth Amendment."

Finally, a determination by the Subversive Activities Control Board that an organization was Communist-front based on evidence of its status six years before the issuance of the board's order could not stand. Evidence of past Communist relationship was not enough; there must be a finding of current status.

In its determination of free speech cases the Warren Court has rarely made reference to the clear and present danger test.

True the contempt case of *Wood* v. *Georgia* was decided on the basis of an absence of "clear and present danger," but this case seems to have been something of an aberration. Like the Hughes Court which pioneered in the judicial protection of freedom of expression from state restraint in 1931 with no reference to clear and present danger, the Warren Court finds the application of unembellished due process to the facts of the cases quite enough.

9

SUMMARY OF ACHIEVEMENTS

There can be little question that the preservation of civil liberty is one of the paramount issues facing the American people today. The problem, in its broadest and most elemental sense, is the age-old one of establishing a satisfactory balance between liberty and authority. In a special way, this has been the persistent problem of constitutional democracy, and it has become vastly more difficult to preserve the freedom of the individual in a society such as that of the United States, which demands so great a measure of power and complex organization in order to insure its efficiency and security. The object of the preceding pages has been to assay the record of the Supreme Court of the United States in safeguarding individual freedom in the significant years since 1937. The purpose of this chapter is merely to summarize some of the judicial achievements of this period.

The major judicial achievements stem from the application of the principle, first enunciated in 1925, that the due process of law clause of the Fourteenth Amendment extends the basic guarantees of the First Amendment into the areas of state and local government. The major part of the progress made by this nation in the field of civil liberties is the product of judicial decisions from 1925 on. It was in this period that a conscious and deliberate attempt was made in Supreme Court decisions to pour practical meaning into specific provisions of the Bill of Rights and the Fourteenth Amendment, such as freedom of speech, press, and assembly, freedom of religion, due process of law, and equal protection of the laws.

Coupled with this significant development was the application, and largely the formulation, of the new doctrines of "clear and present danger" and "preferred status" of First Amendment freedoms. Despite the diversity of judicial opinion with respect to these doctrines, and the fact that they now appear to have been, at least temporarily, abandoned, the record of the Court in sustaining civil liberties in the period from 1937 to 1950 is written largely in the application of these doctrines. Their application to a variety of new situations has been set forth in chapter 3.

It is undoubtedly in the fields of racial discrimination and malapportionment of legislative representatives that judicial protection of basic freedoms has been most far-reaching as well as most dramatic and controversial. Here the Supreme Court has perhaps had its greatest influence in effecting social and political change. While the import of this change is nationwide in scope, it is most significant in the South.

Patterns of segregation in public education, in public transportation, in privately owned public accommodations; and discrimination in voting rights and legislative representation that were thought by most Southerners and by many other Americans to be permanently fixed, have been broken and may even be eliminated before the end of the decade of the seventies. Of course, the courts have not done this alone, as indeed they cannot; but until 1963, they played the role of innovator, insofar as the government was concerned, in all of these movements. It was only after much brave and agonizing work on the part of the courts that the executive and legislative branches of the federal government began to move with decisiveness and vigor. Until the early sixties, then, the legislative and executive branches of the national government and many of the state governments had left largely to the Supreme Court the task of finding new solutions to the long-festering sores of racial discrimination and of deprivation and debasement of voting rights.

In considering the effectiveness of the Court as an instrument of social and political change, it cannot be said that the millennium has arrived for Negro rights, or that discrimination in voting rights either because of race or because of urban residence has been eliminated. But progress has been made. The pattern of racial segregation in education has been broken in every state, and desegregation has been proceeding at a considerably accelerated pace since 1963. In some other fields the degree of desegregation ranges from substantial to complete elimination. Segregation in public transportation has been virtually nonexistent for nearly a decade; in public recreational facilities it is rapidly vanishing under court orders or "voluntarily," and in privately owned public accommodations it was crumbling under court decisions or "voluntarily" under economic pressure, even before the Civil Rights Act of 1964.

Voting rights, both because of race and because of place of residence, are still being restricted, but here, too, modest progress was made even before the Federal Voting Rights Act of 1965. Less than a generation earlier few Negroes could vote in most of the southern states. There is little reason to believe that much of this progress would have occurred without the intervention of the federal judiciary.

It is not too much to say that federal judicial intervention launched two related "revolutions" in mid-twentieth-century America. The first was the establishment of the constitutional right of the Negro to be free from discrimination because of race in public education, in transportation, in public recreational facilities, and from racial discrimination in privately owned public facilities. The second was the establishment of the right to be free from discrimination in the effective exercise of the right to vote either because of race or because of urban residence.

The ultimate destination of these "revolutions" will, of course, be determined by future events. There seems little reason to doubt, however, that the results will be far-reaching, especially in the South where the expanding influence of the Negro in politics is already apparent, and the growing recognition of urban problems on the part of ambitious politicians is impressive. If present trends continue, the South is not far from the day when discrimination, either because of race or because of place of residence, shall find no place in the public policy of any state. For these significant and dramatic changes the Supreme Court blazed the trail; the President and the Congress followed in 1963, 1964, and 1965.

There are sincere and responsible people who feel that regardless of the authority and effectiveness of the courts in bringing about social and political change, it is not appropriate that courts should enter these realms. These are matters "not meet for judicial determination." Certainly few will deny that it would have been more appropriate, and perhaps more effective, if the southern states had taken the initiative and had exerted vigorous leadership in behalf of the constitutional rights of their citizens to be free from racial discrimination in public education, in transportation, and in the exercise of the voting franchise. But they did not. Instead they invoked the dogma of states' rights against the efforts of the national government to protect the civil and political rights of their citizens. Too often they have made a fetish of states' rights to deny the rights of their people.

Even in the face of this prostitution of constitutional theory, the Supreme Court has been slow to act. Consider the two most important cases of the twentieth century, *Brown* v. *Board of Education* and *Baker* v. *Carr*. In each of these cases the Court acted only as a last resort, after the repeated failure to act of other branches of the national government, as well as of the states. In neither case was there a practical political remedy. True, Congress has authority to enforce the equal protection guarantee of the Fourteenth Amendment, but southern congressmen, especially southern senators, have until recently been able to block such action.

If in 1946, when the Supreme Court refused to take jurisdiction in the Colgrove apportionment case, there was hope that rurally dominated state legislatures could be persuaded to respond to reason and justice with respect to legislative apportionment, that hope had vanished by 1962.

Thus in default of responsibility on the part of the states and the political branches of the national government, the federal judiciary has intervened in proper cases to bring about potentially far-reaching social and political changes. In this the Supreme Court was doubtless responding, as Anthony Lewis of *The New*

York Times has pointed out, to a great moral imperative—"a demand of the national conscience" which "had found no way to express itself except through the Supreme Court." [1]

[1] "Historic Change in the Supreme Court," *The New York Times Magazine*, June 17, 1962, p. 38.

TABLE OF CASES

INDEX